Criminal Theory and International Human Rights Law

The development of an international human rights jurisprudence on criminalization is in its relative infancy. Nonetheless, systematic examination of international decisions on acts engaging the criminal law reveals an emerging human rights approach to the acceptability, or not, of criminalization. This book provides an in-depth characterization of the reasoning and principles that underpin those decisions.

The work builds upon and adds value to existing literature by bringing together two fields of study – international human rights law and criminal theory – that usually receive separate treatment. It provides an in-depth analysis of human rights criminalization jurisprudence and presents a systematic identification of underlying reasoning and concepts that influence international human rights decisions on criminalization. The work thus advances both fields independently, as well as providing an example of inter-(sub)disciplinary analysis.

The book will be a valuable resource for academics and students working in the areas of International Human Rights Law, Criminal Law, and Moral Philosophy.

Steven Malby is Head of the Office of Civil and Criminal Justice Reform at the Commonwealth Secretariat, London, and an adjunct lecturer in international human rights law at the University of Essex. He previously worked for the Division for Treaty Affairs at the United Nations Office on Drugs and Crime, Vienna. He qualified as a solicitor in England and Wales, and holds a doctoral degree in law from the University of Göttingen, Germany.

Routledge Research in Human Rights Law

Challenging Territoriality in Human Rights Law
Building Blocks for a Plural and Diverse Duty-Bearer Regime
Wouter Vandenhole

Care, Migration and Human Rights
Law and Practice
Siobhán Mullally

China's Human Rights Lawyers
Advocacy and Resistance
Eva Pils

Indigenous Peoples, Title to Territory, Rights and Resources
The Transformative Role of Free Prior and Informed Consent
Cathal M. Doyle

Civil and Political Rights in Japan
A Tribute to Sir Nigel Rodley
Edited by Saul J. Takahashi

Human Rights, Digital Society and the Law
A Research Companion
Edited by Mart Susi

Criminal Theory and International Human Rights Law
Steven Malby

For more information about this series, please visit: www.routledge.com/Routledge-Research-in-Human-Rights-Law/book-series/HUMRIGHTSLAW

Criminal Theory and International Human Rights Law

Steven Malby

Routledge
Taylor & Francis Group
LONDON AND NEW YORK

First published 2020
by Routledge
2 Park Square, Milton Park, Abingdon, Oxon OX14 4RN

and by Routledge
52 Vanderbilt Avenue, New York, NY 10017

Routledge is an imprint of the Taylor & Francis Group, an informa business

British Library Cataloguing-in-Publication Data
A catalogue record for this book is available from the British Library

Library of Congress Cataloging-in-Publication Data
A catalog record has been requested for this book

ISBN: 978-0-367-18227-4 (hbk)
ISBN: 978-0-429-06021-2 (ebk)

Typeset in Galliard
by Integra Software Services Pvt. Ltd.

Contents

Tables and figures

Tables

Figures

Preface

The aim of this book is to provide a bridge between two legal fields, both of which address the human situation in a fundamental way but have not thus far been examined together. Criminal theory seeks to deliver a critical moral account of when and why the state may use punitive measures with the express stigma of a criminal conviction to deter and punish certain conduct. International human rights law proclaims civil, political, economic, social, and cultural rights for each individual, in pursuit of freedom from fear and want for all. Each field has become a legal specialism in its own right, with its own immense literature, terminology, concepts, and dedicated academics and practitioners. Yet careful analysis of international human rights treaties and case law in particular shows a deep principled concern with, what amounts to, a subject of criminal theory: the rights-based reasons why a state should, can, or should not criminalize certain conduct. This book undertakes a detailed study of this part of international human rights law, with reference to the case law of international human rights courts and tribunals. It asks whether and how such jurisprudence can have value for the development of criminal theory. In order to answer this question, it also contains a discussion of existing approaches to the use of rights within Anglo-American and continental legal theory. In doing so, the book adopts a cross-disciplinary approach that should appeal both to criminal theorists and to international human rights law lawyers.

Each chapter may be read in its own right, but the chapters are intended to build on each other, linking the two fields and developing directions for further research. The book draws, in particular, from analysis of a group of almost 80 cases from the European Court of Human Rights that address matters of criminalization. The underlying reasoning in this group of cases was subject to classification and semi-quantitative analysis. A table at the very end of the book details the cases and their judgment reasoning. References are provided as footnotes to the text in abridged form. A full reference list, including United Nations documents, treaties and legislation, and cases, is provided. Within the book, the terms "criminal theory," "criminal law theory," and "criminalization theory" are used largely interchangeably. The author expresses his sincere thanks to those who provided the professional and personal inspiration for this book, as well as invaluable suggestions and critical review. Thanks are due in particular to

Ms Eva Ignatuschtschenko, Mr and Mrs J. Malby, Mr Reg Pritchard, Dr Anna Alvazzi del Frate, and the author's doctoral supervisors, Prof Kai Ambos and Prof Jörg-Martin Jehle of the Georg-August University of Göttingen. The author also wishes to thank the two anonymous reviewers from Routledge, as well as Ms Alison Kirk and Ms Emily Summers of Routledge for their professional and timely guidance at all stages in the publication process. The views expressed are those of the author only and do not represent the views or endorsement of the Commonwealth Secretariat or any other organization. As ever, any errors that remain are my sole responsibility.

Abbreviations

CAT	Convention against Torture and Other Cruel, Inhuman or Degrading Treatment or Punishment
CEDAW	Convention on the Elimination of All Forms of Discrimination against Women
CPED	International Convention for the Protection of All Persons from Enforced Disappearance
CRC	Convention on the Rights of the Child
CRPD	Convention on the Rights of Persons with Disabilities
ECHR	European Convention on Human Rights
ECtHR	European Court of Human Rights
IACHR	Inter-American Court of Human Rights
IACommHR	Inter-American Commission on Human Rights
ICCPR	International Covenant on Civil and Political Rights
ICCS	International Classification of Crimes for Statistical Purposes
ICERD	International Convention on the Elimination of All Forms of Racial Discrimination
ICESCR	International Covenant on Economic, Social and Cultural Rights
ICMW	International Convention on the Protection of the Rights of All Migrant Workers and Members of Their Families
OP-CRC-AC	Optional Protocol to the Convention on the Rights of the Child on the Involvement of Children in Armed Conflict
OP-CRC-SC	Optional Protocol to the Convention on the Rights of the Child on the Sale of Children, Child Prostitution and Child Pornography
UDHR	Universal Declaration of Human Rights

1 Introduction

If criminal theory and international human rights law were ever considered the sole domain of philosophers, lawyers, and legislators, the critical questions with which they deal have undoubtedly been pushed into the mainstream. The terms "criminalization" and "human rights" are now common parlance. Debates on the criminalization, and perhaps more frequently *de*criminalization, of conduct emerge in the media on a regular basis. Such debates include whether conduct as diverse as forced marriage, squatting, polygamy, possession of narcotic drugs for personal use, and prostitution should or should not be a criminal offence. The criminal law makes headlines around the world when individuals are convicted and incarcerated, or even sentenced to death, for acts such as adultery, blasphemy, and apostasy. At the same time, human rights are often portrayed as at a global juncture, openly questioned by some and lamented as in demise by others, in the context of polarized societies and moves away from global dialogue and multilateralism.

Contemporary phenomena such as the misuse of global information and communications technologies, violent extremism, and terrorism increasingly present complex challenges to safe and peaceful societies. As governments develop new criminal law responses, an expanding reach of criminalization risks threatening the rule of law and a proportionately restrained criminal law. New criminal laws such as encouraging or preparing for acts of terrorism may come up against specific human rights law objections. The need for a principled criminal law, guided by external values and standards, is as great as ever.

Whilst the proper extent and nature of the criminal law have been a topic of intense academic debate from the time of John Locke, Jean-Jacque Rousseau, and Immanuel Kant, recent waves of development of criminal law theory have both reflected and ignited societal concern over the correctness of the scope of criminal liability. The influential 2007 text by Douglas Husak on overcriminalization, for instance, encapsulates an argument that the United States suffers from too much criminal law and too much punishment,[1] a theme subsequently emphasized at the political level by the Over-Criminalization Task Force of the Committee on the Judiciary of the United States House of Representatives.

1 Husak, D., 2007.

Criminal theorists assert that the heart of the problem lies in the absence of a viable account of criminalization. A gap that Husak suggests is perhaps the single most glaring failure of penal theory. The criticism is that theorists, legislators, and judges have had too little to say about the proper scope of criminal law. As noted by Anthony Duff, if not directly about what kinds of conduct should or should not be criminalized, then at least about the considerations that should bear on questions of criminalization, and about the procedures through which such questions should be settled. This includes justification not only as to which acts should count as criminal offences but also as to when and why we should prefer criminalization to other possible ways of responding (or not responding) to such acts. As Duff notes, in a nutshell, we need to be clear about why rape, tax evasion, and driving when uninsured are properly criminal, as well as about why sexual infidelity and rudeness are not.[2]

Recent years have seen a renewed focus on outlining, if not a theoretical framework for criminalization, then at least guiding moral and legal principles for use of the criminal law.[3] Nonetheless, the literature is still far from a settled account of acceptable criminalization. Criminalization theory typically invokes an abundance of terms and concepts, including harm, offence, wrongfulness, morality and moralism, paternalism, culpability, public concern, legal goods, *ultimo ratio* (last resort), deterrence, and retribution. Such concepts may be found in a range of combinations, relationships, and interactions. A number of contemporary commentators have begun to coalesce around the idea that there is no unified, grand theory for criminalization but rather that basic elements may interact to make or deny a case for criminalization. Nonetheless, views on the exact content, place, and interrelationship of individual criminalization concepts remain incredibly diverse.

This perceived lack of clarity in the philosophical account of criminalization is not unrelated to an equivalent criticism made by Dennis Baker: that even the legal boundaries of criminal offences – and specifically their relationship with moral limits – are equally undefined.[4] In practice, such legal limits are often expressed through constitutional limits on the criminal law. Constitutional constraints on the substantive criminal law are found, for example, in the US and German constitutions.[5] Such constraints include the human rights and fundamental freedoms enshrined in most national constitutions. The existence of constitutional rights-based challenges to the criminal law has long been recognized by criminal theorists, who variously have either tried to rationalize criminalization findings of constitutional courts with reference to criminal theory or argued that constitutional rights are unsuitable as the cornerstone of a general theory of criminalization.[6] Whether from

2 Duff, R.A., 2010, pp.16–19.

3 See, for example, Simester, A.P., and von Hirsch, A., 2011; Ashworth, A., and Horder, J., 2013; Matravers, M., 2016.

4 Baker, D.J., 2011, p.1.

5 Bendor, A.L., and Dancig-Rosenberg, H., 2016; Lagodny, O., 1999.

6 Baker, D.J., 2011, pp.245–254; Simester, A.P., and von Hirsch, A., 2011, pp.134–137.

a legal or philosophical perspective, however, a clear area for enquiry emerges: the need for a viable account of criminalization and the potential role of human rights in determining such an account. As López-Rey asserted from the legal-political perspective, over 40 years ago, crime is what is defined by law as such. On the other hand, the definition must take into account the existence of, and respect for, human rights and not merely be the expression of arbitrary power.[7]

This book is concerned with exactly that issue. Whilst human rights take many forms in both the domains of legal positivism and legal theory, the focus here is specifically on human rights as contained in international human rights law. From a global perspective, international human rights law stands as the only common international legal framework that can be applied across a range of modern dilemmas and that aims to clearly delineate state responsibilities and individual entitlements. The rights contained in international human rights law are often the same, or similar, to those protected by national constitutions. International human rights law, as a field in its own right, however, has its own jurisprudence, its own dedicated international mechanisms, and, as this book examines, its own approach to questions of criminalization.

International human rights law cannot be viewed as a substitute for domestic criminal or civil law. However, the positive international obligations of states to ensure realization of human rights will only be fully discharged if individuals are protected by the state, not just against violations of rights by its agent but also against acts committed by private persons or entities that would impair the enjoyment of human rights. This includes in the exercise of due diligence to prevent, punish, investigate, or redress harm caused by private persons or entities. At the same time, however, criminal law and penalties must always themselves avoid violating the rights of individuals. It seems almost self-evident that international human rights law would have something to say about the proper exercise of national criminal law. This book explores the differences between criminal theory and an international human rights law approach to criminalization, and considers whether gains may be achieved at the intersection of the two.

Bringing the two fields together

Whilst international human rights law jurisprudence on matters of substantive criminal law exists, the relationship between international human rights law and criminal theory has not been extensively or systematically explored. Rather, the literature tends to either reflect a broad discussion of a possible place for rights within criminal theory or be limited to examples of the human rights implications of criminalization of limited specific conduct, such as the criminalization of homelessness or HIV transmission.[8] Where legal theorists have attempted to integrate

7 López-Rey, M., 1978, p.11.

8 See, for example, Hörnle, T., 2016; Langley, E.E., and Nardi, Jr., D.J., 2010; Baker D.J., 2009.

a human rights discourse into criminalization theory, they have often not engaged seriously with the framework and lessons of international human rights law. Rather, many criminalization works are completed in isolation from developments in the jurisprudence of international human rights law, preferring instead theories based in welfare rights and deontological moral rights. One major recent initiative aimed at developing a normative theory of criminalization, for example, largely limited its discussion on the place of human rights in criminal theory to that of international criminal responsibility.[9] It is perhaps not surprising that the non-governmental International Council on Human Rights Policy concluded in 2010 that there remains an urgent need for a human rights-based narrative of crime and criminality and responses to crime.[10] In so far as any account of the criminal law must grapple seriously with the concept of wrongdoing, it appears that such a project could benefit significantly from a body of law and thought, such as international human rights law, that proclaims itself to be a foundation of freedom, justice, and peace in the world, as a common standard of achievement for all peoples and all nations.

The limited examination of criminal theory together with international human rights law to date is perhaps all the more surprising in light of the fact that the two fields share a number of common features. From the perspective of underlying legal theory, both the notions of criminalization and human rights concern the idea of constraint on action. The subjects of this constraint are, of course, different: primarily states or public authorities in the case of international human rights law and individuals or groups of individuals in the case of criminal law. Nonetheless, both fields purport to guide their subjects, to a greater or lesser degree through the threat of sanctions for violation, as to an acceptable range of actions. In this respect, both fields share something of a common philosophical heritage from Enlightenment thinkers. The work and philosophy of Immanuel Kant, for instance, are habitually invoked in (separate) academic commentary on human rights and on criminalization.[11] Notwithstanding such elements of common heritage, however, legal philosophical work related to criminalization and human rights tends to remain compartmentalized. The elaboration of capability theory by Sen and Nussbaum, for example, occurred primarily within the language and context of human rights discourse. The theory is rarely discussed in the context of criminalization, despite the importance of criminalization as a constraint on permissible human action.[12] Conversely, well-known concepts that are inherent to many criminalization theories, such as harm theory, find little place within academic discourse on human rights. Indeed, academic commentators who systematically apply legal reasoning or moral and critical

9 Renzo, M., 2013.

10 International Council on Human Rights Policy, 2010, p.v.

11 In the field of human rights, see, for example, Demenchonok, E., 2009. In the field of criminalization, see Richards, D.A.J., 1979b.

12 A number of commentators have recently started to acknowledge the notion of Sen's capabilities in the context of resources to be protected by the harm principle in criminalization theory. See, for example, von Hirsch, A., 2014, p.249.

philosophy in such areas appear for the most part to identify themselves with the field of either human rights or criminalization, but rarely both.

In the positivist legal world, the two bodies of law frequently occupy different positions in the national legal order. Human rights usually benefit from protection at the constitutional level. Criminal offences, on the other hand, can be found in all of primary legislation, in secondary legislation, and at common law. At the international level, both human rights and specific criminal offences are also contained within binding regional and international legal instruments. However, the sociopolitical processes which give rise to such instruments are frequently conducted separately and with little reference to the other field. It is an oft-cited point, for example, that within the United Nations system, international human rights instruments are developed in Geneva, whereas instruments concerning human security are developed in Vienna, frequently with little discussion between the two bodies.[13] Nonetheless, in the positivist legal world, human rights law and criminal law do intersect in a number of circumstances. The criminalization of particular conduct may be tested against a state constitution, where national criminal laws are subject to constitutional protections that include human rights. Some national legislatures conduct specific human rights assessments of proposed criminal legislation. At the regional and international levels, complaints to human rights tribunals can directly concern the compatibility of national criminal law with the international human rights obligations of the state in question.[14] International human rights law includes an implicit duty to punish serious human rights violations through prosecution.[15] A detailed body of law has also arisen around criminal culpability for a limited subset of human rights as a component of international criminal law. Nonetheless, when compared, for example, to the sheer number and depth of judicial decisions on human rights and criminal procedure, jurisprudence on human rights and criminalization is seen, at least at the regional and international levels, to be decidedly limited. It is therefore perhaps unsurprising that few academic commentators have tackled the legal intersections of human rights and criminalization head-on. Of those who do, some take extreme positions, such as the suggestion that the violation of human rights of any kind should be a criminal act.[16] More considered work examines a subset of the criminalization jurisprudence of certain international human rights systems, including the European and the United Nations system.[17] To date, however, the literature lacks detailed analysis of the outcomes and reasoning of such international human rights law criminalization jurisprudence that does exist.

13 Barrett, D., and Nowak, M., 2009.

14 See, for example, *Prince v. South Africa*, UNHRC, concerning the compatibility with the ICCPR of the offence of possessing or using cannabis, and *Kokkinakis v. Greece*, ECHR, concerning the compatibility with the ECHR of the offence of acts of proselytism.

15 Seibert-Fohr, A., 2009.

16 See, for example, Blau, J., and Moncada, A., 2007.

17 See, for example, Bengoetxea, J., and Jung, H., 1991; Ashworth, A., 2013; O'Flaherty, M., and Higgins, N., 2015; Du Hert, P. et al., 2007; Keehn, E.N., 2018.

As a result, bringing the fields of criminal theory and international human rights law together is no easy task. One key reason for this is the fact that international human rights law sits predominantly within the plane of positivist law and *ex post facto* case law. International human rights law consists of treaties and the decisions of international human rights courts and tribunals. Human rights treaties are negotiated positivist text, and the decisions of human rights courts and tribunals are highly context-specific. Where such decisions address the compatibility of a particular criminal offence with international human rights law, they do so from the vantage point of looking back at the offence in law and its application to the facts in practice. By contrast, criminal theory is most usually conducted as a theoretical *a priori* exercise. That is, criminal theory is concerned with an ideal, critical moral approach to what should or should not be a criminal offence, ideally well before any offence is enacted.

In order to analyse whether international human rights law might have any value for criminal theory, it is necessary to distil international human rights law and jurisprudence down to the conceptual level. Fundamental international human rights law principles and concepts can then be compared with the critical moral reasoning of criminal theory. This requires scrutiny of the place of criminalization within international human rights law treaty text, as well as detailed examination of the underlying reasoning of the decisions of international human rights courts and tribunals that address criminalization.

Such an undertaking relies, in particular, on the notion that law has a *dual* nature. Under this approach, the law comprises both a real or factual dimension and an ideal or critical one. The factual dimension is represented by the elements of authoritative issuance and social efficacy, whereas the ideal dimension finds its expression in the element of moral correctness.[18] As applied to international human rights law, dual nature of law theory highlights the connection between human rights as both moral rights and positive rights. In the field of criminal law, as with other national laws, dual nature of law theory, under the Radbruch formula, suggests a threshold of extreme injustice for determining the outermost border of law, beyond which laws are, in some sense, valid but defective.[19] Kai Ambos expresses this as the idea that the positive law ultimately operates with a "legitimacy reservation" that also requires a plausible claim of moral validity.[20]

At the international level, this theoretical approach fits well with the conception of the rule of law. The United Nations definition of the rule of law includes the requirement that laws must be consistent with international human rights norms and standards, fairness, legal certainty, and the avoidance of arbitrariness.[21] Under this approach, law is supreme (in the classically positivist

18 Alexy, R., 2010.
19 Radbruch, G., 1946.
20 Ambos, K., 2013, p.302.
21 United Nations, Security Council, 2004. UN Doc. S/2004/616, para 6.

sense) but – or perhaps *and* – only fully legitimate when it fulfils the substantive requirements of fairness and meets human rights norms and standards. The human rights compatibility requirement in the United Nations rule of law definition plays a role analogous to that of the extreme injustice test. As such, justice is conceived as an ideal of accountability and fairness in the protection and vindication of rights and the prevention and punishment of wrongs. Justice implies regard for the rights of the accused, for the interests of victims, and for the well-being of society at large.

An appeal to dual nature of law theory places emphasis on the fact that whilst international human rights law derives, in positivist terms, from international negotiations and judicial interpretation, it is, at the same time, a product of a historical tradition that owes a great deal to intellectual and philosophical concepts such as natural law, natural rights, autonomy of the person, and human dignity.[22] As expressed by James Griffin:

> The international law of human rights aims, or should aim, at least in part, to incorporate some extra-legal ethical standards. The creators of international law do not, and cannot plausibly say that what they deem to be a human right *is* a human right, that on this subject they are infallible … It is not that over the last fifty years or so the body of treaties and decisions of international courts has grown large enough for those courts now to be able to tell us definitively whether a certain human right exists and what, fairly precisely, its content is. [Rather] … an international court willing to heed expert opinion or considerations of humanity or *jus cogens* is driven to take seriously basic considerations of justice, the meaning of "the dignity of the person", and how justice and rights are related.[23]

It is this approach which facilitates the bringing together of the fields of international human rights law and criminal theory. International human rights jurisprudence does not and cannot examine all acts that may be subject to criminal prohibition. Within some international human rights systems, however, there is now sufficient, consistent case law to undertake analysis of underlying human rights concepts and reasoning that are applied to questions of criminalization. That said, the notion that ideal concepts may underpin international human rights law is one thing to assert, but quite another to identify in practice.

22 Perhaps most clearly argued is the proposition that the Universal Declaration of Human Rights has solid roots in the French Declaration of the Rights of Man and of the Citizen (26 August 1789 and 24 June 1793) through the natural law concept that the individual has rights against the state, through the rule of law requirement that legal rules actually dictate behaviour of all within the state's jurisdiction, and through the social contract that orders society for the common good. See Marks, S.P., 1998, p.511.

23 Griffin, J., 2008, p.54 and 204–205. Reproduced with permission of the Licensor through PLSclear.

Distilling a conceptual framework from the diverse, fact-driven jurisprudence of an international human rights court or tribunal is far from straightforward. Whilst international human rights judges at least aim for consistency of decisions and reasoning, their decisions do not often consciously make reference to conceptual moral frameworks. In addition to its contribution to criminal theory, this book also therefore demonstrates an analytical approach to international human rights law jurisprudence. By classifying and conducting a semi-quantitative analysis of a group of international human rights judicial decisions on criminalization, it demonstrates a technique for identification and analysis of underlying legal concepts and reasoning. To the extent that a conceptual framework is identifiable, the technique offers a route to bringing order and analytical rigour to an otherwise largely unstructured body of case law. This enables new insights and understanding of factors that guide a human rights-based position on criminalization. The differences between this framework and criminal theory are then used to discuss whether international human rights law can either itself provide guiding principles for criminalization or otherwise make a significant contribution to existing criminal theory.

Defining the criminal offence

Whilst some countries benefit from a single, largely definitive penal code, criminalization in other countries can arise from multiple statutes that deal with multiple subject matters and at multiple geographical levels, such as federal and state. Criminal offences may also be contained in secondary legislation, at common law, and from discretionary, or *ta'azir*, crimes in some Islamic legal systems.[24] In Western legal systems, the large spectrum of terminology associated with legal measures of varying types, including words such as crime, offence, legal, indictable, summary and administrative offence, felony, misdemeanour, administrative sanction, and penalty, in particular serves to introduce confusion as to those measures that may be included within the ambit of criminalization. A number of commentators have recognized the significance of this challenge. Susan Klein, for instance, suggests that it is simply impossible, at present, to separate all proceedings into criminal and civil actions, as so many now have a combination of features from both.[25] Nevertheless, some definitions of crime do rely on a focus on the type of proceedings as the determining factor of a crime in law. Under this approach, a crime is defined by reference to the legal consequences of the act. As such, the criminal offence is distinguished, primarily, not as a crime or civil wrong but by virtue of the difference between criminal and civil proceedings. A crime then becomes an act that is capable of being followed by criminal proceedings, having one of the types of outcome known to follow these proceedings.[26]

24 For an introduction to Islamic law, see Bassiouni, M.C., and Badr, G.M., 2002.
25 Klein, S.R., 1999, p.722.
26 Williams, G., 1955, p.123.

Although such definitions on the one hand introduce at least some basis for distinguishing a criminal offence, on the other they arguably simply defer the problem of identification from the level of legal definitions to the level of type of proceedings and sanctions. Further tests have nonetheless been proposed to attach to this definition, including related to the type of procedural rules that govern the legal proceedings, as well as to the distinguishing feature of the sanction. Andreas von Hirsch, in particular, advocates that it is the "censure" that attaches to a criminal penalty which most clearly distinguishes criminal wrongs from other wrongs.[27] International human rights law itself is also able to make a contribution to the point, with jurisprudence under the European Convention on Human Rights (ECHR) Article 6 (Right to a fair trial), for example, providing some guidance as to whether a particular set of proceedings amounts to criminal proceedings for the purposes of fair trial protection. In this respect, European Court of Human Rights (ECtHR) case law tends towards a broadening of the criminal head to all sanctions whose main objective is to deter from future violations of a norm generally perceived as inherently bad or contrary to the common values shared in a democratic society.[28] For the purposes of analysing international human rights jurisprudence on criminalization, and its comparison with criminal theory, however, the focus in this book is on those proceedings that clearly carry the stigma and expressive function of a criminal conviction, rather than coercive sanctions in general.[29]

A conscious exclusion is also made in relation to the general part of the criminal law. Criminal law theorists often refer to the distinction between the general part of the criminal law and the special part of the criminal law.[30] The general part is comprised of rules and principles of the criminal law whose importance and application can be analysed and debated without necessarily referring to a specific crime. By contrast, the special part of the criminal law refers to the particular conduct, situations, and states of mind that are used to define specific offences, such as murder, theft, rape, robbery, and blackmail. Doctrines sometimes argued to reside in the general part of the criminal law, and thus to apply across a range of offences, include the requirement of voluntary action; the principle of causation and interventions between conduct and result; the requirement of a culpable state mind; the operation of defences such as self-defence and duress; and principles related to inchoate offences and accessory liability.

Analysis of the general part of the criminal law is to be found in the European continental perspective, including, in particular Austrian, German, Italian, Portuguese, Spanish, and Swiss legal thinking, in both a classical and, more recently,

27 Von Hirsch, A., 1993, pp.9–12.

28 See, for example, the ECHR cases of *Engel and Others v. The Netherlands; Garyfallou Aebe v. Greece*; and *Jussila v. Finland*. For a general review, see Guinchard, A., 2005.

29 On the expressive function of law in general, see Sunstein, C.R., 1996.

30 Gardner, J., 1998.

post-finalist, structure of the criminal law. Under a post-finalist structure, a crime is considered to consist of the objective and subjective elements of the offence (*Tatbestandsmäßigkeit*) together with a requirement for wrongfulness (*Rechtswidrigkeit*) and culpability (*Schuld*) in a normative sense.[31] Such models suggest that the interaction between the general part and the special part of the criminal law is complex. In particular, depending upon the model applied, mental aspects, such as specific intentions or motives, beliefs concerning the act and situation, and consciousness of the wrong, can be distributed between the special and general parts of the criminal law. As Simester and Shute note, the general part of the criminal law is not simply the set of generalized, directly justiciable doctrines known to criminal law. General part doctrines need not be mandatory, they may be advisory or, for that matter, permissive. Nor is the relationship between the general and special parts uniform or straightforward.[32]

There is no reason, in principle, why a human rights analysis of the general part of the criminal law may not be undertaken. David Richards, for example, examines defences of justification and excuse, as well as other elements of the general part of the criminal law, with reference to a rights-based scheme of autonomous choice and deliberation.[33] The ECtHR, in the context of challenges to criminal convictions, has had occasion to consider the human rights compatibility of strict liability offences.[34] The close interaction between the general part and special part of the criminal law means that it can sometimes be difficult to focus on one part to the exclusion of the other. A human rights analysis of the specific offence of rape, for instance, engages not only issues that are particular to the definition of the specific act but also issues that can be described as belonging to the general part of the criminal law, including the ability of the victim to consent to the act or not, the subjective belief of the perpetrator, as well as strict liability variants of the offence.[35]

That said, the focus of this book is on an analysis of the special part of the criminal law – that is, the range of acts or conduct which may legitimately be made criminal. The rationale for this lies in the particular public, and practical, interest in specific controversial laws, such as the criminalization of homelessness or membership of proscribed organizations. Indeed, international human rights law jurisprudence most usually arises from challenges to specific criminalization and criminal convictions. Similarly, whilst criminal law theorists do not ignore the general part of criminal law, they usually reserve the greater part of their analysis for the acceptability, or not, of specific conduct.

31 Ambos, K., 2007.
32 Simester, A.P., and Shute, S., 2002, p.12.
33 Richards, D.A.J., 1979b, p.1431.
34 See, for example, *Salabiaku v. France*, ECHR, and *Hansen v. Denmark*, ECHR.
35 See, for example, *X and Y v. The Netherlands*, ECHR, and *G v. United Kingdom*, ECHR.

The scope of international human rights law

At its core, international human rights law consists of international customary law and those international treaties that contain human rights and fundamental freedoms concluded under the auspices of the United Nations and regional intergovernmental systems. Whereas the Universal Declaration on Human Rights (UDHR) adopted by the United Nations General Assembly on 10 December 1948 is considered as a foundational international human rights law document, its status as a General Assembly resolution means that it does not, on the face of it, impose binding obligations on states. That said, a number of the provisions of the UDHR arguably do reflect provisions of customary international law. These may include the right to life (UDHR Article 3), as well as prohibitions against slavery (Article 4), torture (Article 5), arbitrary detention (Article 9), and racial discrimination (Article 2).[36] By far the greater body of international human rights legal standards, though, are found in specific international human rights treaties.

Almost exactly 18 years after the UDHR, the International Covenant on Civil and Political Rights (ICCPR) was adopted by General Assembly resolution 2200A (XXI) on 16 December 1966, containing 22 articles setting out civil and political rights for the individual. The Covenant additionally set out two rights of peoples. The same General Assembly resolution also adopted the International Covenant on Economic, Social and Cultural Rights (ICESCR), containing 10 substantive articles with rights of an economic, social, and cultural nature. The 1966 Covenants are accompanied by a further seven core international human rights treaties negotiated under the auspices of the United Nations: the International Convention on the Elimination of All Forms of Racial Discrimination of 1965 (ICERD), the Convention on the Elimination of All Forms of Discrimination against Women of 1979 (CEDAW), the Convention against Torture and Other Cruel, Inhuman or Degrading Treatment or Punishment of 1984 (CAT), the Convention on the Rights of the Child of 1989 (CRC), the International Convention on the Protection of the Rights of All Migrant Workers and Members of Their Families of 1990 (ICMW), the International Convention for the Protection of All Persons from Enforced Disappearance of 2006 (CPED), and the Convention on the Rights of Persons with Disabilities, also of 2006 (CRPD). In addition, Optional Protocols exist to ICESCR, ICCPR, CEDAW, CRC, CAT, and CRPD, creating competencies for communications from individuals claiming to be victims of violations of rights contained in the instruments and covering additional areas such as the abolition of the death penalty, the involvement of children in armed conflict, and the sale of children, child prostitution, and child pornography.

At the regional intergovernmental level, contemporaneously with the preparation of the UDHR, a charter of human rights was proposed in Europe by the Congress of Europe held in The Hague in May 1948. A first draft of what was to become the ECHR was prepared by a committee of the European Movement in 1949. The

36 Hannum, H., 1996.

resultant Convention was opened for signature on 4 November 1950 in Rome, and the ECHR came into effect on 3 September 1953 upon its tenth ratification. The ECHR has been amended and supplemented by a number of additional protocols, which both added additional rights to the original Convention and amended provisions relating to the institutional machinery of the ECHR.

In the Americas, the American Declaration of the Rights and Duties of Man represents the earliest contemporary human rights instrument, having been adopted by the Ninth International Conference of American States, held in Bogotá, Colombia, in 1948. This was followed by the adoption of the American Convention on Human Rights in 1969. Whereas the American Declaration of the Rights and Duties of Man does not hold the status of a treaty, the General Assembly of the Organization of American States has repeatedly recognized that the American Declaration is a source of international obligations for member states of the Organization. In addition, the Inter-American Commission on Human Rights is empowered to consider allegations of violation of rights guaranteed in the American Declaration.

In Africa, the African Charter on Human and Peoples' Rights was unanimously approved by the Organization of African Unity in 1981. A Protocol to the African Charter on the Establishment of an African Court on Human Peoples' Rights was adopted in 1998 and entered into force in 2004. At present, there is no Asia-wide or Oceania-wide intergovernmental human rights system. The Association of Southeast Asian Nations adopted the ASEAN Human Rights Declaration in 2012, however, and the League of Arab States adopted the Arab Charter on Human Rights in 2004. The relationship between the universal international human rights law system of the United Nations and the international human rights law deriving from regional intergovernmental systems is, in many senses, bidirectional. Regional human rights systems may both reflect and influence United Nations human rights instruments. Whilst it is undoubtedly the case, for example, that the European human rights system became influential in its region earlier, the American and African systems have also contributed to the making of the broader international human rights order.[37]

In addition to the provisions of international human rights instruments and treaties themselves, international human rights law is shaped by the jurisprudence of international human rights courts and tribunals. It is the international common law, representing the collective decisions of international tribunals, which provides the soft law interpretative standards that delineate the meaning and application of treaty-based rights.[38] Judgments of international courts and tribunals, such as the ECtHR, do not strictly bind non-parties to the particular case. However, as noted by the European Court in *Pretty*, judgments issued in individual cases establish precedents, albeit to a greater or lesser extent, and

37 See, for example, Huneeus, A., and Madsen, M.R., 2018.
38 Guzman, A.T., and Meyer, T.L., 2010.

a decision in a case could not, in either theory or practice, be framed in such a way as to prevent application in later cases.[39]

Within the United Nations system, treaty bodies are responsible for monitoring implementation of the United Nations international human rights treaties. They produce concluding observations on state party reports and may also receive and consider individual complaints. United Nations treaty body concluding observations differ from judgments of an international court or tribunal in that they are not legally binding on states parties and are developed following a periodic process of state party reporting and dialogue with the relevant treaty-monitoring Committee. Committee decisions in individual cases similarly contain non-legally binding recommendations to the state party. Nonetheless, concluding observations and decisions in individual communications are not without some special status, at least to the extent that they interpret the treaty or consider the treaty obligations of the state party.[40] The combined jurisprudence of an international human rights tribunal or treaty body on a particular issue can therefore be taken as an authoritative expression of the applicable international human rights standards within each international human rights system. Moreover, a certain cross-fertilization can occur between the jurisprudence of different international human rights systems. The African Court on Human and Peoples' Rights, for instance, frequently makes reference to the interpretation of equivalent standards within the United Nations, European, and American human rights systems.[41]

For the purposes of this book, the human rights contained in the nine core United Nations human rights treaties and their protocols, as well as the treaties of the three principal regional human rights mechanisms, together with the authoritative interpretation of their associated international courts and tribunals, are taken as the principal expression of international human rights law to be applied to the question of criminalization. This is not to say that other international law does not exist that may be classified as human rights law. Multilateral treaties agreed under the auspices of organizations such as the International Labour Organization and the United Nations Educational, Scientific and Cultural Organization, including the 1960 Convention against Discrimination in Education, the 1948 Freedom of Association and Protection of the Right to Organize Convention, and the 1999 Worst Forms of Child Labour Convention, for example, also contain human rights protections. Such instruments generally either build on standards in the core United Nations human rights treaties or concern their application in particular circumstances or to specific groups.

This said, the question of what exactly comes within the remit of international human rights law is more than a semantic issue, not least because human rights treaties are often argued to have a special status within international law.[42] The

39 *Pretty v. United Kingdom*, ECHR.

40 O'Flaherty, M., 2006.

41 See, for example, *Lohé Issa Konaté v. Burkina Faso*, African Court on Human and Peoples' Rights, paras 116–166.

42 Mégret, F., 2018.

category of human rights treaties may be larger or smaller depending upon the specific characteristics employed to define the category. These may include rights of petition for individuals, as well as independence of rights from nationality, or reciprocal protection by other states parties to the treaty.[43] Of special relevance to the issue of criminalization is the interface between instruments that contain protections of individual rights and those that prohibit specific acts under threat of penal sanction. International treaties such as the 1926 Slavery Convention and the 1948 Convention on the Prevention and Punishment of the Crime of Genocide, for example, are often viewed as human rights treaties, but do not in fact specify rights of individuals. Rather, they define specific acts and commit states parties to undertake necessary measures to ensure that penalties are imposed in respect of infractions.[44] Whilst their structure is very different to that of the nine core United Nations human rights treaties, their characterization as human rights instruments can probably be traced to the fact that their subject matter strikes at the heart of human life and liberty.

Equally significant is the relationship between international human rights law, international humanitarian law, and international criminal law. Whereas international human rights law is primarily constructed in terms of *state* obligations, international criminal law is concerned with the criminal liability of *individuals*. This applies to the most serious crimes of concern to the international community as a whole, including the crime of genocide, war crimes, and the crime of aggression, but also, under the head of crimes against humanity, a number of acts that represent serious human rights violations, such as enslavement, deprivation of physical liberty, enforced disappearance, and torture.[45] The existence of a continuum between the core international human rights treaties and international instruments that provide for individual criminal liability confirms that the most serious human rights violations are to be subject to criminal sanctions. Indeed, in the 1980s, M. Cherif Bassiouni had already proposed a process of evolutionary development of human rights through enunciative, declarative, prescriptive, enforcement, and, finally, "criminalization" stages.[46] As Bassiouni recognized, however, not all rights will progress through these stages. As such, the focus of this book is *not* on the well-established criminalization of the most serious human rights violations, such as slavery, genocide, and crimes against humanity. Rather, by examining the range of rights and obligations prescribed by international human rights law across its universal and regional systems as a whole, it aims to understand how international human rights law views criminalization in all its aspects – in particular, where criminal law is to be required, tolerated, or constrained.

43 Craven, M., 2000.

44 See Slavery Convention, Article 6, and Genocide Convention, Article 5.

45 See United Nations, 1998. Rome Statute of the International Criminal Court.

46 Bassiouni, M.C., 1982.

2 An international human rights law approach

In promulgating national criminal law, the state, at least in cases of common or conventional crime with identifiable victims, can be considered to reach into and assume competence over a specific set of disputes between individuals. What is, in fact, often a horizontal matter between legal or natural persons, such as when one individual causes physical harm to another, becomes in law a vertical matter between the state and the individual, as the state assumes competence to adjudicate and to sanction the perpetrator. Not all crime types, however, involve such a transformation. Criminal avoidance of state taxes, for example, may already be considered a vertical dispute between the individual and the state. Other crime types may fall somewhere in-between. Whilst a criminal offence of dangerous driving, for instance, often involves specific actual or potential victims, it could also be committed in the complete absence of nearby motorists. A criminal charge in this latter case may be considered partly of a horizontal dispute nature (in so far as a non-defined group of persons is placed at tangible risk of harm) and partly of a vertical dispute nature (in so far as society, represented by state government, is endangered in general). From a theoretical jural relations perspective, the vertical exercise of the criminal law by the state over an individual can be characterized under Hohfeld's scheme of fundamental legal concepts as a "power-liability" relationship. In other words, the state has "dominant volitional control," or the legal power, to effect a particular change of jural relations. In the case of criminalization: to forbid, or require, an individual to act in a particular way under threat of criminal sanctions. The individual's "liability" represents his or her susceptibility to the exercise of this power.[1]

In terms of its application to horizontal and vertical disputes, international law is not dissimilar. At the level of its subjects, primarily states, it assumes competence both over horizontal inter-subject, that is, interstate, disputes, and over state conduct that constitutes a vertical breach of international community obligations in general.[2] In determining whether state conduct falls short of such

1 Hohfeld proposed that fundamental juridical relations could be characterized by four sets of relations: right–duty; liberty–no-right; power–liability; and immunity–disability. Hohfeld, W., 1913, 1917.

2 Cassese, A., 2005, pp.270–272.

standards, international law, and particularly international human rights law, is also sometimes required to reach in to the national level, in order to examine actions attributable to state authorities that affect individuals.[3] International human rights law specifically envisages this piercing of the veil of sovereignty, including by purporting to allow individuals, and sometimes groups of individuals, to benefit from certain rights-based protections that it asks states to protect. Breaches of such state obligations are not generally considered to constitute state crimes, although they may entail legal consequences for international wrongful acts of a state.[4]

Where the state action under scrutiny is the promulgation or application of national criminal law, the application of international human rights law thus involves the "superimposition" of one system – that of international law – on that of another – the national criminal law. This process raises many questions, however, concerning the exact interaction between the two legal plains. Does international human rights law impose limits on national criminalization, for instance, by virtue of the fact that the individual has an international law right not to be criminalized for certain conduct? Or is it rather because the state has an obligation not to prohibit particular acts?[5] Alternatively, does international human rights law bestow individual international rights not to be criminally harmed by others? Or even duties not to harm others? And, if so, is it these exact rights and duties that must be enforced by the state through criminal law? The possibilities are diverse and, to some extent, overlapping. Serious engagement with such questions is, however, important. The precise way in which international human rights law is understood affects the way in which questions about its application to criminalization are framed and, in turn, the answers received.

Subjects and violations

An oft-cited feature of international law is that the fundamental or primary subjects of international law are not, traditionally, individuals but states.[6] As characterized by Antonio Cassese, it is the state that possesses full legal capacity in the international sphere, and hence the ability to be vested with rights, powers, and obligations.[7] From the Hohfeldian perspective, international law, and thus international human rights law, contains a mix of right–duty, privilege–no-right, and power–liability correlatives that operate between states, depending upon the nature of terms agreed within bilateral and multilateral treaties, as well as the accepted rules of customary international law. At the national level, states give effect to their international commitments either through automatic standing incorporation of international rules into

3 See, for example, United Nations, Human Rights Committee, 2004a. UN Doc. CCPR/C/21/Rev.1/Add.13, para 10–16.

4 Cassese, A., 2005, p.269 and 241.

5 See, for example, Baker, D.J., 2011.

6 Oppenheim, L., 1905, p.19.

7 Cassese, A., 2005, p.71.

national law (often associated with monist systems) or by legislative incorporation (in dualist systems), whereby international rules become applicable within the state legal system only if and when the relevant parliamentary authorities pass specific implementing legislation.[8] Whilst this is the clear traditional position, Cassese also concedes that, in the 20th century, and increasingly after the Second World War, other poles of interest and activity, including national liberation movements and individuals, have gained a limited international status in some circumstances.[9]

When it comes to the particular position of individuals under international human rights law, it is though neither simple nor straightforward to argue that international human rights law with its heavy employment of the treaty form creates legal rights and obligations for individuals.[10] Indeed, under the traditional view, individuals would *not* acquire independent international legal rights under human rights treaties such as the International Covenant on Civil and Political Rights (ICCPR) or International Covenant on Economic, Social and Cultural Rights (ICESCR) at all. Rather, individuals would be solely dependent upon the recognition of claims by the contracting state through its domestic legal system.[11] Critics of this view, on the other hand, point to international complaints mechanisms associated with a number of forms of international human rights law that may be accessed by individuals, including, not least, the possibility of individual complaint to the European Court of Human Rights (ECtHR) and Inter-American Commission on Human Rights (IACommHR).[12] They also highlight the fact that the language of some instruments appears to feasibly ascribe rights directly to individuals. The ICCPR, the European Convention on Human Rights (ECHR), and the American Convention on Human Rights, for instance, use formulations such as "every human being has ...," "everyone has ...," "everyone shall ...," and "no one shall ...," suggesting some direct attribution of individual rights (and duties) by international law.[13] The traditionalist, though, is able to respond that, by contrast, instruments such as the International Convention on the Elimination of All Forms of Racial Discrimination (ICERD) and Convention against Torture and Other Cruel, Inhuman or Degrading Treatment or Punishment (CAT) do not use the language of individual rights. Rather, they express rights through the concomitant obligations of states parties, using language such as "states parties shall ..." and "each state party shall ...."[14] Neither side wins conclusively through a linguistic argument alone, and it is likely that the difference is more cosmetic than substantive.[15]

8 *Ibid.*, pp.220–221.
9 *Ibid.*, pp.71–72.
10 Addo, M.K., 2010, p.193.
11 United Nations, Human Rights Committee, 2004a. UN Doc. CCPR/C/21/Rev.1/Add.13.
12 Addo, M.K., 2010, pp.193–196.
13 See, for example, ICCPR, Articles 9 and 17, and ECHR Articles 5, 8, 9, 10, and 11.
14 See, for example, ICERD, Articles 2(2), 4, and 6, and CAT Articles 2, 3, 4, 5, and 9 to 16.
15 Orakhelashvili, A., 2001, p.268.

National law interpretations of international law also show divergence. Some lines of authority from the US courts suggest that binding international (in this case, customary) human rights law can confer rights on individuals.[16] By contrast, in the United Kingdom, the courts have consistently held that international law alone cannot directly represent a source of individual rights and obligations enforceable in the national courts.[17] It should be carefully noted at this stage that, whilst closely related, the question of whether the individual enjoys international rights under international law remains strictly separate from the question of remedies and from the modality of implementation of international law at the national level. The existence of one or more states with national legal systems that recognize an individual right derived from international law may be evidence of a piece of international law that directly confers rights on individuals. It does not, however, prove the existence of an international individual legal right, in the sense that the individual may be considered a subject of international law. The modality of implementation sits firmly within the discretion of each state and its own national law. By contrast, the position of individuals under international law is itself a separable point of international law.

Whilst the point may appear academic, it is pivotal to a consistent analysis of the relationship between international human rights law and criminalization as exercised through national law. The most appropriate approach to applying international human rights law to matters of national criminal law is one based on the perspective of state obligations, rather than individual rights. This approach has the result that from the international legal perspective, it makes more sense to speak, *sensu stricto*, of the international human rights law obligations of a state not to prohibit a certain conduct by means of the national criminal law than it does to invoke a putative international right of the individual not to be criminalized for a particular act. Equivalently, international human rights law provisions that require states parties to ensure that specific acts are offences in national criminal law are best characterized as state obligations, rather than as international individual rights to enjoy criminal protection from a specific act.

This said, there are myriad circumstances where the individual is able to practically exercise his or her human rights, in the sense of initiating a valid legal challenge to his or her non-enjoyment of them, either because the state offers a mechanism of national legal recourse or because the individual has access to an international complaints mechanism. As such, the legal contours of the state obligation are driven, not least, by the rights-based claims of individuals, wherever these are successful in reaching national or international tribunals. Such challenges require the national court or international mechanism to assess whether the facts of the particular situation reveal a violation of the human right. In line with the focus on state obligations, the majority of this assessment is carried out, not solely with respect to the impact on the individual victim or others but also with respect to the extent of the obligation of the state. Thus,

16 Kedian, M.K., 1999.
17 Higgins, R., 1992, p.1272.

the well-known approach of the ECtHR begins with the identification of a *prima facie* interference of a right of an individual but quickly introduces the state perspective. The initial complaint concerns the facts such as they apply to individuals – whether the retired businessman of Greek nationality arrested more than 60 times for proselytism or the young Jehovah's Witness prosecuted for evading compulsory military service.[18] However, whether an interference with a right amounts to a violation is determined not only with reference to the specific situation of the applicant but also with respect to the particular actions, or inactions, of the state itself in a wider context. For rights that may be legitimately subject to limitations, this involves ascertaining whether the state exercised its discretion, within a certain margin of appreciation accorded to it, reasonably, carefully, and in good faith, and whether in light of the case as a whole, the reasons adduced by national authorities are relevant and sufficient to justify a restriction that meets a legitimate aim and is proportionate to a pressing social need, upon an acceptable assessment of the relevant facts.[19] The legitimate range of choices of the respondent state in this respect is narrowed or widened, not with reference to the situation of the complainant but, at least in ECtHR jurisprudence, by considering the views of other Council of Europe member states in the form of a common European consensus test. Thus, in the case of the Jehovah's Witness prosecuted for evading compulsory military service, the ECtHR, in determining that such a criminal offence could not correspond to a pressing social need, placed particular weight on the fact that almost all member states which ever had, or still have, compulsory military service had introduced alternatives to service, in order to reconcile the possible conflict between individual conscience and military obligations.[20] In a very real sense, the right of the individual – in particular, the contours of its content and its violability – is described not solely by the effect on the individual himself or herself but by the nature and extent of the corresponding state obligation. An individual may be go hungry, yet there be no violation of the right to food. An individual may be killed, yet there be no violation of the right to life.

As such, whilst there is, in many ways, a strong link between the individual as a rights-holder and the state as a duty-bearer in the correlative Hohfeldian sense of legal relations, at the same time, it is clear that the relationship between the state and individual in international human rights law is more complex.[21] Whereas Hohfeld imagines a perfect reciprocal relationship between rights and duties in a "claim right" sense, as noted by Michael Addo, the effect of permissible limitations on rights contained within international human rights treaties exposes these rights to uncertainties that can inflex rights into privileges and liberties.[22] From

18 *Kokkinakis v. Greece*, ECHR, and *Bayatyan v. Armenia*, ECHR.

19 See, for example, *Mamère v. France*, ECHR, and *Lindon, Otchakovsky-Laurens and July v. France*, ECHR.

20 *Bayatyan v. Armenia*, ECHR, para 123.

21 Hohfeld, W., 1913, 1917.

22 Addo, M.K., 1997, p.11.

a legal relations theory perspective, this means that international human rights law contains elements of a number of different juridical relationships. As a result, at the very least, the right–duty relationship of international human rights law as between individual and state must be understood with reference to asymmetrical factors that affect one of the correlatives by acting on the other. Under international human rights law, for instance, an individual cannot understand the nature of his or her "right" to freedom of expression without reference to all of the circumstances in which the state may curb its duty to respect the right, including having regard to the extent to which other states curb their own duties in equivalent circumstances.

This state of affairs is recognized in conceptual-legal discussions of the nature of rights and obligations at the international level. Arjun Sengupta, then independent expert on the right to development, for example, speaks of rights that become "norms" of behaviour or action of the agents, such as other individuals, the state, or the international community, who can contribute to the fulfilment of those rights.[23] In other words, the right is assessed with reference to the actions of the state as duty holder. Importantly, the state norms of behaviour entail both negative and positive obligations – that is, not only obligations not to interfere in the exercise of rights but also obligations to take the necessary measures to safeguard a right. Violation of international human rights law occurs in the first case from preventing or limiting the exercise of the right through positive action, and in the second case, from inaction or passivity on the part of the state. A common formulation within the United Nations human rights system, in particular as regards economic, social, and cultural rights, that reflects this position is that the state has obligations to respect, protect, and fulfil human rights.[24]

Applying international human rights law to criminalization

When it comes to the question of criminalization, a focus of international human rights law on the obligations of the state entails the principle of respect for the sovereignty of states to do as they choose within their sovereign bounds.[25] This includes in matters of national criminal law. As such, states may, in principle, promulgate any criminal law they so wish, unless such action is incompatible with a specific state obligation under international law. Where this obligation is one of international human rights law, the restriction can be described as a Sengupta norm of behaviour, representing the counterpart to the specific right of the individual listed in the international human rights instrument. The norm may require a state not to criminalize certain conduct, where, for example, criminalization falls outside of the state's legitimate range of action, as defined by the margin of appreciation. The norm may be

23 United Nations, General Assembly, 2000. UN Doc. A/55/306, para 8.
24 International Commission of Jurists, 1997.
25 See United Nations, General Assembly, 1981. UN Doc. A/RES/20/2131. See also *United Kingdom v. Albania*, ICJ, and *Nicaragua v. United States*, ICJ.

ambivalent towards criminalization, such as where both criminalization and non-criminalization are within the margin of appreciation. The norm may even require criminalization, where the use of criminal law to prohibit certain conduct is required by positive obligations under international human rights law. In other words, national criminal laws may be required, tolerated, or constrained by the international human rights law obligations of the state. This dual, or even triple, interaction of human rights with criminal law has been described as the shield and sword function of human rights.[26] As noted by Françoise Tulkens, human rights have both a defensive and an offensive role, a role of both neutralizing and triggering the criminal law.[27]

With respect to a particular criminalization question, the compatibility of the existence, or absence, of a particular criminal law with international human rights law must therefore be assessed on a right-by-right basis, taking into account the contours and nature of the (positive and negative) state obligations under each separate human right contained in applicable international law. In effect, the international human rights tribunal must start from a neutral position on the criminalization question, until it can be demonstrated that a particular right requires or prohibits criminalization.[28] In other words, for each possible act – be it rape, assisting suicide, blasphemy, or defamation – the criminalization, or lack of criminalization, must be tested separately against state obligations under relevant rights that may be engaged – non-exhaustively, for instance, the right to life, the right not to be subjected to torture or to inhuman or degrading treatment or punishment, the right to liberty and security, the right to respect for private and family life, and rights to freedom of thought, conscience, religion, and expression. As a result, criminal laws may thus at the same time infringe certain rights but not others.[29] This is not inconsistent. It is, rather, a logical result of the discrete structure of international human rights law, comprising, as it does, collections of individual rights and correlative state obligations, largely in treaty form.

Theoretically, a particular criminalization issue could be assessed *in abstracto* against a range of rights and corresponding state obligations. In practice, however, this process occurs when the particular rights-based claim of an individual, or group of individuals, is successful in reaching a national or international tribunal. Thus, the human right compatibility assessment is most usually conducted *in concreto*, with reference to not only the particular national criminal law, or absence of law, but also the facts to which the law, or its absence, is applied. In some cases, an applicant may directly or indirectly allege that the national criminal law itself is incompatible with international law.[30] In other cases, the challenge may relate

26 Tulkens, F., 2011, p.577. Tulkens notes that this phrase is commonly attributed to Christine Van den Wyngaert.

27 *Ibid.*, p.579.

28 See United Nations, Commission on Narcotic Drugs and Commission on Crime Prevention and Criminal Justice, 2010. UN Doc. E/CN.7/2010/CRP.6 – E/CN.15/2010/CRP.1, para 14.

29 *Ibid.*, para 19.

30 See, for example, *S.A.S. v. France*, ECHR; *Friend, the Countryside Alliance and Others v. United Kingdom*, ECHR; and *Norris v. Ireland*, ECHR.

solely or primarily to the way in which the law has been applied.[31] In either case, international human rights courts and tribunals tend to prefer to conduct their analysis within the confines of the facts at hand. The ECtHR, for example, has recalled on a number of occasions that its jurisdiction is confined to examining the application of a national law in a specific case and that it cannot consider in the abstract the compatibility of such law with the Convention.[32] The United Nations Human Rights Committee has also noted that it is not called upon to criticize in the abstract laws enacted by states parties.[33]

The *in concreto* approach creates a particularly diverse international human rights jurisprudence on criminalization. A challenge to a specific criminal conviction, or the lack of one, often necessitates some consideration of the underlying criminal law in human rights terms. Yet human rights tribunals do not always speak directly to the human rights compatibility of the law itself. In some cases, it can be assumed that the criminal law is legitimate with respect to international human rights law, insofar as the tribunal does not find an impugned conviction to violate any right.[34] In other cases, the finding of a violation may be with reference only to the particular facts of the impugned conviction, and not to the underlying criminal law itself – with the result that nothing can be said about the human rights compatibility of the criminalization *per se.* This said, there are instances where international human rights tribunals have conducted analysis verging on the abstract consideration of the criminal law in isolation. In the European Court case of *A, B and C v. Ireland*, for example, the Court was called upon to consider an Article 8 challenge brought by three women who had travelled abroad for an abortion due to prohibitions on abortion for health and well-being reasons in Ireland. Whilst the Court recounted the specific circumstances of each of the three women, it used the opportunity to consider more broadly the proportionality of the abortion prohibitions with respect to the right to private life and rights invoked on behalf of the unborn.[35]

Even further in the direction of *in abstracto* analysis, in both *Modinos v. Cyprus* and *Norris v. Ireland*, the European Court was asked to consider the compatibility of criminal laws on homosexual relations in private between consenting male adults with the Convention, in the absence of any enforcement action against the complainants and no real prospect of the law actually being applied. The Court held, in *Norris*, that the Convention entitles individuals to contend that a law violates their rights by itself, in the absence of an individual measure of implementation, if they "run the risk" of being directly affected by it. The Court went on to conclude that

31 See, for example, *Osman v. United Kingdom*, ECHR; *Beganović v Croatia*, ECHR; and *M. C. v. Bulgaria*, ECHR.

32 See *Acmanne and others v. Belgium*, ECHR. See also *Salabiaku v. France*, ECHR, and *Wingrove v. United Kingdom*, ECHR.

33 United Nations, Human Rights Committee, 1996. UN Doc. CCPR/C/58/D/550/1993, para 9.3.

34 See, for example, *Müller and others v. Switzerland*, ECHR; *Perrin v. United Kingdom*, ECHR; and *Gough v. United Kingdom*, ECHR.

35 *A, B and C v. Ireland*, ECHR, para 222–242.

a law which remains on the statute book, even though it is not enforced in a particular class of cases for a considerable time, may be applied again in such cases at any time, if, for example, there is a change of policy.[36] Similarly, in *Modinos*, the Court, noting that there was no guarantee that action will not be taken to enforce the law, considered that the existence of the prohibition continuously and directly affected the applicant's private life.[37] Whilst the logic of the Court is clear in such cases, at the same time, the notion of a victim at risk of being directly affected by a law represents a significant exception to the general principle against *in abstracto* consideration of laws. In principle, therefore, at least wherever a criminal law applies to an identifiable group of persons, it may be possible for the Court to engage in *in abstracto* consideration of the law, absence a specific set of individual facts concerning its application. Overall, in applying an international law approach to criminalization, the position of international human rights law must be constructed from specific treaty provisions and the interpretive case law of international human rights courts and tribunals. Such case law is driven primarily by the facts at hand, but sometimes leads courts and tribunals to engage in broader and more theoretical discussion.

A note on human rights and human duties

Its name notwithstanding, individual duties are not unknown to international human rights law. With the notion of human duties gaining little traction in recent years, there is a tendency to overlook the importance placed on duties within the drafting of contemporary international human rights law treaties. The earliest modern instrument, the American Declaration of the Rights and Duties of Man of 1948, for instance, contains a whole chapter on duties. It specifies duties such as the duty of every person to aid, support, educate, and protect his minor children (Article 30); the duty of every person to acquire at least an elementary education (Article 31); the duty of every person to vote in the popular elections of the country of which he is a national (Article 32); the duty of every able-bodied person to render whatever civil and military service his country may require for its defence and preservation (Article 34); and the duty of every person to pay the taxes established by law for the support of public services (Article 36).

Similarly, in reviewing the first drafts of what was to become the Universal Declaration of Human Rights (UDHR), it is clear that the nascent Human Rights Commission gave serious consideration to the relationship between individual rights and duties. Article 1, for example, of the draft outline of an International Bill of Rights presented by the United Nations Division for Human Rights in June 1947 referred to a duty of loyalty to the state and to the international society, and called upon everyone to accept their just share of responsibility for the performance of social duties and such common sacrifices as may contribute to the common good.[38] The

36 *Norris v. Ireland*, ECHR, paras 31–33.
37 *Modinos v. Cyprus*, ECHR, para 24.
38 United Nations, Economic and Social Council, 1947b. UN Doc. E/CN.4/AC.1/3. Article 1.

same draft also included a duty to perform socially useful work and a duty towards society to present information and news in a fair and impartial manner.[39] Approving of the general sentiment of the notion of duties, members of the Human Rights Commission noted that it was a question of establishing the rights of the human being and at the same time demanding his acceptance of the corresponding obligations.[40] Other delegations observed that it was of no use seeking to define personal freedom entirely detached from the obligation of those individuals either to the state or to voluntary organizations.[41] The UDHR as finally promulgated created two duties for individuals and one duty for society: the duty to act towards one another in a spirit of brotherhood (Article 1); (unspecified) duties of the individual to the community (Article 29); and the duty of society to protect the family (Article 16). By the time the binding ICCPR and ICESCR were adopted by the General Assembly in December 1966, however, only a weak reference to specific duties remained in the fifth preambular paragraph common to both covenants.[42]

Theoretically, individual duties derived from international human rights law, such as duties to the community, could be one approach via which international human rights law may possibly intersect with national criminal law. Such a duty may require, for instance, the state to enact criminal laws for enforcement of the individual obligation. Under the American Declaration, for example, it is not perhaps outside of the bounds of reasonable analysis to imagine that a state may argue a justified criminalization of failure to vote, to render military service, or to pay taxes, with reference to the duties contained in Articles 32, 34, and 36 of the American Declaration.

Whilst the drafters of the UDHR, and of a limited number of other instruments such as the American Declaration, grappled seriously with the issue of human duties, the prevailing trend in international human rights law since has seen a waxing and waning of interest in the issue. The first serious study of Article 29 of the UDHR was conducted in 1980 by Erica-Irene Daes, Special Rapporteur of the (then) United Nations Sub-Commission on Prevention of Discrimination and Protection of Minorities.[43] Twenty years later, the Sub-Commission again appointed one of its members, Miguel Alfonso Martínez, to undertake a study on the issue of human rights and human responsibilities.[44] In 2003, Martínez presented a pre-draft declaration on human social responsibilities to the Commission on Human Rights.[45] Member state reactions to the

39 *Ibid.*, Articles 6, 18, and 37.
40 United Nations, Economic and Social Council, 1947c. UN Doc. E/CN.4/AC.1/3/Add.1, p.5.
41 *Ibid.*, p.6.
42 ICCPR and ICESCR, common preambular para 5: "Realizing that the individual, having duties to other individuals and to the community to which he belongs, is under a responsibility to strive for the promotion and observance of the rights recognized in the present Covenant."
43 Daes, E-I., 1990.
44 United Nations, Sub-Commission on the Promotion and Protection of Human Rights, 2000. UN Doc. E/CN.4/2001/2.
45 United Nations, Commission on Human Rights, 2003. UN Doc. E/CN.4/2003/105.

pre-draft declaration were divided. On the one hand, governments proposed that the pre-draft declaration could be seen as an extension and development of the fundamental international legal instruments in the field of human rights. On the other hand, many countries expressed the view that the pre-draft declaration was contrary to the principles on which the international human rights system is built. In particular, countries objected to the idea that a state could determine which, if any, rights an individual can enjoy in return for the exercise of responsibilities, on the basis that to do so would be fundamentally inconsistent with the basic concepts of human rights, according to which human rights are universal and inalienable.[46] Following this round of comments by states, a proposal of the United Nations Commission on Human Rights to request Mr Martínez to prepare a new initial version of the pre-draft declaration was rejected by the Economic and Social Council at its 38th meeting in July 2005, effectively putting an end to the initiative.[47]

The question of specific individual duties may no longer be one of particular relevance to international human rights bodies, courts, and tribunals. Nonetheless, as a general corollary of rights, duties can still be seen to play some role in an international human rights law approach to criminalization. In the context of limitations on rights, for example, the exercise of rights such as the right to freedom of expression, according to the ICCPR, carries with it special duties and responsibilities.[48] This (arguably, individual) duty is linked to the permissibility of state restrictions on the right, not only for the protection of matters such as national security, public order, and public health but also for respect of the rights or reputations of others.[49] As noted by Erica-Irene Daes, one key duty of the individual under international human rights law is thus to exercise ones' rights to the extent that they do not infringe on the rights and freedoms of others.[50] This principle can be traced back to some of the founding influences on contemporary international human rights law. The French Declaration of the Rights of Man of 1789, for example, stated that

> liberty consists in the freedom to do everything which injuries no one else: hence the exercise of the natural rights of each man has no limits *except those* which assure to the other members of the society the *enjoyment of the same rights*. These limits can only be determined by law.[51]

As noted by the Human Rights Council Advisory Committee, individuals may be regarded as having a responsibility not to cause human rights violations against other individuals.[52] To some extent, of course, the problem is one of

46 United Nations, Commission on Human Rights, 2005a. UN Doc. E/CN.4/2005/99, paras 3 and 26.
47 United Nations, General Assembly, 2005. UN Doc. A/60/3/Rev.1, p.83.
48 ICCPR, Article 19(3).
49 ICCPR, Article 19(3)(a) and (b).
50 Daes, E-I., 1990, p.10.
51 French National Constituent Assembly, 1789, Article 4.
52 United Nations, General Assembly, 2012. UN Doc. A/HRC/22/71, para 30.

semantics – whether one speaks of the duty of an individual not to exercise his or her rights such that they infringe the rights of others or the right of the other not to have his or her own rights infringed.

Whichever way the point is expressed, the perspective of exercising rights in a manner that does not infringe on the rights of others represents an important factor taken into consideration by international human rights bodies in reaching decisions on the acceptability of criminalization. Where the criminal law restricts, for example, the right to freedom of expression of one individual, in order to protect the right to private life of another, the human rights acceptability of that criminal law requires consideration of the extent to which the law constrains the exercise of the right, having regard to the nature and scope of both rights. For the human rights court or tribunal, this balance will involve a range of factors, including the seriousness of the infringement of the right of the other individual. If the court or tribunal finds the criminal law to be acceptable from a human rights perspective, in a very real sense, this aligns with enforcement of a duty to exercise the right to freedom of expression in a restrained and considerate manner.

Summary

International human rights law, and its application to criminalization, is considered as best viewed from the perspective of state obligations, in line with the position of states as the primary subjects of international law. Whilst individual claims before international human rights courts and tribunals represent the starting point for (usually) *in concreto* consideration of human rights violations, the subsequent analysis is often state-centric and driven by the contours of state obligations. Especially in the European human rights system, state obligations are delineated also with reference to the practice of other states. As complaints to human rights tribunals often concern the application of criminal law, human rights jurisprudence on criminalization is often one step removed from direct consideration of the criminal law *per se*, involving consideration of both a particular law and its application to a set of facts. Human rights jurisprudence does not therefore enjoy the liberty of *in abstracto* reasoning to the same extent as employed by criminal law theorists. Rather, the overall position of international human rights law on matters of criminalization must be constructed from the human rights compatibility of specific criminalization contexts inherent in the decisions of international courts and tribunals. Such decisions show that human rights have a role in both neutralizing and triggering the criminal law. The framework of international human rights law, as an area of international law in general, presents certain constraints in the manner in which jurisprudence is generated and in the perspective from which human rights questions are best answered. Once these points have been recognized and well defined, the framework shows potential for effective criminalization analysis alongside that of traditional criminalization theory.

3 Rights in criminal theory

Criminal law theory has enjoyed a period of intellectual vitality over the last few decades. Nonetheless, when it comes to attempts to theorize the special part of the criminal law, a number of contending theories still abound, with comparatively little agreement as to the most effective approach. Contemporary theories do not differ appreciably from those debated almost 150 years ago: chiefly, constrained utilitarianism represented by the harm principle, and legal moralism.[1] Within criminalization literature, comparatively few legal theorists have invoked rights as a component of a developed criminal theory. Certainly none have done so using the human rights of international human rights law. This is despite the fact that the idea that in committing a crime the offender does not just violate the law but potentially also the rights of the individual victim is centuries old. In German legal thought, for example, Feuerbach pointed out in 1801 that many crimes involved violations of individual rights.[2]

One critical issue in this respect is the particular notion of rights that is understood and applied by legal theorists. Perhaps the most common approach is to employ a conception of rights grounded in Kantian moral theory. Such conceptions use a theory of claim rights, whereby rights are viewed as horizontal claims that one individual has against another or against society in general. David Richards, writing in the 1970s and 1980s, for example, grounds much of his work on criminal theory within the framework of the neo-Kantian moral theories of John Rawls and Alan Gewirth.[3] In doing so, Richards invokes a form of morality based on the deontological concept that what is morally right cannot be defined in terms of whether something maximizes goodness in the world, but rather in terms of whether it expresses respect, on fair terms to all, for a person's capacity for autonomy.[4] For Richards, human rights are thus forms of coercive claim justified by the principle of autonomy. Under this approach, Richards holds that the minimum boundary conditions for criminalization must

1 Lacey, N., 2009, p.937.
2 For a general review of German legal theory in English language, see Dubber, M.D., 2005.
3 Rawls, J., 1971; Gewirth, A., 1978.
4 Richards, D.A.J., 1981b, p.251.

be directed by a set of general moral principles of obligation, duty, and correlative "human rights."[5]

A key role of Richards' human rights is to place particular constraints on the imposition of criminal penalties in line with the imperatives of respect for autonomy and the treatment of all persons as equals. Richards applies this particular conception of rights to questions such as the (de)criminalization of prostitution and of certain forms of drug use.[6] The work of David Richards represents, at least in English language literature, one of the first detailed attempts at the introduction of a rights-based discourse into general criminalization theory. Nonetheless, the end results of Richard's reasoning often have something of an *ex post facto* sense about them. In respect of the question of (de)criminalization of drug use, for example, Richards argues that higher-order interests in freedom and rationality identify respect for choices to use drugs as an aspect of personal dignity worthy of protection under the constitutional right to privacy.[7] Richards reaches this conclusion after consideration of traditional arguments for drug use based on harm to self and to others, paternalism, and societal moralism. In essence, Richards effectively draws a connection between well-established criminal theory arguments and a rights-based vision of autonomy, mutual concern, respect, and the right to create one's own life on terms fair to all.

Joel Feinberg, writing a few years after Richards, links his notion of rights to the concept of harm, originally conceived by Mill, and which plays a central role in many criminalization theories.[8] In Feinberg's 1984 work *Harm to Others*, he holds that the subset of harms which should be considered for criminalization can be defined in a sequential manner: as those that (i) represent a setback of interests that; (ii) wrong the victim, in; (iii) a morally indefensible manner.[9] In other words, unlike Mill, Feinberg does not believe that harm alone is sufficient for criminalization. Rather only those harms that are wrong in a morally indefensible manner should attract criminal sanctions. The next step in Feinberg's argument is to define wrongfulness as a setback of interests that is at the same time a violation of the victim's *rights*. In order to define a point of reference that is external to the criminal law, Feinberg clarifies that he is, in this context, referring to moral rights rather than legal rights – that is, rights that are independent of and antecedent to law, a conception strongly reminiscent of the doctrine of natural rights.[10]

In other words, for Feinberg, it is always a good reason in support of criminalization that the restriction would probably be effective in preventing harm to a person that, at the same time, wrongs him or her by violating his or her rights. As Feinberg acknowledges, this raises the question as to whether the definition presupposes the

5 Richards, D.A.J., 1979b, p.1414.
6 Richards, D.A.J., 1979a; Richards, D.J., 1981a.
7 Richards, D.A.J., 1981a, pp.676–677.
8 Mill, J.S., 1974 (originally published 1859), and Feinberg, J., 1984, 1985, 1986, 1988. Hereinafter: "Feinberg, *Harm to Others*;" "Feinberg, *Offense to Others*;" "Feinberg, *Harm to Self*;" and "Feinberg, *Harmless Wrongdoing*."
9 Feinberg, *Harm to Others*. p.106.
10 *Ibid.*, p.111.

existence of a complete moral system. If what is criminal is to be defined in part with reference to what is a violation of natural or moral rights, then what is moral must first be defined. Feinberg argues that this challenge can be overcome by an appeal to basic *welfare* interests as the basis for the rights – which if violated in the context of a setback of interests constitute wrongful harm and therefore warrant criminalization. Feinberg does not go to great lengths to define such welfare rights nor to establish thresholds of violation. Holding that nothing as elaborate as a complete moral system is required, Feinberg refers simply to welfare rights as the moral rights to life, minimal health, economic sufficiency, political liberty, and so on. In Feinberg's scheme, wrongful harm thus occurs by invading one of the welfare interests whose maintenance at a minimal level is a necessary condition for the advancement of any other interests at all.[11]

More recent use of rights in criminalization theory, such as proposed by Tatjana Hörnle, similarly relies on a theory of claim rights, defined by what Hörnle describes as "important spheres of liberty."[12] Whilst Hörnle explicitly recognizes the existence of positive constitutional rights, she holds, in the same vein as Feinberg, that criminalization theory cannot be anchored in a simple, genuinely positivistic way and seeks rather to identify moral rights that can serve as the entrance decision of criminalization theory, being the fundamental question for which protective purpose criminal prohibitions may be used. Whereas Hörnle, Feinberg, and Richards follow the, quite defensible, route of seeking to identify an autonomous concept of rights that can be employed in criminalization theory, at the same time, this approach risks missing out on potential gains from the field of international human rights law – not only from its positivist jurisprudence but also from its underlying legal theory and philosophy. Hörnle recognizes, for example, the human rights catalogue in a constitution as a relevant point of reference but is largely persuaded by the criticism that national positive law is too limited and that criminalization theory needs to work with the concept of rights of others in a wider sense. In later chapters, this book argues that international human rights law offers exactly that opportunity. The construction of a theory of rights for the purposes of criminalization theory need not rely on *de novo* identification of which rights should be recognized and which collective interests are of high importance but, rather, can be informed by, and draw from, the concepts and principles of international human rights law.

Use of rights in criminal theory – Feinberg's welfare interest rights

Amongst the legal theorists who employ conceptions of rights, Joel Feinberg in his four-part work, *The Moral Limits of the Criminal Law*, represents the most developed integration of rights into criminal theory. Being committed to a liberal approach, Feinberg starts from the idea of "liberty-

11 *Ibid.*, p.112.
12 Hörnle T., 2014, p.184.

limiting principles" as a requirement for criminalization, where liberty is understood as the absence of legal coercion. To this end, Feinberg proposes a number of liberty-limiting (or coercion-legitimizing) principles, which he defines as a consideration that is always a morally relevant reason in support of penal legislation. Feinberg acknowledges the existence of a number of potential liberty-limiting principles, including harm, offense, paternalism, moralism, benefit, and perfectionism. His starting point, expressed in a commitment to a liberal position on the moral limits of the criminal law, is that only the harm and offense principles, duly clarified and qualified, between them exhaust the class of good reasons for criminal prohibitions. This is in contrast to what Feinberg describes as the extreme liberal position that only the harm principle provides a good reason in support of criminal prohibition. In this context, Feinberg describes the harm and offense principles as follows:

> *The Harm Principle:* It is always a good reason in support of penal legislation that it would probably be effective in preventing (eliminating, reducing) harm to persons other than the actor (the one prohibited from acting) *and* there is probably no other means that is equally effective at no greater cost to other values.
> *The Offense Principle:* It is always a good reason in support of a proposed criminal prohibition that it is probably necessary to prevent serious offense to persons other the actor and would probably be an effective means to that end if enacted.[13]

For Feinberg, a liberty-limiting principle is not, however, a sufficient condition for criminalization, because in any given case its purportedly relevant reason may not weigh heavily enough on the scales to outbalance the standing presumption in favour of liberty. In the case of Feinberg's liberty-limiting harm principle, for example, considerations that must also be weighed on the scales include the magnitude of the harm, the probability of harm, the relative importance of the harm, and the extent to which a criminal prohibition limits the options open to an individual. Feinberg refers to these considerations (and others) as "mediating maxims" for application of the liberty-limiting principles. As Feinberg's work progresses, through *Harm to Others, Offense to Others, Harm to Self,* and *Harmless Wrongdoing*, his view evolves and Feinberg concludes his enquiry with an endorsement of a somewhat broader "cautious liberalism." Feinberg's cautious liberalism holds that only the harm and offense principles state reasons that are always good, and frequently decisive, for criminalization. It concedes, however, that legal moralism states reasons that are sometimes (but rarely) good for criminalization.[14] Feinberg's general notion of liberty-limiting principles largely survives in contemporary criminalization literature. Commentators such as Simester and von Hirsch, for

13 Feinberg, *Harm to Others*, pp.26–28. Reproduced with permission of the Licensor through PLSclear.
14 Feinberg, *Harmless Wrongdoing*, p.324.

example, broadly start from the position that criminal law limitations on freedom of action require principled justification.[15] There is significant diversity, however, in the principles that legal theorists are prepared to accept. Feinberg's offense principle, for instance, is often divisive, with some theorists supporting the need for a separate offense principle of one form or another and others arguing that such a principle is unnecessary or undesirable.[16] A distinction is also often made between the legal moralists' single-element wrongfulness account, and dual-element accounts, based on combinations of harm and wrongfulness.[17] In this regard, continued recognition of the role of both harm *and* wrongfulness in criminalization theory is an important validation of the significance of Feinberg's approach.

The centrepiece of Feinberg's criminalization scheme is, without doubt, his harm principle: that the subset of harms which should be considered for criminalization are those that represent a setback of interests that wrong the victim in a morally indefensible manner. With respect to the interests that may be set back, Feinberg observes that "interests" consist of all those things in which one has a stake. He distinguishes between passing wants (such as to go to a movie), which do not qualify as interests, and higher level wants, which are to be considered as interests. These interests include instrumental wants (such as to get exercise), welfare interests (such as in emotional stability), and focal aims (such as writing a book).[18] To set back such an interest is, according to Feinberg, to reverse its course or to put it in a worse condition than it was formerly in. In Feinberg's scheme, in order to support the possible use of criminal sanctions for a particular conduct, the conduct must itself *produce* the setback of interests. As Kai Ambos highlights, Feinberg's harm principle is therefore traditionally thought of as a consequentialist principle focusing on the effects of the conduct to be prohibited.[19] Whilst Feinberg acknowledges a range of interests that can be, or risk being, set back by actions or omissions, he limits his harm principle to one particular type of interest – that of welfare interests. This has the effect of excluding instrumental wants and focal aims from the harm principle. He does so with a view to requiring that conduct which may be criminalized not only produce harm but also be *wrongful* in the sense of morally indefensible. Feinberg holds that an element that is always present when one person wrongs another is the violated *right* of the victim. Accordingly, Feinberg argues that one person, A, can be said to wrong another, B, when B's set-back interest is one that he has a right to have respected.[20] His next step is to identify welfare interests as the grounds for valid rights claims. In other words, harm, for the

15 Simester, A.P., and von Hirsch, A., 2011, p.19.

16 See, for example, Simester, A.P., and von Hirsch, A., 2002; Simester, A.P., and von Hirsch, A., 2011, pp.118–122; Alexander, L., 1994.

17 See, for example, Duff, R.A., 2007.

18 Feinberg, *Harm to Others*, p.59.

19 Ambos, K., 2015, p.314.

20 Feinberg, *Harm to Others*, p.107.

purposes of Feinberg's harm principle, is a setback of interests that wrongs the victim by violating his or her welfare rights. In his final work, *Harmless Wrongdoing*, Feinberg describes this as $harm_1$: "A adversely affects B's interest," and $harm_2$: "A adversely affects B's interest and in so doing wrongs B (violates B's right)."[21] Only $harm_2$ is harm for the purposes of Feinberg's harm principle.

As regards the nature of welfare interest rights, Feinberg focuses on welfare interests whose maintenance at a minimum level is a necessary condition for the advancement of any other interests at all as the basis of rights claims. He describes these welfare interests as interests in the necessary means to his more ultimate goals, whatever the latter may be.[22] Feinberg's shortlist of welfare interest rights consists of a moral right to life, minimal health, economic sufficiency, political liberty, and so on. His longer explanation covers interests in the continuance for a foreseeable interval of one's life, and the interests in one's own physical health and vigour, the integrity and normal functioning of one's body, the absence of absorbing pain and suffering or grotesque disfigurement, minimal intellectual acuity, emotional stability, the absence of groundless anxieties and resentments, the capacity to engage normally in social intercourse and to enjoy and maintain friendships, at least minimal income and financial security, a tolerable social and physical environment, and a certain amount of freedom from interference and coercion. Feinberg also appears to later add an interest in privacy to this list, which he defines as the absence of physical intrusions upon solitude and the absence of unpermitted disclosure of intimacies.[23]

There is much in Feinberg's broad concept of welfare rights that is reminiscent of neo-Kantian approaches, such as those developed by Gewirth and Rawls. A central contention in Gewirthian moral theory, for example, is that agents need both freedom and well-being, as it would be impossible to act towards those agent's purposes without these necessary conditions of agency.[24] Gewirth argues that, on pain of self-contradiction, each agent must accord to each other the same generic rights to freedom and well-being that he necessarily claims for himself.[25] Gewirthian theory is itself sometimes invoked as a basis for harm analysis. Alex Stevens suggests, for instance, that harms can be seen as acts and conditions that infringe on rights to the freedom and well-being that we all need as agents – essentially reproducing Feinberg's scheme in terms of Gewirthian generic rights.[26] In the same way as Feinberg's welfare interests are required as the necessary condition for the advancement of any other interests at all, and Gewirthian generic rights are required for purposes, so Rawls, in the context of justice, places the emphasis on the necessary means or primary goods required to enable the exercise of moral powers and the pursuit of final ends.[27] Rawls

21 Feinberg, *Harmless Wrongdoing*, p.xxviii. Reproduced with permission of the Licensor through PLSclear.
22 Feinberg, *Harm to Others*, p.37 and 111.
23 *Ibid.*, p.61 and 204.
24 Gewirth, A., 1996.
25 Gewirth, A., 1982.
26 Stevens, A., 2001.
27 Rawls, J., 1971.

summarizes these primary goods as the basic liberties (freedom of thought and liberty of conscience), freedom of movement and free choice of occupation, powers and prerogatives of offices and positions of responsibility, income and wealth, and the social bases of self-respect.[28] In addition to drawing from Gewirth's rights to freedom and well-being, Feinberg's welfare interest rights also reflect some elements of Rawlsian goods, most notably, economic sufficiency.[29]

Within the neo-Kantian line of reasoning, equivalently to Gewirth, Feinberg is also committed to the principle that his welfare rights cannot be violated where a person consents to an infringement. Feinberg holds clearly that no one can rightly intervene to prevent a responsible adult from voluntarily doing something that will harm only himself, for such a harm is not a "wrong," and also that one person cannot properly be prevented from doing something that will harm another when the latter has voluntarily assumed the risk of harm himself through his free and informed consent.[30] Feinberg's harm principle accordingly rejects any form of hard paternalism as a good reason for criminalization.

Challenges with welfare interest rights

Whilst Feinberg's welfare interest rights show a degree of internal consistency and sit within a defensible legal philosophical heritage, they also suffer from some significant challenges. The first of these is that welfare interest rights are not violated until they are brought below a tolerable minimum level.[31] As a result, they do not well account, for example, for the fact that the criminal law often protects minimal invasions of interests. Welfare interest rights cannot provide a good reason, for instance, for the criminalization of assault where there is no injury, or injury that is transient or trifling.[32] In reality, as Feinberg himself recognizes, "the law of burglary protects not only the pauper who would be ruined by the theft of his welfare check, but also the millionaire for whom a thousand-dollar bill has less utility than a penny has for a child."[33] In the latter case, almost all legal systems recognize this as a crime, despite the fact that the act may not bring a Feinberg welfare interest right below its tolerably minimum level. Secondly, welfare interest rights can be too narrow a basis for criminalization, insofar as they protect only those interests considered as the necessary or vital means to more ultimate goals.

Simester and von Hirsch recognize these shortcomings and build on Feinberg's concept of welfare interests in the context of the harm principle to

28 Rawls, J., 1980, p.526.

29 Feinberg, *Harm to Others*, p.111.

30 *Ibid.*, p.115.

31 *Ibid.*, p.206.

32 Under English law, any injury that is more than "transient or trifling" can be classified as actual bodily harm. The statutory crime of common assault includes where there is no injury or injuries which are not serious occur. See Crown Prosecution Service, Undated.

33 Feinberg, *Harm to Others*, p.63. Reproduced with permission of the Licensor through PLSclear.

suggest that the kind of adverse effect that should count as harm should rather be the impairment of some "resource."[34] Von Hirsch invokes both Rawls and Amartya Sen to argue that a resource may be characterized as constituting an asset or capability.[35] Von Hirsch has in mind assets in the sense of the Rawlsian conception of goods and capabilities from Sen's notion of a person's capacities to exercise skills or to undertake specified courses of conduct. Von Hirsch claims that the concept of resources extends beyond Feinberg's welfare interests, in the sense that it is not only basic assets or capabilities that count but also more particular assets, such as miscellaneous personal possessions, that contribute importantly to the quality of a person's life. It is of course the case that, unlike Feinberg, Simester and von Hirsch view the impairment of resources primarily at the level of harm, rather than wrongfulness (in the form of a violation of Feinberg's welfare interest rights). Nonetheless, the end result, at least for immediate harms, is largely equivalent. Von Hirsch, for example, further equates the intrusion on the resources of a person that occurs in immediate harm also with wrongfulness, in the same way as Feinberg. He states that, in the case of immediate harms, the attribution of wrongfulness is derived from the infringement of a "normative claim" to the resource.[36]

To some extent, Feinberg in fact extends his concept of rights in the direction of Simester and von Hirsch's resources. In addition to linking wrongfulness with welfare interest rights, Feinberg allows that if a given ulterior interest, or focal aim, is such that it can be invaded directly, and another person does so indefensibly, then that would also constitute a wrong.[37] In particular, Feinberg includes ulterior goals that simply extend elements of welfare beyond minimal levels within the class of interests that can ground rights claims for the purposes of wrongful harm. This allows him to apply an exception to core welfare interest rights and to find a good reason for criminalization of all theft (and not just theft that affects welfare rights). His argument is part pragmatic, in that there would be enormous practical difficulties in attempting to apportion degrees of protection according to the actual seriousness of harm. It is also theoretical, insofar as Feinberg asserts that each individual has a general security of property and liberty interest in deciding how accumulated funds are to be spent that is deserving of protection.[38]

A similar extension is also required in the second part of Feinberg's work, *Offense to Others*. Within his overall criminalization scheme, Feinberg distinguishes offense from harm, in that acts which may shock sensibility, alarm, disgust, frustrate, or cause unpleasant sensations cannot be said to set back interests in the sense of the harm principle. As such, offended states of mind, even intense ones, are not in themselves harms. Feinberg therefore requires a separate principle to provide a good reason for criminalization of acts such as

34 Simester, A.P., and von Hirsch, A., 2011, p.36.
35 Von Hirsch, A., 2014. p.249.
36 *Ibid.*, p.252.
37 Feinberg, *Harm to Others*, p.112.
38 *Ibid.*, p.63.

insult or obscenity. As set out above, Feinberg's second liberty-limiting principle is thus that it is always a good reason in support of a proposed criminal prohibition that it is probably necessary to prevent serious offense.

In the same way as for harm, Feinberg requires that only acts causing "wrongful" offense (as opposed to all offense) can qualify for criminalization. Feinberg again links wrongfulness in the context of offense to a violation of rights, explaining that the offense-causing action must be "a wrong" to the offended party, in short, a violation of his rights.[39] Feinberg does not, however, explicitly rely on a welfare-based argument in this regard. Rather, his invocation of rights in *Offense to Others* appears to be in the sense of a generic right of others to be free of offended states. This right is not characterized as a welfare interest right, as Feinberg is not convinced that it is plausible to attribute to most people an independent, non-instrumental interest in being unoffended. Instead, the right may be most accurately characterized as another example of an ulterior interest, or focal aim, that can be invaded directly and hence ground a finding of wrongfulness. In practice, this has the effect in Feinberg's offense principle of creating a requirement for an individual victim with a personal grievance, who can complain that he or she witnessed an offense and suffered a violation of his or her rights as a result.

Simester and von Hirsch view Feinberg's construction of wrongful offense as insufficient. They argue that the violation of an interest to be free of unoffended states is not enough, by itself, to also establish the wrong. In their book *Crimes, Harms, and Wrongs*, Simester and von Hirsch hold rather that offense is a wrong when the behaviour violates a victim's "right" to be treated with due consideration and respect.[40] They further propose that harm is also required in order to justify the criminalization of offense. They maintain, nonetheless, that the harm and offense principles are separate, insofar as in the harm principle, harm, its gravity and likelihood, is the driving force behind the decision to criminalize. Conversely, in the offense principle it is the conduct's offensiveness that provides the initial impetus towards criminalization, which is why one might take seriously the possibility of criminalizing mere offence, whilst simultaneously rejecting the possibility of criminalizing behaviour that is purely a moral wrong.[41] The distinction here between mere offence and mere immorality derives, importantly, from the rights-based notion of the conduct being other-affecting. That is, the wrongdoing in offensive conduct generates a tension between the victim's right to be treated with respect and the perpetrator's interest in being able to express herself freely.

This last point hints at a further challenge faced by the rights-based conception of wrongfulness that Feinberg employs: the difficulty in its application to acts where no individual victim can be clearly said to have his or her welfare rights violated. As Hamish Stewart argues, this sometimes has the result in

39 Feinberg, *Offense to Others*, p.68.
40 Simester, A.P., and von Hirsch, A., 2011, p.117.
41 *Ibid.*, p.119.

Harm to Others that the wrongfulness element of Feinbergian harm tends to drop out, or be taken for granted, with the idea of rights tending either to become simply instrumental to the prevention of setbacks of interests or to be insufficiently analysed.[42] In many senses, this quite valid criticism arises as a result of the way in which Feinberg conceives of rights within his notion of welfare interest rights. In *Harm to Others*, it is clear that Feinberg's rights are of the form where "A has a right" can be understood as "A can assert a claim."[43] This is a claim directed against one's fellow citizens prior to and independent of any claim of enforcement against the state. Feinberg thus conceives of rights as "individual claim rights" that may be violated by individuals to whom claims are addressed and who hold corresponding duties. In other words, rights, for Feinberg, are inextricably linked with specific "horizontal" claims of individuals against individuals. In this sense, the horizontal act between individuals which constitutes a setback of interests that wrongs the victim by violating his or her welfare interest rights provides the good reason for the vertical intervention of the state through criminalization. The right thus has a double character: a claim against all other citizens to their non-interference and a claim against the state to its protection. In this sense, Feinberg's welfare interest rights are aligned with the Gewirthian approach of will or choice rights that give rise to both negative and positive rights (to freedom and well-being) against others, as opposed to mere interests.

The challenge with claim rights, however, is that for acts such as non-payment of taxes or breaches of other regulatory systems, it is difficult to argue that the breach of a regulatory rule by an individual violates another individual's moral right to life, minimal health, economic sufficiency, political liberty, and so on, or risks bringing it below a tolerable minimum level. This makes it challenging to establish both harm and wrongfulness under Feinberg's scheme, in order to provide a good reason in favour of criminalization in such cases.

In the same way as the exception made for *de minimis* theft of property, Feinberg requires a workaround in order to apply his criminalization scheme. Whilst Feinberg commences his work with the disclaimer that it does not apply to *mala prohibita* offences, he is nonetheless well aware of the challenge of regulatory offences and attempts to address it in *Harm to Others*. He considers the problem predominantly in terms of accumulative harms, where single occurrences of an act (such as non-payment of taxes) up to a threshold may not noticeably set back any interests (that is, be effectively harmless), but general performance would be harmful, in the sense that it would set back a public interest.[44] The public interest itself may be viewed either as a collection of specific interests of the same kind possessed by a large and indefinite number of private individuals (an interest that each has in his own X) or as a common, widely shared specific interest (that each

42 Stewart, H., 2001, p.67.
43 Chwaszcza, C., 2010, p.336.
44 Feinberg, *Harm to Others*, pp.225–232.

has in one and the same X).[45] Feinberg argues that it is a good reason for criminalization if a sufficient number of persons would have an interest in engaging in the conduct, thereby breaching a threshold of setback to the public interest, or if all have an interest in the conduct, but the majority would refrain from that conduct out of a sense of a civic virtue.[46]

The argument can be followed as regards the setback of interests. There is a good reason under this scheme, for example, in support of criminalization of non-payment of taxes. Many persons have an interest in retaining a higher proportion of their income, but wide-scale non-payment of taxes would set back each individual's interest in the enjoyment of critical government services, including garbage collection, street lighting, police protection, and law and order, whether viewed in the first or second sense of public interests described above. The problem, however, is that, at least in *Harm to Others*, Feinberg effectively drops the part of his criminalization scheme that associates wrongfulness with the violation of an individual's welfare interest right. In the case of non-payment of taxes, Feinberg is silent on the point of wrongfulness. For the regulatory offence of environmental pollution, Feinberg specifically moves the wrongfulness requirement from a breach of welfare interest rights to a simple violation of an authoritative scheme of allocative priorities already in force.[47] As pointed out by Stewart, in Feinberg's scheme of aggregative and accumulative harms, conduct can thus be defined as harmful for the purposes of penal law even if it is not independently wrongful.[48]

Part of the challenge here for Feinberg is that the setback of the public interest likely does not also amount to a violation of any one individual's claim right to life, minimal health, economic sufficiency, or political liberty. Feinberg actually recognizes as such in *Harmless Wrongdoing*, when he concedes that it is not immediately evident that anybody can claim that his own rights have been violated each time a person causes a public harm.[49] In other words, in the case of public harms, no one individual can be said to breach any reciprocal duty to another not to infringe their welfare-based claim right. Feinberg's claim rights, however, require the notion of a linked duty. As Christine Chwaszcza notes, asserting a valid claim under a claim right system implies that the claim is acknowledged by those who are bound by it.[50] Strict application of Feinberg's scheme to a public cumulative-harm-type act would require recognition of a web of reciprocal claim rights and duties, as between individuals, that defined violations dependent in whole or part upon the accumulative acts of the whole. This would represent, if not a departure from, then at least a complex

45 *Ibid.*, p.222.
46 *Ibid.*, p.243.
47 Feinberg, *Harm to Others*, p.244.
48 Stewart, H., 2001. p.54.
49 Feinberg, *Harmless Wrongdoing*, p.33.
50 Chwaszcza, C., 2010, p.336.

reformulation of, Feinberg's commitment to the concept of causal and indefensible invasions of welfare rights.

Feinberg's solution to this challenge is found divided between *Harm to Others* and *Harmless Wrongdoing*. In *Harm to Others*, Feinberg argues that, in the context of public accumulative harm, wrongful must mean "unlawful," as judged by a regulative agency applying rules in accordance with specified requirements of fairness and efficiency.[51] In other words, where the state identifies that general performance of an act would be harmful, in the sense that it would cumulatively set back a public interest, and devises rules to distribute or limit engagement in that act accordingly, then breach of those rules is *per se* wrongful. Feinberg further justifies and slightly broadens the argument to public harm in general in *Harmless Wrongdoing*. He suggests that

> the publicly harmful acts set back, or rather *threaten* to set back … convergent interests … When public harms are committed *we* are wronged, and the public grievance is *our* grievance. I have a grievance as an individual because *we* have a grievance as a group.[52]

That is, the wrongfulness of acts that cause or risk public harm derives from the violation of each individual's interest in the shared convergent interest. Such an approach goes some way to explaining why Feinberg holds that breach of a regulatory rule is, in itself, wrongful, provided that the regulatory rule has, as its aim, the prevention of public harm. Feinberg's workaround has some efficacy, but of course represents a significantly different approach to that of the claim right system originally invoked to identify wrongfulness in the case of *mala in se* crimes.

Contemporary writers, such as Tatjana Hörnle, do not elaborate to any great extent on the exact nature of the rights that they envisage employing within their approach to criminalization theory. Nonetheless, Hörnle's approach, being based on intrusions into spheres of liberty, seems to also imply rights in the nature of Feinberg's claim rights. Certainly, Hörnle finds it necessary to speak of both protective rights and important collective interests as two components of a rights-centred approach. In the same vein as Feinberg, Hörnle acknowledges the challenges of identifying genuine collective interests that deserve protection through criminalization. She emphasizes that a complete theory of criminalization must discuss which collective interests deserve protection by the criminal law, without necessarily opening the door to criminalization of vague public goods such as public morals and public peace.[53] In this regard, neither does Feinberg's approach, insofar as it allows

51 Feinberg, *Harm to Others*, p.230.

52 Feinberg, *Harmless Wrongdoing*, p.33. Reproduced with permission of the Licensor through PLSclear.

53 Hörnle, T., 2016, pp.304–305.

for public harms, necessarily provide a clear set of guiding principles for delineating which particular shared interests may best qualify for protection by the criminal law. Its acknowledgement of that need, however, remains consistent with contemporary objectives of criminal law theory.

Finally, commentators such as Simester and von Hirsch point to challenges around the application of Feinberg's harm principle in the case of "remote harms," whereby welfare interests may be violated not immediately but remotely. They note that this is an implicit feature of a number of offences, including prophylactic offences such as supplying weapons.[54] Applying Feinberg's scheme – under which wrongful harm derives from a setback of interests and the violation of an individual's welfare right by another – is complex in such situations. One possible line of reasoning, however, runs as follows. In the case of an act such as supply of a firearm, the supply itself does not set back interests and thus does not cause harm *per se*. There is of course a risk, however, that the weapon may ultimately be used by a purchaser for harm (such as injury by gunshot). This (remote) risk of harm cannot easily be used to justify an offence of sale, however. This is because the seller does not violate the welfare right of any eventual victim, due to the intervening act of the subsequent purchaser and user of the weapon, and hence the sale itself is not wrongful. In other words, despite the remote risk of harm, no wrongfulness can be attributed under the reciprocal claim right system as between the seller and the victim.[55] As a result, there would be no clear argument under Feinberg's scheme for an offence of sale of weapons. Dennis Baker captures something similar to this idea by the proposition that a normative connection is required between the remote harmer's isolated conduct and the primary harm in order to limit criminalization of remote harms to cases involving fairly imputable harm and wrongdoing.[56] Thus for Feinberg, and Baker, there are inherent challenges in justifying criminalization of acts linked with remote harms. Von Hirsch addresses this problem by arguing that a dual-element harm and wrongfulness theory could justify criminalization of remote harms due also to a normative involvement between the present (harmless) conduct and the eventual harmful choices of actors further down the causal chain.[57] This line of reasoning benefits, in particular, from a reciprocal constraint approach to harm and wrongfulness, as opposed to Feinberg's more tightly tied construction of wrongful harm.

Overall, Feinberg's welfare interest rights can fulfil a role in providing a good reason towards criminalization of core interpersonal offences, such as homicide, false imprisonment, and assault. This is on account of the consequentialist setback of interests to persons affected by the act that at the same time constitutes a violation of their welfare rights. A focus on wrongful harm in terms of a violation

54 Simester, A.P., and von Hirsch, A., 2011, p.79.
55 Simester and von Hirsch argue to the same effect. *Ibid.*, p.80.
56 Baker, D.J., 2007.
57 Von Hirsch, A., 2014, p.252.

of welfare interest rights in the nature of claim rights, however, suffers a number of limitations. These include, at least, in the case of *de minimis* theft of property; in the area of offense, obscenity, and outrage; in the case of acts where no individual victim can be clearly said to have his or her welfare rights violated; and in the case of remote harms, in particular prophylactic-type offences.

Rights, wrongfulness, and harm

Within Feinberg's scheme, welfare interest rights are used primarily to define his understanding of "wrongfulness" – at least in the context of an act that also causes harm or offense. A violation of a welfare interest right is equated with wrongful harm or wrongful offense that in turn represents a good reason for criminalization. In this regard, Feinberg's theory places harm or offense as the primary gateways that also require wrongfulness, as defined by a violation of welfare interest rights. Importantly, under Feinberg's scheme, a welfare rights violation alone is thus insufficient to provide the good reason for criminalization. In other words, where one individual violates the welfare interest right of another, such as a moral right to life, minimal health, economic sufficiency, and political liberty, there is not, alone, a good reason in favour of criminalization. The production of harm or offense is also required.

Feinberg does not examine in depth the mode or contours of violation of his welfare interest rights as between individuals. Throughout *Harm to Others*, Feinberg identifies a welfare interest right violation in the context of a number of specific acts. These include a violation of security of property, in the context of theft; continued life, in the context of homicide; the interest in liberty, in the case of false imprisonment, kidnapping, hijacking, and forcible detention; the interest in a functioning body, as regards assaults; and the interest in avoiding severe suffering or being free of extreme pain, which Feinberg refers to in the context of torture. These examples are, of course, all cases where the act also causes harm, resulting in a good argument for criminalization. Despite the lack of full development of Feinberg's welfare interest rights, their place in his criminalization scheme does at least broadly align with the situation of international human rights law. It is not the case, for instance, that the violation of all rights recognized by international human rights law must be protected by the criminal law. For those serious human rights violations that are commonly associated with penal sanctions, such as violations of the right to life or right to be free from cruel, inhuman, or degrading treatment, these almost certainly result in harm under Feinberg's conception of it.

Amongst modern theorists, Tatjana Hörnle's work on rights as a central concept in criminalization envisages rights as claims that protect resources which humans need to effectuate whatever their personal choice of a "good life" might be.[58] In this regard, Hörnle holds that legal rights which deserve to be

58 Hörnle, T., 2016, p.304.

protected with the means of the criminal law can only demand from others that they abstain from intruding into an individual's sphere of liberty.[59] She lists bodily integrity, sexual autonomy, and property as important rights that are tied to the sphere of liberty and what it means to be a person, and from which the protection from others' intrusions should be considered intrinsically valuable.[60] It is possible that Hörnle's rights could in practice be wider than Feinberg's welfare interest rights, due to her greater emphasis on individual choice, as opposed to antecedent needs. Unlike Feinberg, however, who favours utilizing rights to restrict the set of harms that can legitimately be criminalized, Hörnle seems to prefer replacing a harm-focused approach largely with a rights-based approach. Instead of using harm as the initial gateway to criminalization, Hörnle emphasizes the incursion in to the individual's personal sphere of liberty as the threshold and precondition for criminal law to react.[61] As such, Hörnle is one of the few theorists to propose that rights can in fact act as the primary filter for acceptable criminalization. Hörnle does not go to great lengths to further define the contours of her liberty rights or the way in which they may be violated. In this regard, her proposals certainly raise further questions about the way in which a potentially wide range of liberty-based rights could be used to define acceptable criminalization, including outside of the interpersonal sphere.

Whilst Feinberg's welfare interest rights, and presumably Hörnle's liberty rights, are central to their understandings of wrongfulness, such a step is comparatively rare within criminal theory. Almost all criminal theorists accept that an act must be wrongful in order to justify criminalization. Theorists disagree, however, over exactly how wrongfulness is to be defined and its relationship to other concepts. Similar to Feinberg, criminal theorists such as von Hirsch emphasize the importance of wrongdoing together with harm. Von Hirsch, who does not rely on a notion of rights violation to define wrongfulness, however, views harm and wrongdoing as "reciprocal" constraints, rather than sequential constraints as Feinberg does. Under this approach, interlocking requirements of harmfulness and wrongfulness help restrict the reach of offence prohibitions. Von Hirsch argues, for example, that one can employ the wrongfulness requirement to restrict the criminalization of conduct having remote harmful consequences by requiring that there also must be a present wrongful act. Conversely, one can use the harmfulness requirement as a means for restricting the criminalization of wrongful acts.[62] Duff goes further to argue that rather than search for a suitable refined master principle, whether based on rights or not, the proper task for a theory of criminalization is, rather, to assemble and clarify the different kinds of consideration that should be relevant in different contexts.[63]

59 Hörnle T., 2014, p.184.
60 *Ibid.*, p.185.
61 Ambos, K., 2017, p.609.
62 Von Hirsch, A., 2014, p.250.
63 Duff, R.A., 2010, p.20.

Schonsheck, for example, considers actions as having to pass successfully and successively, through "filters," with passing through all filters entailing that an action can be justifiably made criminal.[64] Duff views these as "gates."[65] By contrast, Andrew Ashworth identifies general principles and values that ought to be considered when deciding whether or not to make conduct criminal, but does not purport to describe relationships, sequences, or relative weights for such principles within a criminalization scheme.[66]

As regards the principle of wrongfulness in particular, Simester proposes wrongfulness as a baseline for determining whether conduct is eligible for criminalization.[67] In this role, wrongfulness is necessary, but not necessarily sufficient for criminalization. It is merely one essential criterion of justified criminalization. "Bare wrongfulness," according to Simester and Edwards, consists of the simple idea that when, all things considered, one ought not to do it. It does not rely, as Feinberg does, on the concept of violations of rights or breaches of duty. Rather, Simester describes bare wrongfulness as conduct the reasons *for* which are defeated by the reasons *against*.[68] Bare wrongfulness is of course open to the criticism that it has little to say about which acts count as wrongful. Du Pois-Pedain argues, for example, that the approach of bare wrongfulness requires a "filler morality" in order to make it capable of doing some work for regulatory objectives.[69] Edwards and Simester answer that there is utility in a bare wrongfulness constraint as a first filter and assert that it is not empty, but rules out proscription of an enormous array of act types, with which there is nothing wrong. In particular, they highlight that following the establishment of a *pro tanto* case for criminalization under bare wrongfulness, a number of other filters must be applied. They do not claim to identify all such filters through which a legitimate criminal law must pass, but do suggest that both the effectiveness principle and the harm principle (in a non-Feinbergian sense) must be satisfied.[70]

Whilst the normative content, or lack thereof, of Simester's bare wrongfulness may well present some challenges, the approach of separating wrongfulness from other filters, such as harm or effectiveness, has merit. Simester and von Hirsch assert, for instance, that some actions are wrongs prior to, and in virtue of, any harm that they may cause. They suggest that a range of important offences exist where the wrong is not, in the first instance, grounded in any consequential harm.[71] They refer, for example, to perjury, which they claim directly

64 Schonscheck, J., 1994.
65 Duff, A., 2014.
66 Ashworth, A., and Horder, J., 2013. Ashworth's key principles are the principle of individual autonomy, the principle of welfare, and the harm principle and public wrongs.
67 Simester, A.P., 2012.
68 Edwards, J.R., and Simester, A.P., 2014, p.172.
69 Du Bois-Pedain, A., 2014, p.159.
70 Edwards, J.R., and Simester, A.P., 2014, p.176 and 178.
71 Simester, A.P., and von Hirsch, A., 2011, p.50.

criminalizes an intrinsic rather than instrumental wrong (the act of not telling the truth), which is committed even if no one is even momentarily deceived. By contrast, being logically committed to the harm principle as his primary gateway, Feinberg prefers to place perjury within his category of *mala prohibita* derivative-artificial crimes, and to emphasize a "public harm" in the sense of an actual or risked setback to the public interest in an institution's functioning and health, as a result of not telling the truth.

The example serves to highlight different characterizations of the same act within criminalization theory. It also draws attention, however, to the possibility of harm-independent wrongs that are deserving of criminalization and begs the question as to how these should be identified. Whilst von Hirsch primarily favours a dual-element harm and wrongfulness theory, he concedes that it is not impossible that in some special situations wrongfulness alone might possibly be a sufficient standard.[72] Similarly, whilst Feinberg is initially committed to the harm and offense principles as the only good reasons for criminalization, his inquiry in *Harmless Wrongdoing* aims to determine exactly that point: whether it can be morally legitimate for the state, by means of the criminal law, to prohibit certain types of action that cause neither harm nor offense to anyone, on the grounds that such actions constitute or cause evils of other kinds – in other words, whether acts can be wrong without causing harm or offense. Feinberg considers four main categories of acts as candidates for potential harmless wrongdoing: acts that fail to preserve a traditional way of life; acts against morality; exploitative acts; and acts that degrade the human character.[73] He is not ultimately convinced that any of these present a good argument for criminalization. Nonetheless, Feinberg is not completely unmoved by the arguments of legal moralism. By the end of his fourth and final volume of *The Moral Limits*, Feinberg reiterates his commitment to the harm and offence principles as the only always good reasons for criminalization, but acknowledges that the need to prevent evils of any description is at least "some" kind of reason, putting at least some amount of weight, however slight, on the decisional scales.[74] Feinberg suggests, in this regard, that in certain extraordinary circumstances, the prevention of "free-floating" non-grievance evils (often, consented-to acts), in particular acts related to the enjoyment and creation of human suffering, may sometimes, though rarely, be a good reason for criminalization – a position he terms "cautious liberalism."

Interestingly, whilst Feinberg is, at least in principle, committed to welfare interest rights as the basis for wrongfulness in acts that cause harm or offense, his welfare interest rights feature to a lesser extent within his analysis in *Harmless Wrongdoing*. Most usually, Feinberg invokes the claim nature of his welfare interest rights in *Harmless Wrongdoing* simply to argue that even where an act produces a setback of

72 Von Hirsch, A., 2014, p.255.
73 Feinberg, *Harmless Wrongdoing*, p.124.
74 *Ibid.*, p.321.

interests (harm), any non-coercive consent to the act means that there is no wrongful harm. Quite rarely does Feinberg analyse whether a (non-harmful) act wrongs an individual with reference to the nature or extent of a violation of the others rights, above and beyond the issue of consent.[75] This is significant, not least because it represents another aspect in which welfare interest rights face challenges in their consistent application across Feinberg's criminalization theory. If wrongfulness in criminal theory genuinely is to be equated with a violation of rights, then it might be expected that rights-based arguments could also be analysed in the case of acts that do not clearly result in harm or offense. Of course, Feinberg is generally reluctant to concede that wrongdoing (right-violating) which does not produce harm could present a good reason for criminalization in any event. Indeed, part of the challenge in understanding exactly how Feinberg's scheme can be applied lies in the fact that Feinberg tends to analyse *either* the harm (the setback of interests) *or* the wrong (the violation of welfare interest rights) in different contexts across *The Moral Limits*, but not usually the relationship between the two. As Hamish Stewart points out, Feinberg could be clearer about the source and the role of rights in his analysis. He contends that Feinberg's theory would benefit from better identification of the role of the right in structuring relationships between individuals or between the individual and the state, as well as an account of which rights can be limited in the cause of preventing setbacks to interests and under what circumstances.[76]

As theorists continue to explore a possible place for rights within criminal theory, much needs to be done to bring clarity to criminalization frameworks. Multiple issues arise, including whether rights should function, as proposed by Hörnle, as a first gateway in their own sense or whether rights are to be equated with wrongfulness, and if so, the independence of that wrongfulness from other considerations, such as harm. It is clear, for example, that there is a significant difference between the sense of bare wrongfulness employed by Edwards and Simester and the wrongfulness linked with a rights violation. The nature and definition of rights employed are also critical. Feinberg's own use of welfare interest rights as a key criterion for criminalization places his theory open to the charge that it is, at the same time, *both* too narrow a basis *and* too wide a basis for delineating the criminal law. Feinberg finds it necessary to extend welfare interest rights to include ulterior interests that can be invaded directly and indefensibly, in order to account, for instance, for criminalization of minimal theft that does not appreciably set back interests.[77] Feinberg also requires significant extensions to his core theory in order to argue for criminalization of a number of acts such as air pollution, tax evasion, defamation and insult, duelling, and gladiatorial fights to the death. These modifications include the construction of accumulative harms, the idea of a right to be free of offended states, and the concept of free-floating evils loosely related to the enjoyment and creation

75 See, however, Feinberg, *Harmless Wrongdoing*, p.231, 248, and 326.
76 Stewart, H., 2001, pp.65–66.
77 Feinberg, *Harm to Others*, p.243.

of human suffering. On the other hand, Feinberg's formulation of welfare interest rights as horizontal claim rights, together with the inclusion of broad interests such as economic sufficiency, has the potential to capture a wide range of acts that may not usually be subject to the criminal law. Unfair dismissal of an employee, for example, would likely set back interests and, at the same time, conceivably qualify as an interference with a right to economic sufficiency, generating an argument, at least on the face of it, for criminalization of an act more usually subject to civil remedies.

Further notions of rights – continental legal theory

In addition to the work of Anglo-American theorists, the notion of rights in criminal theory also features, in a different guise, in continental criminal theory. An important line of reasoning, originally developed as an antithesis to rights theory, is the German *Rechtsgut* concept. The *Rechtsgut* concept is most usually attributed to Birnbaum, who argued, in 1834, that Feuerbach's view of crime as a violation of subjective rights was too narrow, as it could not account for a great many criminal statutes, such as those covering unethical and irreligious acts, which were not concerned with violations of individual rights at all and yet were not considered to be any less criminal as a result.[78] Birnbaum's argument is of course familiar from Feinberg's own analysis under his welfare interest rights–based theory, which, like Feuerbach, does not account for legal moralism. In contrast to a rights-based theory, Birnbaum therefore proposed that instead of a violation of individual rights (*Rechte*), a crime was to be regarded as a violation of or a threat to goods (*Güter*) protected by the state. As Ambos points out, the *Rechtsgut*-concept was thus developed mainly as an abstract normative concept referring to *values*, with the materialization of those values in social realities taken, at best, as a background fact.[79] In other words, Birnbaum's legal goods included the values of the day, with little consideration of whether these in fact represented critical moral values or not.

Following the introduction of the *Rechtsgut* idea, the exact nature of its legal goods has been famously disputed in German academic literature and discussion on *Rechtsguttheorie.*[80] Depending upon the account of *Rechtsgut* adopted, goods protected by law can represent a wide range. Jescheck and Weigand, for example, identify *Rechtsgut* as "life goods" (*Lebensgüter*) that are indispensable for the coexistence of humans in the community, as well as deep-rooted ethical convictions of society.[81] This can include, amongst others, human life, personal

78 Dubber, M.D., 2005, p.687.

79 Ambos, K., 2015, p.307.

80 Views on the concept of legal good are represented by, amongst others, Jescheck, Weigend, and Roxin. See Jescheck, H.-H, and Weigand, T., 1996; Roxin, C., 1998. See also Hefendehl, R., *et al.*, (eds), 2003.

81 Dubber, M.D., 2005, p.684.

freedom of action and movement, bodily integrity, property, wealth, the incorruptibility of public officials, traffic safety, the constitutional order, the public peace, and the external security of the state. Claus Roxin aims to capture the essence of such legal goods as all facts or established goals that are necessary for the free personality development of the individual, the realization of his or her civil rights, and the functioning of a political system which is based on these objectives.[82] Such definitions provide a somewhat tighter concept than that originally conceived by Birnbaum and are not dissimilar in nature to Rawlsian primary goods, with the addition, at least by some theorists, of certain ethical convictions of society that form part of the legal order, such as a prohibition against cruelty to animals.[83]

The fluid nature of the *Rechtsgut* concept means that it has been used to justify a number of different criminalization results. Historically, the concept has been employed to argue for the expansion of criminal law beyond the protection of individual rights to the protection of communal goods, societal interests, and eventually the state itself. Markus Dubber notes, for example, that by the late 19th century, legal goods became, under Karl Binding, "interests of the law," transforming law from a means to an end in itself. As such, if crime was thought to violate any right, it was not the rights of individuals but the state's right to obedience.[84]

By contrast, recent application of *Rechtsguttheorie*, such as that by Claus Roxin, has perhaps a more limited effect on the criminal law. Roxin describes nine consequences arising from his concept of *Rechtsgut*.[85] These include that unethical conduct, violations of societal taboos, and the violation of the dignity of humankind do not in themselves constitute a violation of, or a threat to, legal goods and thus cannot alone form the basis for criminalization. This is because such principles lack the nature and value that conditions for individual development have. In other words, they are neither needed to realize fundamental liberties nor are particularly valuable for the existence of the state that ensures such liberties.[86] Further consequences also include that none of; objects of protection that are too abstract or predominantly symbolic, deliberate self-harm, or the protection of feelings alone qualify as *Rechtsgüter* and hence cannot, by themselves, form the basis of criminalization.[87] Applying such principles, Roxin argues that public health (*Volksgesundheit*) and public peace (*öffentlicher Friede*) are not legal goods, and that criminal laws in these areas must instead be justified with reference to the protection of individuals and of peaceful coexistence. In the area of self-harm and paternalism, Roxin rejects hard

82 Roxin, C., 2006, pp.16–17, quoted in English by Lauterwein, C.C., 2016.
83 Dubber, M.D., 2005, p.684.
84 *Ibid.*, pp.687–688.
85 Lauterwein, C.C. 2016, pp.15–18.
86 Ambos, K., 2015, p.305.
87 Lauterwein, C.C., 2016, pp.16–18.

paternalism as not being a concern of the state, and hence not a legal good, but, like Feinberg, accepts soft paternalism. Offended states of mind are further rejected as a basis for criminalization based on the idea that the function of the criminal law is the maintenance of coexistence, not of human co-sentiment, although Roxin does allow for feelings of fear and discrimination.[88]

In principle, Birnbaum's original concept of *Rechtsgut*, as a combination of the ideas of justice, law, rights, and goods, was quite different to the solely rights-based approach of Feuerbach.[89] Importantly, for example, the *Recht* in Birnbaum's *Rechtsgut* is not the *Recht* that is violated in Feuerbach's view of crime. The former is "the law," whilst the latter is a "right," in the form of individual rights.[90] Thus, whilst an individual right protected by the law, such as freedom of movement, can itself be a legal good, and therefore form part of *Rechtsgut*, the argument for criminalization under *Rechtsgut* does not arise due to the nature of the value as a *right* in itself, but rather from its value to individuals and the functioning of the community as a whole. Lauterwein similarly notes that, according to Roxin, criminal laws which violate principles such as equality, freedom of opinion, or freedom of religion cannot, accordingly, be justified under *Rechtsguttheorie*.[91]

The recognition of some (if not many) rights by *Rechtsgut*, as well as the Rawlsian approach of Roxin to interpretation of the *Rechtsgut* theory, raises the question as to whether a concept of legal goods has anything to add to Feinberg's principles. Roxin, after all, reaches many similar conclusions to Feinberg on the basis of *Rechtsgut*, including a general rejection of legal moralism and paternalism. Kai Ambos argues, in the context of application to international criminal law, that the *Rechtsgut* concept can add something significant to harm theory. He notes that harm theory is traditionally consequentialist in nature, focusing on the effects of the conduct to be prohibited, whereas *Rechtsgut* is a deontological theory that focuses on critical moral duties. As such, Ambos proposes that *Rechtsgut* can correspond, to some extent, to the role of Feinberg's welfare interest rights in defining a subclass of setbacks of interest (harms) that always present a good reason in favour of criminalization.[92] Under such a combined harm-*Rechtsgut* concept, it is conceivable that only a setback of interests to a legal good or perhaps a setback of interests that *also* represented a violation of, or threat to, a legal good would present a good reason in favour of criminalization.

It could well be the case that such an approach would not encounter some of the workarounds that Feinberg is forced to employ. Using legal goods in place of welfare interest rights, for example, has the immediate advantage of not being bound by the limitations of Feinberg's conception of rights as individual claim rights that may only be violated by individuals to whom claims are

88 *Ibid.*, p.18.
89 Regarding translation of the term *Recht*, see Fletcher, G.P. 1985.
90 Dubber, M.D., 2005, p.686.
91 Lauterwein, C.C., 2016, p.15.
92 Ambos, K., 2015., p.315.

addressed and who hold corresponding duties. It will be recalled that the limitations of individual claim rights are a primary source of Feinberg's need to find workarounds for *mala prohibita* offences, such as non-payment of taxes and other aggregative and accumulative harms. Whilst some intangible interests, such as public order, may themselves only be "apparent" legal goods, *Rechtsguttheorie* usually recognizes *Kollektivrechtsgüter*, such as a functioning judiciary, a stable currency, and safe road traffic, that benefit multiple individuals.[93] Under a combined harm-*Rechtsgut* approach that included *Kollektivrechtsgüter*, the legitimacy of a crime such as tax evasion could be accepted on the grounds that intentional non-payment of taxes sets back, or harms, the collective good of a redistributive wealth system, provided for by law and integral to securing peaceful coexistence. Such an approach may not, in practice, be so different to that proposed by Simester and von Hirsch, who suggest that the kind of adverse effect that should count as harm should be the impairment of some *resource*.

Whilst today's *Rechtsguttheorie* no longer accepts the legal moralism of Birnbaum's *Rechtsgut*, the theory may, nonetheless, also offer support towards criminalization of some "free-floating evils" that trouble Feinberg. In so far as some conceptions of *Rechtsgut* recognize deeply rooted ethical convictions of society that are adopted by the legal order, the concept could support, for instance, criminalization of Feinberg's (arguably legal moralist) stubborn counterexamples, such as the gladiatorial contest.[94] In such a case, it is possible to conceive of a setback to the putative legal good of non-glorification of violence, being a moral principle of a peaceful society, as a reason in support of criminalization. Such approaches raise a multitude of issues, including, as with harm theory, matters of the *extent* to which a legal good must be set back in order to cross the criminal threshold, as well as the borderline between legal moralism (where morals alone would not count as a legal good) and genuine ethical convictions of society that are reflected in the legal order. Caution must certainly be exercised, though. The notion of legal goods undoubtedly provides the potential for criminal protection against a wider range of acts than those proscribed by Feinberg's welfare interest rights in the form of individual claim rights. Such an approach may be more consistent with modern criminal law, with its reach into environmental, financial, health and safety, and regulatory fields. At the same time, though, criminalization theory also requires the ability to clearly constrain use of the criminal law to punish conduct that is simply unpopular with the prevailing moral standards of a particular community. Roxin's account of *Rechtsgut* argues that the concept could indeed play this role. To be successful, however, any alternative to Feinberg's theory will need to address the challenge of being both a sufficiently wide *and* yet sufficiently narrow approach for delineating the criminal law.

93 Lauterwein, C.C., 2016, p.19.
94 Dubber, M.D., 2005, p.684, and Feinberg, *Harmless Wrongdoing*, p.328 onwards.

Summary

Whereas rights feature in a relatively limited set of approaches to criminalization, their nature and role in those criminal theories where they do appear are diverse. In Anglo-American thought, rights are invoked by Joel Feinberg in the sense of welfare interest rights to define wrongful harm as a good reason in support of criminalization. Feinberg's welfare interest rights are described as the basic requisites of a man's well-being, including moral rights to life, minimal health, economic sufficiency, and political liberty. These rights are in the nature of claim rights, being horizontal claims of individuals against other individuals. In this sense, Feinberg's welfare interest rights both reflect some elements of Rawlsian goods and align with the Gewirthian approach of will or choice rights that give rise to both negative and positive rights against others, as opposed to mere interests. Feinberg's claim rights have the general feature that they cannot be violated where a person freely consents to an infringement.

Whilst wrongful harm is used by Feinberg to explain the criminalization of a range of acts that universally are criminal offences, such as theft, homicide, false imprisonment, and assault, Feinberg's underlying welfare interest rights suffer from a number of challenges. These include the problem of minimal invasions of interests, difficulties faced where no individual victim clearly has his or her welfare rights violated, and their application in the case of remote harms. Within Feinberg's criminalization scheme, a violation of welfare interest rights functions as a criterion for identifying the subset of wrongful harms that qualify as crimes. Other theorists adopt different approaches to wrongfulness, however, including the idea of bare wrongfulness as a first filter for criminalization, and harm and wrongfulness as reciprocal constraints on each other, without reference to the notion of rights. A number of questions arise within such lines of thought, including whether rights should function, as proposed by Hörnle, as a first gateway in their own sense or whether rights are to be equated with wrongfulness, and if so, the independence of that wrongfulness from other considerations, such as harm.

Continental criminal law theory equally offers a rich source of discussion on rights and criminalization, beginning with the work of Feuerbach in the 19th century. In German legal thought, the *Rechtsgut* concept, whilst originally developed as an antithesis to a rights-based theory of criminalization, nonetheless today represents a deontological approach that includes consideration of rights. Importantly, however, these are not rights of the individual claim right nature, but rather legally protected rights of value to both individuals and the community. In principle, such an approach, perhaps used in conjunction with a harm filter, may not encounter some of the challenges faced by welfare interest rights in respect of *mala prohibita* offences and genuine non-grievance evils. Nonetheless, the concept of *Rechtsgut* remains highly fluid and stretches beyond solely notions of rights.

4 Crime and criminalization obligations in international human rights law

Legal literature frequently conveys mixed messages regarding the relationship between international human rights law and the criminal law. One leading text on the criminal law, for example, recently concluded that the European Convention on Human Rights (ECHR) does not have widespread relevance to the substantive criminal law.[1] In stark contrast, others propose that the violation of human rights of any kind is a criminal act or practice – exemplifying how far apart the views of academics in this area can be.[2] In addition, intersections between international human rights law and criminalization are often intermingled and not always clearly distinguished from a broader narrative on human rights and crime in general. This broader narrative includes human rights discourse on crime and security, the concept of the right to security of person, crime investigatory and prosecutorial obligations, and the rights of victims of crime.[3] Issues of criminalization form part of these areas to varying extents. Where criminalization is also discussed in such contexts, criminalization requirements may not always be differentiated from law enforcement and criminal justice operational requirements. Moreover, there is little discussion of how and why some human rights require protection through criminalization but not others. Or why some crimes, such as trafficking in persons or domestic violence, are often spoken of as human rights violations but not others, such as shoplifting or car theft. In short, academic literature rarely provides a clear, compelling overview of international human rights law, crime, and criminalization.

This chapter provides a structure for understanding an international human rights law approach to criminalization within the broader crime and human rights narrative. A good starting point for this endeavour is found in the 2013 work of Andrew Ashworth on *Positive Obligations in Criminal Law*. Ashworth concludes his work with a chapter on human rights and positive obligations to create particular criminal offences. His chapter is far from a complete treatment

1 Ashworth, A., and Horder, J., 2013, p.81. Although Ashworth and Horder concede that it has had some effect on approaches to defining offences.

2 Blau, J., Moncada, A., 2007.

3 See International Council on Human Rights Policy, 2003; Powell, R.L., 2008; Seibert-Fohr, A., 2009; Mégret, F., and Calderón J-P.S., 2015.

of human rights and criminalization, not least because Ashworth limits himself to consideration of a comparatively small number of cases and does not examine negative obligations not to criminalize. Nonetheless, the chapter opens with a useful characterization of human rights positive obligations in the broad area of crime and criminalization, drawing especially from the European human rights system. In doing so, Ashworth identifies three key human rights positive obligations. He characterizes these as positive obligations in respect of: (i) criminal law provisions; (ii) preventive operational measures; and (iii) effective machinery for investigation of complaints.[4]

The first of these directly concerns criminalization. The latter two, on the face of it, appear to concern primarily practical or operational responses to crime. In practice, however, these obligations often subsume a positive criminalization obligation. In order to develop as complete a picture as possible, however, two further obligations must be added to Ashworth's scheme. The first of these is a general positive obligation in the area of crime prevention and control – a general security of person obligation. The second is a negative human rights obligation not to criminalize.

Table 4.1 reproduces Ashworth's three positive obligations, along with these two additional human rights obligations. Ashworth's existing positive obligations correspond to numbers two, three, and five.[5] The description of these obligations is exactly as formulated by Ashworth, although the italicized title is assigned for the purposes of this book. The additional general security of person obligation is inserted at number one.[6] The negative obligation not to criminalize certain acts is inserted at number four.[7] Together, the scheme aims to cover all key crime, criminalization, and human rights intersections identifiable in international human rights jurisprudence.

Table 4.1 represents the broadly distinguishable state obligations in the area of crime and criminalization that can be derived from international human rights law. The exact nature and content of many of the obligations remain the subject of academic debate and can also differ as between different international human rights systems. As such, Table 4.1 is a generic frame, rather than a definitive statement of international human rights law. Considerable conceptual overlap exists between almost all of the five obligations and especially between the four positive obligations.

Out of the five obligations deriving from international human rights law, numbers three and four most directly concern criminalization – in the form of the sword and shield criminalization functions of international human rights law, respectively. These two obligations are the focus of this book as a whole. Whilst the positive criminalization obligation is represented as a separable obligation in Table 4.1, it is in fact inextricably connected with the general security of person obligation, as well as the

4 Ashworth, A., 2013, p.198.

5 Ashworth, A., 2013, p.198. Used by permission of Bloomsbury Publishing Plc.

6 See Organization of American States, Inter-American Commission on Human Rights, 2009; International Council on Human Rights Policy, 2003; Powell, R.L., 2008.

7 See *Norris v. Ireland*, ECHR, para 46, and *Şükran Aydin and Others v. Turkey*, ECHR, paras 55–56.

Table 4.1 Five Crime, Criminalization, and Human Rights Obligations

1	*The general security of person obligation*: The obligation to guard against general impunity, to address underlying causes of violent crime, and to provide basic protection against violent crime;
2	*The specific crime prevention obligation*: The obligation, in certain well-defined circumstances, to take preventive operational measures to protect an individual whose right is at risk from the criminal acts of another individual (*Ashworth*);
3	*The positive criminalization obligation*: The obligation to secure a right by putting in place effective criminal law provisions, backed by law enforcement machinery for the prevention, suppression, and sanctioning of breaches of such provisions (*Ashworth*);
4	*The negative criminalization obligation*: The obligation to exercise criminalization discretion, within a certain margin of appreciation, reasonably, carefully, and in good faith, for the purposes of a legitimate aim and in a manner that is proportionate to a pressing social need; and
5	*The general crime investigatory obligation*: The obligation to have in place effective machinery for investigating complaints of human rights violations, combined with the duty to ensure that there is a thorough and effective investigation capable of leading to the identification and punishment of those responsible (*Ashworth*).

specific crime prevention and general crime investigatory obligations. This is the case, in particular, where these other obligations imply criminalization as a prerequisite for human rights-based operational or procedural obligations in the area of crime prevention and criminal justice. Careful examination of these other obligations (one, two, and five in Table 4.1) aids an appreciation of the place of criminalization within the wider human rights and crime narrative. It is also necessary in order to understand some of the legal mechanisms and context which give rise, specifically, to a positive criminalization obligation within international human rights law.

The general security of person obligation

Across the United Nations and regional human rights systems, legal rights to security of person show considerable variation in terms of substantive content and facets of security protected.[8] Increasingly, however, both international human rights jurisprudence and literature contain a number of common arguments that strongly link, or even characterize, crime and insecurity as a human rights issue.[9] The core of these arguments usually amounts to the assertion that

8 Powell, R.L., 2008, pp.17–51.

9 See, for example, Organization of American States, Inter-American Commission on Human Rights, 2009; Powell, R.L., 2008; Snodgrass-Godoy, A., 2005.

the state has an obligation to provide basic protection against – usually, violent – crime and that the individual holds a corresponding broad right to security of person. Such arguments are particularly developed in the Americas region.

In the early nineties, commentators such as Elias began to argue, from a criminological perspective on failed political and economic democracy as underlying causes for crime, that crime *is* a human rights violation. But, equally, that crime *results* from the violation of human rights produced by unjust political and economic arrangements.[10] In a similar vein, other commentators attack a distinction between common crime and human rights violations. Snodgrass-Godoy, in the context of violence during and following political transition in Central America, for example, discusses the "razor's edge" between crime and human rights, arguing that in recent decades these boundaries have become blurred in many parts of the world, making it sometimes impossible to separate the two.[11] The Inter-American Commission on Human Rights (IACommHR) 2009 *Report on Citizen Security and Human Rights* also highlighted that insecurity generated by crime and violence in the Americas placed the observance and enjoyment of human rights at stake.[12]

Drawing out clear arguments from a general notion that crime somehow violates human rights is challenging. Many specific crimes indeed do engage interests that are also protected by international human rights law. On the other hand, recent rights and security dialogue comes close to arguing not only that some crimes violate human rights but that crime *in general* violates human rights. Elias, for example, argues that the widespread existence of crime in society is both symptomatic and constitutive of human rights violations. The IACommHR as well as the non-governmental International Council on Human Rights Policy develop the intersection between crime and human rights in this direction, based on an obligation to provide "basic security." The International Council concluded, in 2003, for example, that states have an obligation to provide basic security to the people they govern. This obligation was said to flow from the rights to life, physical integrity, freedom of movement, and others.[13]

A certain tension exists, however, as to whether a general security of person obligation exists independently or is rather merely the sum of the effect of a number of underlying rights. The Inter-American Commission has stated that the right to security from crime or interpersonal or social violence is not expressly protected under the international system of human rights law, but nevertheless asserts that the right to such protection "can be inferred" from the obligation of the state to guarantee the security of the individual, as set forth in Article 3 (Right to life, liberty and security of person) of the Universal Declaration of Human Rights (UDHR), Article 1 (Right to life, liberty and security of person) of the

10 Elias, R., 1991.

11 Snodgrass-Godoy, A., 2005.

12 Organization of American States, Inter-American Commission on Human Rights, 2009, para 35.

13 International Council on Human Rights Policy, 2003, pp.17–18.

American Declaration of the Rights and Duties of Man, Article 7 (Right to personal liberty and security) of the American Convention on Human Rights, and Article 9 (Right to liberty and security) of the International Covenant on Civil and Political Rights (ICCPR).[14]

The Inter-American Commission thus appears, on the face of it, to pull these elements together into a distinct, aggregate general security of person obligation that could, in principle, be applied to all crime types. In other words, since violent and criminal conduct is considered an affront to human rights, the state is under a general obligation to guarantee the security of the individual. The individual thus enjoys a concurrent right to security from crime. On closer examination, however, the Commission retains, at the same time, a focus on the separate, constituent rights.[15] Having asserted that a (presumably, distinct) right to security can be inferred, the Commission then uses the language of "those" human rights that are related to citizen security. It tightly links the general security obligation to a "normative core" of rights that is characterized as particularly vulnerable to criminal or violent acts. The Commission continues by reviewing the links between citizen security and a range of separate rights, including the right to life, the right to personal liberty and security, the right to privacy and to have one's honour respected and dignity recognized, the right to freedom of expression, assembly, and association, and the right to the peaceful use and enjoyment of one's property.[16] This ambiguity over the existence or not of a distinct, aggregate security of person obligation introduces, in turn, questions with respect to whether crime in general constitutes a human rights violation, as opposed to only a certain, limited subset of crimes that engage specific individual rights. Where the Inter-American Commission speaks in broad terms of the obligation to prevent, deter, and suppress violent and criminal conduct, this suggests obligations in respect of crime in general. On the other hand, if the obligation is, in practice, not more than the sum of obligations under individual rights, then the general security of person obligation becomes limited to those crimes that specifically engage those particular rights. The problem is that the range of rights found in international human rights law does not necessarily cover the vast breadth of conduct that may potentially be subject to the criminal law. Whilst privacy-based rights can go some way towards a human rights position on the criminalization (or decriminalization) of diverse conduct linked with the private sphere in general, it is far from clear that all conduct potentially subject to criminal sanctions clearly engages individual human rights to the extent that a general human rights preventative obligation arises.

Indeed, in practice, the general crime, security, and human rights discourse of the Inter-American Commission and International Council is in fact largely

14 Organization of American States, Inter-American Commission on Human Rights, 2009, p.6.

15 The Inter-American Commission report notes that at the second meeting of experts, held in Bogota, Colombia, on 18 September 2008, reference was made to the need to determine whether there is a specific human right to security from violence and crime or whether one should look to a combination of rights that can be violated in situations of citizen insecurity. *Ibid.*, p.6, footnote 13.

16 *Ibid.*, pp.41–91.

a discourse on specific crime types – violent threats to life, serious assault, kidnapping, rape, and, to a limited extent, crimes against property, these being the criminal conduct that represent the most direct affront to rights to life and liberty, as well as to freedom from cruel, inhuman, or degrading treatment. A right to security from such acts is developed in the Americas through decisions of the Inter-American Court and Commission, such as *Velásquez Rodriguez*, *Goiburú*, *Cotton Field*, and *Jessica Gonzales* – most of which concern situations of intentional homicide, enforced disappearance, and violence.[17] Such decisions reiterate the principle that the state can have international responsibility for an illegal act of a private person which violates human rights, on the basis of a lack of due diligence on the part of the state to prevent the violation or to respond to it.[18] They emphasize the state obligation to combat impunity and to investigate human rights violations and to prosecute and punish those responsible.[19] They further clarify that the state must prevent the liberty of the individual being violated by the actions of public officials and private third parties, and must also investigate and punish acts that violate this right.[20] Such requirements can include an obligation of prevention to put in place a general policy to prevent violence, as well as coordinated and effective responses to violence.[21]

The result of a focus on the specific interests protected by international human rights law – such as life, expression and association, and freedom from discrimination, torture, inhuman or degrading treatment, slavery, and forced labour – is that the general security of person argument is particularly strong for certain crimes that engage a number of such interests. In the Americas, for example, the Inter-American Convention on the Prevention, Punishment and Eradication of Violence against Women (the Bélem do Pará Convention) affirms that crime involving violence against women constitutes a violation of their human rights and fundamental freedoms, and specifically asserts that every woman has the right to be free from violence in both the public and private spheres. The characterization of violence against women as a human rights violation is especially premised on the link between discrimination and violence against women, as well as the protection of the right to life. Such provisions represent reinforced obligations in respect of a particular crime type.[22] Thus, under the Bélem do Pará Convention, any act or conduct, based on gender, which causes death or physical, sexual, or psychological harm or suffering to women, whether in the public or the private sphere, is subject to the prevention, punishment, and eradication obligations of the Convention. The Convention obliges states parties to pursue policies to prevent, punish, and eradicate such violence, as well as to apply

17 *Velásquez Rodriguez*, IACHR; *Goiburú et al. v. Paraguay*, IACHR; *González et al. ("Cotton Field") v. Mexico*, IACHR; and *Jessica Lenahan (Gonzales) et al. v. United States*, IACommHR.

18 *Velásquez Rodriguez*, IACHR, para 172.

19 *Goiburú*, IACHR, paras 129 and 164.

20 *Cotton Field*, IACHR, para 247.

21 *Cotton Field*, IACHR, para 282, and Jessica *Lenahan (Gonzales)*, IACommHR, para 170.

22 Organization of American States, Inter-American Commission on Human Rights, 2009, pp.18–20.

due diligence to prevent, investigate, and impose penalties for violence against women. Such obligations include the promulgation of an appropriate legal framework for protection that is enforced effectively, prevention policies and practices that allow effective measures to be taken, and a prevention strategy that prevents risk factors and strengthens institutions that provide an effective response.[23]

The general security of person obligation, as well as a reinforced obligation in the case of particular crimes, has broad implications for criminalization. Whilst the contours of the right are far from clear, individuals, at least in the Americas, can be assumed to have a general right to security from crime or interpersonal or social violence. The corresponding state obligation requires a legal framework to meet the need to prevent or suppress crime and violence, and to develop criminal procedure and prison management.[24] The implication from this framework is that it must involve criminalization. At this point, the argument becomes somewhat circular. It does not advance the analysis much, for example, to assert that the Inter-American Commission requires security from crime, which must, in turn, be achieved through criminalization. In addition, perhaps unsurprisingly, the Inter-American Commission in discussing the right to security does not speak directly of security from crimes that less obviously engage specific rights, such as financial or fraud-based offences, or health and safety, environmental, or labour offences. Whilst reference to crime in general in the security of person obligation does not strictly rule out such offences, their inclusion in any general security obligation could be hard to reconcile with the Inter-American Commission's focus on individual right violations.

Nonetheless, the general security of person obligation highlights the importance of criminalization in protecting key areas identified by the Inter-American Commission as pertaining to issues of citizen security. If the rights at stake in public policy on citizen security identified by the Inter-American Commission are taken as a guide to those interests that pertain to a right to security from crime or interpersonal or social violence, then criminalization should protect a range of interests including life, liberty, privacy, honour, dignity, expression, assembly, association, participation in government, and peaceful use and enjoyment of property. This conclusion does not provide details about the exact conduct that should, or should not, be criminal. It does, however, set out broad areas that pertain to a human rights understanding of security, and hence to criminalization, as well as general obligations to prevent, deter, and where necessary suppress acts of violence and crime.

The specific crime prevention obligation

In addition to a general security of person obligation, international human rights law also defines a specific crime prevention obligation to take operational measures, in certain well-defined circumstances, to protect an individual whose

23 *Cotton Field*, IACHR, para 258.

24 Organization of American States, Inter-American Commission on Human Rights, 2009, para 57.

right is at risk from the criminal acts of another.[25] The boundary between the general security obligation and the specific crime prevention obligation is not absolute and significant overlaps exist. In broad terms, however, the general security obligation can be considered to draw primarily from Inter-American jurisprudence, whilst the specific crime prevention obligation is based mostly on European jurisprudence. This said, it is also the case that the Inter-American system recognizes many of the elements of the European specific crime prevention obligation applicable in individual situations of criminal risk, as one component of its general crime prevention obligation.[26]

The specific crime prevention obligation can be traced back to the ECtHR case of *Osman*, which established the principle that the European right to life (ECHR Article 2) may imply a positive obligation on authorities to take preventive operational measures to protect an individual whose life is at risk from the criminal acts of another.[27] The extent of the obligation is summarized in the ECtHR case of *Van Colle*. According to *Van Colle*, not every claimed risk to life can entail a Convention requirement to take operational measures to prevent that risk from materializing. In order to find a violation of the positive obligation to protect life, it must be established that the authorities knew or ought to have known, at the time, of the existence of a real and immediate risk to the life of an identified individual from the criminal acts of a third party and that the authorities failed to take measures within the scope of their powers which might reasonably have been expected to avoid that risk.[28]

On this basis, the European Court has found, for example, that national authorities failed to take adequate steps to protect a women from being killed by her son-in-law, despite a number of years of domestic violence and complaints to the police and prosecuting authorities.[29] A comparable test of whether the state authorities should have known that the victims were in a situation of imminent risk, and whether the authorities undertook reasonable measures to protect them from those acts, has also been applied by the Inter-American Commission on Human Rights. The Inter-American Commission thus similarly found that authorities had failed to exercise the necessary due diligence in protecting a mother and her three daughters from domestic violence and killing by a perpetrator with a criminal history and subject to a restraining order.[30]

Whilst the *Osman* test of real and immediate risk was originally formulated in the context of ECHR Article 2 (Right to life), the Court has applied an equivalent standard for Article 8 (Right to respect for private and family life) in cases

25 Ashworth, A., 2013, p.198.

26 See, for example, *Jessica Lenahan (Gonzales) et al. v. United States*, IACommHR, paras 132 to 170.

27 *Osman v. United Kingdom*, ECHR, para 115. See also *Mahmut Kaya v. Turkey*, EHCR, para 85; *Keenan v. United Kingdom*, ECHR, para 89; and *Paul and Audrey Edwards v. United Kingdom*, ECHR, para 54.

28 *Van Colle v. United Kingdom*, ECHR, para 88.

29 *Opuz v. Turkey*, ECHR.

30 *Jessica Lenahan (Gonzales) et al. v. United States*, IACommHR, para 137.

involving homicide. Thus, in *Osman* itself, as well as *Van Colle*, the Court found that the fact that the authorities could not have known that there was a real and immediate risk to life, in addition to leading to a finding of no violation under Article 2, equally supported a finding that there was no breach of any positive obligation implied by Article 8 to safeguard physical integrity.[31] In one non-lethal Article 8 case, involving threats and physical violence, the Court did not apply the *Osman* test, but focused on the, more generic, need for active state involvement in the victim's protection.[32] On the other hand, in the Article 3 non-lethal case of *Milanović* concerning threats and physical assault, the Court again rehearsed the *Osman* test and found that the state had failed to take any reasonable and effective steps to prevent the applicant's repeated ill-treatment, notwithstanding a real, immediate, predictable, and continuing risk.[33]

Whilst the majority of the specific crime prevention obligation jurisprudence arises in the context of criminal homicide, the few non-lethal cases do provide some basis for Ashworth's broader characterization of the specific crime prevention obligation in terms of protection from criminal acts in general, as opposed to protection from loss of life.[34] Nonetheless, as with the general security of person obligation, there is a clear absence of international jurisprudence on the specific crime obligation beyond the area of violent crime. It is interesting to speculate, for example, whether, and if so what, specific operational, crime prevention obligations may arise under Article 8 in the face of a real and immediate risk to a specific individual or individuals of, for instance, non-violent crimes of theft of personal identifying information or identity fraud. At present, whilst European jurisprudence does not, in principle, exclude a specific crime prevention obligation arising in respect of any criminal act that also engages a substantive Convention right, the obligation is only delineated through case law in respect of crimes such as homicide and serious bodily assault. In this respect, whereas the Inter-American Commission has explored the possibility of a broad, almost free-standing, general security of person obligation, the European specific crime prevention obligation cannot easily be separated from the specific provisions of Articles 2 (Right to life), 3 (Prohibition of torture), and 8 (Right to respect for private and family life) and the constraints of the *Osman* real and immediate risk test.

The European specific crime prevention obligation nonetheless has relevance to the issue of criminalization. This is so, in particular, by virtue of the fact that many cases that invoke the specific prevention obligation also refer to the required criminal law framework. *Osman* itself, for example, introduces the positive obligation to take preventive operational measures to protect an individual whose life is at risk by recalling that the state has a primary duty to secure the

31 *Osman v. United Kingdom*, ECHR, para 128 and *Van Colle v. United Kingdom*, ECHR, para 108.

32 *Bevacqua and S. v. Bulgaria*, ECHR, paras 65, 83, and 84.

33 *Milanović v. Serbia*, ECHR, paras 89 to 90.

34 Ashworth, A., 2013, p.198.

right to life by putting in place "effective criminal-law provisions" to deter the commission of offences against the person.[35] The existence of the relevant criminal law (of murder and manslaughter) was not in dispute in *Osman*. The case was primarily about whether the authorities had failed to appreciate and act upon an alleged serious threat to the physical safety of an individual who was subsequently killed. Nonetheless, the fact that *Osman* handles the Article 2 positive requirement for criminal law provisions almost in the same breath as preventative operational requirements has tended, to some extent, to secure a place for *Osman* as an authority on criminalization, as well as on the specific crime prevention obligation.[36] Indeed, Ashworth himself cites *Osman* and *Van Colle* as his authority for the positive criminalization obligation (as well as the specific crime prevention obligation), notwithstanding the fact that the substantive criminal law was not at issue in either *Osman* or *Van Colle*.[37]

The effective criminal-law provisions requirement of *Osman* has been referred to by the European Court in more than sixty-five other judgments. The vast majority of these cases cite this requirement within the context of an alleged violation of Article 2, arising either from a failure to take preventive operational measures to protect an individual whose life is at risk from the criminal acts of another (the specific crime prevention obligation) or to conduct a prompt, impartial, and effective investigation.[38] In almost all of these cases, the sufficiency of the criminal law provisions was not in issue. Nonetheless, the European Court habitually introduces an examination of the effectiveness of law enforcement machinery and the sufficiency of preventive operational measures with a reference to the *Osman* requirement to put in place effective criminal-law provisions. Depending upon the Article at stake (usually, Article 2 (Right to life) or Article 3 (Prohibition of torture)), the Court variously describes this as a requirement to put in place effective criminal-law provisions to deter grave acts, to deter the commission of offences against personal integrity, or to deter offences against the person.[39]

The Court's introductory recital in such cases is significant for a number of reasons. In the first place, it confirms that acts suffered by victims that engage a specific crime prevention must be a criminal offence. Accordingly, where the Court finds, for example, that circumstances of serious bodily assault, murder, or serious domestic violence engage the European specific crime prevention obligation, it also confirms a criminalization obligation in respect of these acts, through use of the *Osman*

35 *Osman v. United Kingdom*, ECHR, para 115. See also *Opuz v. Turkey*, ECHR, para 128; *Mastromatteo v. Italy*, ECHR. 24 October 2002, para 67; and *Paul and Audrey Edwards v. United Kingdom* ECHR, para 54.

36 See, for example, Lazarus, L., 2012.

37 Ashworth, A., 2013, p.198, footnote 10.

38 Some cases also cite the requirement within the context of ECHR Article 3 (see, for example, *O'Keefe v. United Kingdom*, ECHR; *Çelik v. Turkey (no.2)*, ECHR; and *Đurđević v. Croatia*, ECHR) and Article 8 (*Van der Heijden v. The Netherlands*, ECHR).

39 *O'Keefe v. United Kingdom*, ECHR, para 148; *Çelik v. Turkey (no.2)*, ECHR, para 34; and *Perevedentsevy v. Russia*, ECHR, para 91.

effective criminal-law provisions wording. This, in itself, does not tell us a great deal about the range of acts that should constitute criminal offences. As with the general crime prevention obligation, in practice, the range of judgments that cite *Osman's* effective criminal-law provisions are limited to core criminal acts of violent offences against the person. Nevertheless, as jurisprudence on the specific crime prevention obligation expands, the Court's examination of specific operational requirements may yet, at the same time, yield further conclusions on criminalization.

Secondly, the common recital of a criminalization obligation in cases concerning the effectiveness of law enforcement machinery and the sufficiency of preventive operational measures serves to highlight the interconnectedness between criminal law and its implementation in practice. This is a theme which arises from all of the general crime prevention obligation, the specific crime prevention obligation, and a general crime investigatory obligation. Whilst criminalization can be addressed, to some extent, as a separable issue, it is also the case that criminalization conclusions are often embedded in cases that concern some or all of these other obligations. Any analysis of criminal theory and international human rights law must take full account of this broader context.

The general crime investigatory obligation

Ashworth defines the general crime investigatory obligation as the duty to have in place effective machinery for investigating complaints of human rights violations, combined with the duty to ensure that there is a thorough and effective investigation capable of leading to the identification and punishment of those responsible.[40] This obligation derives specifically from the jurisprudence of the ECtHR. At the same time, however, the general crime investigatory obligation, out of the three obligations discussed in this chapter, is most clearly identifiable across almost all international and regional human rights systems, albeit in somewhat different forms. In formulating the obligation, the United Nations, European, and Inter-American human rights systems variously place emphasis on the obligation to investigate, to bring to justice, to prosecute, and to punish human rights violations, as well as to provide a remedy for victims of violations.

In legal terms, the general crime investigatory obligation is complex. Its exact content and legal nature deserve, and have received, academic analysis in their own right.[41] Whilst – in order to emphasize its particular relevance to crime and criminalization – the obligation is referred to here as the general "crime" investigatory obligation, the obligation in fact attaches to acts constituting infringements of individual human rights, rather than crimes.[42] In the terms summarized by Ashworth,

40 Ashworth, A., 2013, p.198.

41 See, in particular, Seibert-Fohr, A., 2009.

42 Ashworth characterizes it as an obligation attached to "criminal acts." Ashworth, A., 2013, p.198.

the obligation is thus, most correctly, a "human rights violation investigatory obligation." Nonetheless, within this context, the obligation identifies a subset of serious human rights violations in respect of which criminal investigation, prosecution, or punishment is required. For these human rights violations, the obligation can properly be described as a crime investigatory obligation.

In the same way as the general security of person obligation and the specific crime prevention obligation, the general crime investigatory obligation often subsumes a concomitant positive criminalization obligation. A typical form of argument in human rights jurisprudence is: government X should have [investigated]/[prosecuted]/[punished]/[brought to justice those responsible for]/[provided an effective remedy for] treatment Y, experienced by Z. Where an international human rights tribunal finds that this is the case, this often also implies – depending upon the exact nature of the obligation – that conduct Y constitute a criminal offence in state X. Whilst a pure "investigatory" obligation, for example, may not necessarily demand criminalization of the impugned act, a "prosecutorial" obligation would do so.

Understanding the legal basis for the general crime investigatory obligation is important for an appreciation of the reasoning and rationale behind many international human rights cases on criminalization. In broad terms, three different distinct, yet sometimes overlapping, legal bases can be identified from which a human rights duty to investigate, prosecute, or punish may be derived. The first possible legal justification flows from the general overarching obligations contained in international human rights treaties to "respect and ensure" or to "secure" the rights contained therein.[43] The United Nations Human Rights Committee, for example, derives a duty to "bring to justice" and to "punish" perpetrators of human rights violations arising from Articles 2(1) and 2(2) of the ICCPR.[44] This duty to punish is a duty of prevention for the purposes of "general" human rights protection. The obligation is thus procedural and requires the existence of an effective law machinery, rather than its specific application in individual instances of human rights violation. In this respect, the duty has significant overlaps with the general security of person obligation and its focus on a crime prevention and criminal justice system. The duty to bring to justice or to punish does not necessarily demand a criminal process and punishment, however. Rather, the scope of the duty depends upon the substantive right at issue, as well as the gravity of the particular act.[45] Admonition and disciplinary measures, including removal from office in the case of public officials, may be sufficient in the case of less serious violations. As such, the Committee generally views criminalization and prosecution as mandatory only in the case of serious human rights violations.

43 ICCPR, Article 2(1); American Convention on Human Rights, Article 1(1); and ECHR, Article 1.
44 Seibert-Fohr, A., 2009, p.15, footnotes 23 and 24.
45 *Ibid.*, pp.200–202.

The second possible legal justification derives from procedural obligations ascribed to individual substantive rights. In the European system, ECHR Article 2 (Right to life), for example, incorporates a procedural limb that confirms a specific duty to "investigate" deaths that may have occurred in breach of the Convention.[46] The ECtHR, in *Kaya v. Turkey*, clarified that the obligation to protect the right to life under Article 2 of the ECHR, read in conjunction with the general duty under Article 1, ECHR, required, by implication, that there should be some form of effective official investigation when individuals were killed.[47] The essential purpose of such an investigation is to secure the effective implementation of the domestic laws which protect the right to life. In the case of a death suspected to be resulting from use of force, this involves taking reasonable steps to secure the evidence concerning the incident, including, *inter alia*, eyewitness testimony, forensic evidence, and, where appropriate, an autopsy providing a complete and accurate record of injury and an objective analysis of clinical findings, including the cause of death. The Article 2 investigatory obligation applies whether the death is caused by state agents or private individuals. Even in respect of acts resulting in death, however, the Article 2 procedural investigatory requirement does not automatically require a criminal investigation in every case. In *Mastromatteo*, the ECtHR highlighted that the form of investigation may vary according to the circumstances and, in particular, in the sphere of negligence, a civil or disciplinary remedy may suffice.[48] An important difference between procedural obligations arising under substantive rights and duties arising as a matter of general human rights protection is that the former constitutes an obligation that can be enforced by individual claim, whereas the latter is a measure of implementation owed to society at large.[49]

As a result, there is significant overlap between procedural obligations ascribed to individual substantive rights and the third legal justification for the general crime investigatory obligation, the human rights duty to provide for an effective remedy. ECHR Article 13, for example, provides for the right to an effective remedy before a national authority. Similarly, ICCPR Article 2(3) obliges states parties to ensure that any person whose rights or freedoms are violated shall have an effective remedy. As remedial obligations provide a necessary remedy for the wrong suffered, they are accompanied by enforceable individual rights. General Comment 31 of the United Nations Human Rights Committee emphasizes that an investigation into allegations of violations is part of ensuring an accessible and effective remedy.[50] In this respect, purely disciplinary and administrative

46 *McCann and Others v. United Kingdom*, ECHR, para 161, and *Kelly and Others v. United Kingdom*, ECHR, paras 94–98.

47 *Kaya v. Turkey*, ECHR, para 86.

48 *Mastromatteo v. Italy*, ECHR, para 89.

49 Seibert-Fohr, A., 2009. pp.127–128.

50 United Nations, Human Rights Committee, 2004a. UN Doc. CCPR/C/21/Rev.1/Add.13, para 15.

remedies cannot be deemed to constitute adequate and effective remedies within the meaning of Article 2(3) of the Covenant, in the event of particularly serious violations of human rights.[51] Whilst the state has the obligation to investigate and, if possible, to prosecute in such circumstances, the Committee has clarified that the right of the individual victim is limited to the investigation itself, rather than a right to require prosecution and punishment of suspected perpetrators. By contrast, the Inter-American Commission and Court have explicitly interpreted the remedial obligation of Article 25 of the American Convention on Human Rights in a more expansive manner than both the United Nations Human Rights Committee and the ECtHR. In the Inter-American system, remedies are not only limited to the investigation of a violation but also extend to a requirement for criminal "punishment" in the case of serious human rights violations.[52]

The diversity of argument across human rights tribunals as to the rationalization of obligations to investigate and/or prosecute in international human rights law demonstrates the lack of a clear theoretical approach to this area. Nonetheless, the subset of human rights for which the general crime investigatory obligation indicates criminalization is required is similar, in broad terms, to that also identified by the general security of person obligation and the specific crime prevention obligation. Recall that the general security of person obligation is constructed primarily in respect of crimes such as violent threats to life, serious assault, kidnapping, rape, and, to some extent, crimes against property. These represent the criminal conduct that most directly constitutes an affront to the rights identified by the Inter-American Commission as those human rights that are related to citizen security. Similarly, the specific crime prevention obligation to take preventive operational measures to protect an individual whose right is at risk from the criminal acts of another individual is most clearly expressed in the case of acts such as serious bodily assault, murder, and serious domestic violence or core criminal acts of violent offences against the person. The general crime investigatory obligation also requires criminal measures in the case of serious human rights violations, in particular the right to life.

Overall, the question whether punishment in the sense of criminal prosecution is required depends on the affected right and on the seriousness of the particular violation. Whereas international human rights law requires the prosecution or punishment of serious or grave human rights violations, it follows that less serious violations can adequately be addressed by non-criminal matters. These may include civil, administrative, or disciplinary sanctions, or, for public officials, removal from office. Jurisprudence of the United Nations Human Rights Committee confirms that punishment of private individual perpetrators is required in order to effectively secure fundamental human rights in the case of grave abuses

51 *Bautista de Arellana v Colombia*, UNHRC, para 8.2. See also *José Antonio Coronel and others v. Colombia*, UNHRC, para 6.2.

52 Seibert-Fohr, A., 2009 pp.24–25.

such as large-scale murder, domestic violence, serious cases of female exploitation, and trafficking in women and children. For the ECtHR, an obligation to criminalize arises under substantive rights where essential aspects of a fundamental right are at stake, as in the case of murder, rape, and serious breaches of personal integrity.[53]

Taken together, the general security of person obligation, the specific crime prevention obligation, and the general crime investigatory obligation provide a range of legal routes towards a positive criminalization obligation. Whereas Ashworth identifies the positive criminalization obligation as a separable duty, it is clear that criminalization can also be implied or explicitly demanded through these other obligations. This is indicative of the fact that criminalization jurisprudence derives from *in concreto* cases where the issue of criminalization is intimately connected with duties to investigate, to sanction, and to provide redress for victims.

Summary

This chapter identified general points of intersection in international human rights law with issues of crime and criminalization. It started from five crime and criminalization obligations that can be derived from international human rights law: (1) the general security of person obligation; (2) the specific crime prevention obligation; (3) the positive criminalization obligation; (4) the negative criminalization obligation; and (5) the general crime investigatory obligation.

In addition to direct criminalization obligations, broader crime prevention and investigation obligations under international human rights law also create a range of routes to a *de facto* criminalization requirement. Some systems, such as the Inter-American human rights system, come close, under a general security of person obligation, to establishing a justiciable right to freedom from violent crime that includes a requirement for a legal framework for the suppression of crime and violence. Other systems, such as the European human rights system, in the context of a more operational specific crime prevention obligation, require the establishment of effective criminal law provisions, at least in the cases of serious threats to life and bodily integrity. Across international human rights law as a whole, a general crime investigatory obligation further obliges states to put in place mechanisms for effective investigations that may frequently subsume a positive criminalization obligation, at least in the case of serious human rights violations. As the criminalization findings of international human rights courts and tribunals are most often derived from concrete cases, as opposed to reasoning in the abstract, a detailed understanding of the legal routes to criminalization outcomes is critical to a correct analysis of international human rights law jurisprudence.

53 *Ibid.*, p.33 and 113.

5 Criminalization in human rights treaties

Perhaps unsurprisingly, given the political nature of the treaty negotiation process and the latitude granted to states through the wording of treaty articles, very few provisions of the nine core international human rights treaties in fact address criminalization directly. This is not to say that criminalization does not feature in treaty law in general. Instruments sometimes referred to as the "suppression" conventions, such as the United Nations Convention against Transnational Organized Crime, the United Nations Convention against Corruption, and the Single Convention on Narcotic Drugs, for instance, oblige states parties to enact a range of criminal offences in national law.[1] In addition, a continuum exists between core international human rights law and international instruments that provide for individual criminal liability for the most serious human rights violations. Besides international criminal law itself, treaties such as the 1926 Slavery Convention and the 1948 Convention on the Prevention and Punishment of the Crime of Genocide contain criminal law provisions. This body of law creates well-established criminalization requirements for the most serious human rights violations.

By contrast, where the core United Nations human rights proscribe certain acts, they rarely provide specifically for penal sanctions. Rather, they more commonly use general language such as "no one shall" or "prohibit." The International Covenant on Civil and Political Rights (ICCPR), for example, in three cases obliges states parties to "prohibit" certain conduct – Article 8 (Slavery), Article 20 (Propaganda for war and advocacy of national, racial, or religious hatred), and Article 26 (Non-discrimination). It is not immediately apparent on the face of such treaty language alone whether such prohibition requires the creation of a criminal offence in national law or not.

In some cases, subsequent interpretation is clear. In respect of the prohibition on non-discrimination in ICCPR Article 26, for example, the Human Rights Committee has clarified that it is for states parties to determine appropriate measures to implement the relevant provisions, without mention of any requirement for use of criminal law.[2] Other cases, such as ICCPR Article 20, however,

1 See Boister, N., 2002, 2003.
2 United Nations, 2008. UN Doc. HRI/GEN/1/Rev.9 (Vol. I), para 4.

are less clear cut. On the one hand, the *travaux préparatoires* suggest that the original intention of member states was that ICCPR Article 20 would not require criminalization of propaganda for war or advocacy of national, racial, or religious hatred.[3] Thirty years later, in 1983, General Comment 11 of the Human Rights Committee on Article 20 broadly maintained this position.[4] Subsequent developments, though, suggest a move towards the use of criminal sanctions. The Human Rights Committee recommended in 2011, for example, the adoption of legislative reforms needed to "criminalize" any advocacy of national, racial, or religious hatred constituting incitement to discrimination, hostility or violence and the imposition of "criminal penalties" on any person making statements whose effect is the incitement to such acts, in violation of Article 20 of the covenant.[5] The United Nations Special Rapporteur on Freedom of Religion has also recommended that any advocacy of national, racial, or religious hatred that constitutes incitement to discrimination, hostility or violence must be vigorously investigated and that perpetrators must be "prosecuted" in accordance with international human rights law.[6] At the same time, however, the Human Rights Committee and the Special Rapporteur do not always refer to the need for criminal sanctions when discussing Article 20. The recent Rabat Plan of Action on the prohibition of advocacy of national, racial, or religious hatred that constitutes incitement to discrimination, hostility or violence emphasized that criminal sanctions related to unlawful forms of expression should be seen as "last resort" measures to be applied only in strictly justifiable situations.[7] Whilst the prohibition may therefore require criminalization in many, if not all, contexts, it is apparent that criminal laws must be enacted carefully, having regard to the circumstances of the statement, the identity of the speaker, his or her intent, the content or form of the statement, and the extent of the speech. In sum, it is clear that the "prohibit" language of ICCPR Article 20 remains somewhat ambiguous, even with interpretative authority.

Use of the term "prohibit" is indicative of the style of international human rights treaties of remaining largely open in the treaty text itself as to whether criminalization is required in the case of proscribed conduct, even to the extent that the same language may have different subsequent interpretations. In the case of the ICCPR, in addition to the four uses of the word "prohibit," the Covenant includes the phrase "no one shall" some 14 times, without specifying the modality of how this state of affairs should be brought about. Similarly, the ECHR and its Protocols includes one use of the phrase

3 During work on the draft Covenant in 1953, member states noted, in respect of advocacy of national, racial, or religious hatred and violence, that the phrase "shall be prohibited by the law of the State" was chosen in preference to the phrase "constitutes a crime and shall be punished under the laws of the State." See Bossuyt, M.J., 1987, p.405.

4 UNHRC General Comment 11 provides that for Article 20 to become fully effective, there ought to be a law making it clear that propaganda and advocacy as described in Article 20 are contrary to public policy and providing for an appropriate sanction in case of violation.

5 United Nations, Human Rights Committee, 2011a. UN Doc. CCPR/C/TGO/CO/4, para 9.

6 United Nations, General Assembly, 2009. UN Doc. A/HRC/13/40/Add.3, para 69.

7 United Nations, Human Rights Committee, 2013a. UN Doc. A/HRC/22/17/Add.4, para 22.

"is prohibited" and 14 uses of the phrase "no one shall," with no mention in any article of either a specific requirement for criminalization or the specific exclusion of criminalization. Indeed, across all of the nine core international human rights treaties and their protocols, as well as the treaties of the three regional human rights mechanisms, specific provisions requiring criminalization are found in only five cases. In no case do international human rights treaties specifically prohibit an act from being a criminal offence under national law.[8] The five specific provisions on criminalization relate to acts of torture; enforced disappearance; incitement to racial, and ethnic discrimination and violence; sale and sexual exploitation of children; and recruitment and use in hostilities of children. The provisions are worth reproducing in full:[9]

1. International Convention on the Elimination of All Forms of Racial Discrimination (ICERD), Article 4:

   [States Parties] (a) Shall declare an *offence punishable by law* all dissemination of ideas based on racial superiority or hatred, incitement to racial discrimination, as well as all acts of violence or incitement to such acts against any race or group of persons of another colour or ethnic origin, and also the provision of any assistance to racist activities, including the financing thereof… .(b) [States Parties] … shall recognize participation in … organizations [which promote and incite racial discrimination] and [such] activities as an offence punishable by law.

2. Convention against Torture and Other Cruel, Inhuman or Degrading Treatment or Punishment (CAT), Article 4:

   Each State Party shall ensure that all acts of torture are *offences* under its criminal law. The same shall apply to an attempt to commit torture and to an act by any person which constitutes complicity or participation in torture.

3. Optional Protocol to the Convention on the Rights of the Child on the Involvement of Children in Armed Conflict (OP-CRC-AC), Article 4:

   States Parties shall take all feasible measures to prevent … recruitment and use [in hostilities of persons under the age of 18 years by armed groups that are distinct from the armed forces of a State], including the adoption of legal measures necessary to prohibit and *criminalize* such practices.

8 Although ICCPR Article 11 implies as such through its proscription on imprisonment on the grounds of inability to fulfil a contractual obligation.

9 Extracts from ICERD, CAT, OP-CRC-AC, OP-CRC-SC and CPED reprinted with the permission of the United Nations.

4. Optional Protocol to the Convention on the Rights of the Child on the Sale of Children, Child Prostitution and Child Pornography (OP-CRC-SC), Article 3:

> Each State Party shall ensure that, as a minimum, the following acts and activities are fully covered under its *criminal or penal law*, whether such offences are committed domestically or transnationally or on an individual or organized basis: (a) In the context of sale of children as defined in article 2: (i) Offering, delivering or accepting, by whatever means, a child for the purpose of: a. Sexual exploitation of the child; b. Transfer of organs of the child for profit; c. Engagement of the child in forced labour; (ii) Improperly inducing consent, as an intermediary, for the adoption of a child in violation of applicable international legal instruments on adoption; (b) Offering, obtaining, procuring or providing a child for child prostitution, as defined in article 2; (c) Producing, distributing, disseminating, importing, exporting, offering, selling or possessing for the above purposes child pornography as defined in article 2 … Subject to the provisions of the national law of a State Party, the same shall apply to an attempt to commit any of the said acts and to complicity or participation in any of the said acts.

5. International Convention for the Protection of All Persons from Enforced Disappearance (CPED), Articles 4 and 25:

> Each State Party shall take the necessary measures to ensure that enforced disappearance constitutes an *offence* under its criminal law and
>
> Each State Party shall take the necessary measures to prevent and punish under its *criminal law*: (a) The wrongful removal of children who are subjected to enforced disappearance, children whose father, mother or legal guardian is subjected to enforced disappearance or children born during the captivity of a mother subjected to enforced disappearance; (b) The falsification, concealment or destruction of documents attesting to the true identity of the children referred to in subparagraph (a) above.

It is notable that all of these criminalization instances occur within the United Nations human rights treaties. None of the primary regional human rights treaties, such as the American Convention on Human Rights, the ECHR, or the African Charter on Human and Peoples' Rights, contain any article specifically requiring or prohibiting criminalization. This is the case despite the fact that a number of such treaties contain provisions in the same or similar areas. The prohibition of torture, for instance, is accepted as a matter of customary international law and even as a peremptory *jus cogens* norm and is contained within Article 3 of the ECHR, Article 5(2) of the American Convention on Human Rights, and Article 5 of the African Charter on Human and Peoples' Rights. None of these provisions, including also the prohibition on torture contained in ICCPR Article 7, however, specifically require criminalization of torture, even when adopted around a similar time to CAT, such as in the case of the African Charter on Human and Peoples' Rights.[10]

On the face of it, it is not therefore immediately apparent why, amongst the multiplicity of prohibitions in international human rights law – including many acts that could be perpetrated by third parties, such as arbitrary deprivation of life; slavery; servitude; forced labour; or arbitrary detention – only the five above acts are made subject to criminal measures as a matter of international human rights treaty wording alone. With respect to slavery, for example, all of the ICCPR, ECHR, and the American Convention on Human Rights simply state that no one shall be held in or subject to slavery, despite the fact that the 1926 Slavery Convention highlighted the importance of severe penalties for acts of slavery almost 40 years previously.[11] It should be noted that this is not to say that international human rights law is inconsistent. In line with the Slavery Convention, both the ECtHR and the Human Rights Committee highlight the importance of legislation classifying slavery as a criminal offence.[12] It is merely that the treaty wording itself is not explicit on the issue. The question of why this should be the case turns on two main issues – firstly, the general nature of state obligations as conceived under contemporary international human rights law, and secondly, the individual context of each human rights-based prohibition.

It is clear that, in general, regulation of the substantive content of national criminal law was not considered as a primary aim of contemporary international human rights law at the time of formulating the new United Nations human rights machinery. That this should have been the case, however, in fact represented something of a departure from parts of the body of earlier declarations of rights from which the philosophy, reason, and morality of contemporary international human rights law were derived. Texts such as the 18th century French Declaration of the Rights of Man and Citizen and the 18th century Constitution of the United States with its 18th and 19th century amendments include a greater concern for substantive criminal law than was ultimately reflected in the Universal Declaration of Human Rights (UDHR) and the subsequent core human rights treaties. Article 5 of the French Declaration of the Rights of Man and Citizen of 1789 stated that law can only prohibit such actions as are hurtful to society – reflecting almost exactly a key tenet of criminalization theory.[13] The French Declaration of 1795 also touched upon substantive criminal law through its assertion that those who incite, promote, sign, execute, or cause to be executed arbitrary acts are guilty and ought to be punished.[14] Within the French Declarations, provisions on the substantive content of criminal law are found alongside individual rights, such as rights to liberty, equality, security,

10 CAT was adopted on 10 December 1984 by General Assembly resolution 39/46, and the African Charter on Human and Peoples' Rights was adopted on 27 June 1981.

11 ICCPR, Article 8; ECHR, Article 4; American Convention on Human Rights, Article 6.

12 *Siliadin v. France*, ECHR; *C.N. v. United Kingdom*, ECHR; United Nations, Human Rights Committee, 2013d. UN Doc. CCPR/C/MRT/CO/1, paras 4 and 17.

13 French National Constituent Assembly, 1789, Article 4.

14 French National Constituent Assembly, 1795, Article 9.

and property; provisions of governance, such as a requirement for legal delegation in order to exercise any authority or fill any public function; and procedural requirements, such as for only such penalties as are strictly necessary and proportionate to the offense and a prohibition on laws with retroactive effect. In this way, some of the precursors to contemporary international human rights law contained not only rights and duties for the individual and the community but also provisions that reflected a broad societal, philosophical, and governance perspective.

When it came to early work on the formulation of the UDHR in 1946, the concept of "human rights" was subject to somewhat of a more specific interpretation. The original mandate of the United Nations Commission on Human Rights, bestowed by the Economic and Social Council in February 1946, provided that the work of the Commission should be directed towards submitting proposals, recommendations, and reports to the Council regarding, amongst others, an international bill of rights.[15] This reflected the Charter power for the Economic and Social Council to make recommendations for the purpose of promoting respect for, and observance of, human rights and fundamental freedoms for all. At its first session, the nuclear Commission on Human Rights decided that work on an international bill of rights might also substantively cover other items in the Commission's mandate, including international declarations or conventions on civil liberties, the status of women, freedom of information, and similar matters; the protection of minorities; and the prevention of discrimination on grounds of race, sex, language, or religion.[16] Aiming to fulfil this mandate, the earliest proposals submitted by states for an international bill of rights focused primarily on entitlements that could be directly claimed by individuals against the state. A first draft declaration on human rights submitted by Cuba in February 1946 expressed all of its provisions in terms of rights of "every human being." It included rights found in the French Declaration of 1795, such as to liberty, equality, security, immunity from arbitrary arrest, and participation in government, as well as economic and social rights, such as to education, work, food, and health.[17] It did not, however, contain duties for individuals, nor did it include the general principles of the French Declaration concerning governance or the criminal law. Such documents quickly set the tone for which issues would come to be considered as "human rights" matters. Tellingly, the Australian member of the Commission during its first session asked, What is seen when one speaks of human rights? He went on to answer his own question as having in mind issues such as minorities, nationalities, statelessness, rights of options, property, and discrimination,[18] thereby crystalizing a conception of rights that focused on specific issues, as distinct from a broader theory of governance, use of law, and the social contractarian elements of the French Declaration. By 1947,

15 United Nations, Economic and Social Council, 1946a. UN Doc. E/27, para 2.
16 United Nations, Economic and Social Council, 1946c. UN Doc. E/38/Rev.1, para I.
17 United Nations, Economic and Social Council, 1946b. UN Doc. E/HR/1, Articles 7 to 14.
18 United Nations, Economic and Social Council, 1947c. UN Doc. E/CN.4/AC.1/3/Add.1; United Nations, Economic and Social Council, 1947a. UN Doc. E/CN.4/SR.2.

a documented outline of an international bill of rights included criminal law only in contexts such as use of the death penalty, fair trial without undue delay, rights to legal defence, and protections against self-incrimination. When substantive criminal law was referred to during early discussions of the Commission, there appears to have been little in-depth consideration of its content as a human rights issue. In general, the Commission rather seemed to apply an assumption that the proper content of the criminal law could be broadly identified and agreed. During discussions in 1947, for instance, one proposed amendment to the draft declaration referred to acts which, at the time of their commission, were regarded as criminal by virtue of the "general principles of law" recognized by civilized nations.[19]

As a result, the foundational UDHR referred only to the criminal law in the context of the right to a fair and public hearing in the determination of any criminal charge (Article 10), as well as an exception to the right to seek and enjoy asylum in the case of prosecutions genuinely arising from non-political crimes (Article 14). Against this background, some 17 years later, the first United Nations human rights treaty to be concluded, ICERD, introduced, at the same time, the first human rights treaty criminalization obligation by requiring states parties to declare a range of actions related to racial hatred, violence, and discrimination as offences punishable by law.

Criminalization obligations in human rights treaties

ICERD Article 4

ICERD drew substantially from the earlier 1963 United Nations Declaration on the Elimination of All Forms of Racial Discrimination, which encouraged states to criminalize incitement to or acts of violence against any race or group of persons of another colour or ethnic origin. States that advocated for reference to criminalization in the draft declaration held that it was essential in the fight against discrimination, creating effective practical measures and a real rule of conduct.[20] Other delegations argued that such provisions were not suitable for inclusion in such an instrument and could be interpreted as an undue restriction of freedom of speech.[21] Tensions ran high in this regard, with one delegation stating, on conclusion of the declaration, that it did not think that the delegation could, in good faith, say that it would pass a special law to prosecute and punish "under criminal law" every person who uttered a remark capable of being interpreted as advocacy of racial discrimination.[22] The inclusion of criminalization provisions in the declaration on racial discrimination, however, set

19 United Nations, Economic and Social Council, 1947d. UN Doc. E/CN.4/SR.37, p.13.
20 United Nations, Economic and Social Council, 1963. UN Doc. E/CN.4/SR.37; United Nations, General Assembly, 1963. UN Doc. A/PV.1261, paras 58–61.
21 United Nations, Economic and Social Council, 1963. UN Doc. E/CN.4/857, p.75.
22 United Nations, General Assembly, 1963. UN Doc. A/PV.1261, para 153.

a strong precedent for the subsequent ICERD. Accordingly, some of the first texts of the draft convention already included proposals that it should be an offence to commit, or to incite to commit, an act of violence against another person on the grounds of race, colour, or ethnic origin. Other proposals included an obligation to "penalize" all incitement to racial discrimination resulting in or likely to cause acts of violence, as well as to recognize all incitement to racial discrimination and racial hatred as an offence "punishable under law." The Third Committee of the General Assembly amended a further revised proposal to that finally adopted as Article 4 of ICERD in December 1965.

Whilst ICERD was adopted by majority vote of the General Assembly, a number of countries made statements following its adoption that were specifically critical of the criminal law requirements of Article 4. Many states subsequently made declarations or reservations pertaining to ICERD Article 4 on becoming party to the Convention. These focused predominantly on either reaffirming the primacy of rights to freedom of opinion and expression, as contained in UDHR Articles 19 and 20, or on reserving the requirement to enact such legislation if the need arose.[23] Most recently, the Committee on the Elimination of Racial Discrimination has provided useful clarification on the scope of the criminalization requirements of Article 4. General Recommendation 35 of the Committee on combatting racist hate speech recommends that the criminalization of forms of racist expression should be reserved for serious cases, to be proven beyond reasonable doubt, whilst less serious cases should be addressed by means other than criminal law, taking into account, *inter alia*, the nature and extent of the impact on target persons and groups.[24] This interpretation places a limiting effect on the criminalization of Article 4 and brings the article towards greater convergence with ICCPR Article 20 (Prohibition on advocacy of national, racial or religious hatred that constitutes incitement to discrimination, hostility or violence), which does not contain a clear criminalization requirement on the text alone. CERD General Comment 35 also notes that the application of criminal sanctions under ICERD Article 4 should be governed by principles of legality, proportionality, and necessity, with clear reference to HRC General Comment 34 on freedoms of opinion and expression.[25] In addition, in identifying forms of conduct that may constitute dissemination or incitement offences punishable by law under Article 4, CERD draws strongly from the principles of the Rabat Plan of Action on the prohibition of advocacy of national, racial, or religious hatred that constitutes incitement to discrimination, hostility

23 See, for example, declarations and reservations made by Antigua and Barbuda, Bahamas, Barbados, Belgium, Fiji, France, Grenada, Italy, Japan, Malta, Nepal, Monaco, Papua New Guinea, Switzerland, Tonga, and United Kingdom (United Nations Treaty Collection, 2019).

24 United Nations, Committee on the Elimination of Racial Discrimination, 2013. UN Doc. CERD/C/GC/35, para 12.

25 United Nations, Human Rights Committee, 2011b. UN Doc. CCPR/C/GC/34, paras 22–25 and 33–35.

or violence – a document framed largely within the context of ICCPR Article 20. The combined effect of such developments is the nuancing, or tempering, of the criminalization provision of ICERD Article 4. The textual contrast – in terms of the absence of criminalization – with the related provisions of ICCPR Article 20 adopted just one year later remains. However, the largely political considerations that gave rise to each text, and the differences between them, have gradually experienced reconciliation around the criminalization of intentional, serious statements that constitute threats or incitement to racial or ethnic discrimination, hostility, or violence.

CAT Article 4

Whilst the process leading to ICERD Article 4 contained some degree of controversy, the next criminalization provision to be adopted within international human rights treaty law, CAT Article 4, in 1984, achieved a higher level of consensus. In the context of international humanitarian law, common Article 3 of the 1949 Geneva Conventions had already provided a prohibition on torture in the case of persons taking no active part in hostilities in conflicts not of an international character. This prohibition was included in the grave breaches regime of the Geneva Conventions, in respect of which High Contracting Parties are obliged to undertake to enact any legislation necessary to provide effective penal sanctions for persons committing, or ordering to be committed, grave breaches. The Fifth United Nations Congress on the Prevention of Crime and the Treatment of Offenders held in Geneva in September 1975 included in its discussions the protection of detainees against torture and other inhuman treatment.[26] The Congress considered a draft declaration initiated by the Netherlands and Sweden on protection from torture, which was subsequently adopted as the Declaration on the Protection of All Persons from Being Subjected to Torture and Other Cruel, Inhuman or Degrading Treatment or Punishment, by the General Assembly in December 1975. Article 7 of the Declaration stated that each state shall ensure that all acts of torture, as well as acts constituting participation in, complicity in, incitement to, or an attempt to commit torture, are offences under criminal law.

Torture under the 1975 Declaration was restricted to acts intentionally inflicted by or at the instigation of a public official, as opposed to the broader formulation that included "with the consent or acquiescence" of a public official or other person acting in an official capacity, ultimately used by CAT. Nonetheless, the criminalization provisions of Article 7 of the 1975 Declaration survived, almost word for word, in the form of CAT Article 4. Criminalization was included in Article 7 of a draft international convention against torture prepared by Sweden in 1978, which was used as a basis for the work of an open-ended Working Group on a Draft Convention against Torture and Other Cruel,

26 See United Nations, 1976. UN Doc. A/CONF.56/10, para 260.

Inhuman or Degrading Treatment or Punishment, established by the Economic and Social Council in 1983.[27] The Working Group submitted its proposed draft convention to the General Assembly in 1984, resulting in the adoption of CAT by General Assembly resolution 39/46 of 10 December 1984. Throughout this process, there is no record of divergent views on inclusion of the requirement to ensure that all acts of torture are offences under criminal law. The 1984 report of the Working Group, for example, refers to a certain lack of consensus on the issue of the forms of jurisdiction attaching to the criminal offence of torture, but not on the point of criminalization itself.[28] Unlike the situation with respect to ICERD Article 4, this is reflective of the higher degree of pre-existing consensus on criminalization of torture in national law prior to development of the international instrument.

OP-CRC-AC Article 4 and OP-CRC-SC Article 3

For over 15 years, torture and incitement to racial discrimination and violence remained the only criminalization requirements contained directly in international human rights treaties at the global level. This changed in the year 2000, with the adoption of two optional protocols to the Convention on the Rights of the Child.

OP-CRC-AC requires states parties to criminalize the recruitment or use in hostilities of persons under the age of 18 years by armed groups that are distinct from the armed forces of a state. OP-CRC-SC creates a requirement for the criminalization of a number of specific acts constituting elements of the sale of children, child prostitution, and child pornography. As optional protocols to an existing convention, both of these areas were already addressed in broad terms by the primary instrument, the Convention on the Rights of the Child. CRC Article 38, for example, requires states parties to refrain from recruiting any person who has not attained the age of 15 years into their armed forces, as well as to take all feasible measures to ensure that persons who have not attained the age of 15 years do not take a direct part in hostilities. CRC Articles 35 and 34 require states parties to take measures to prevent the sale or traffic of children, as well as their exploitative use in prostitution and pornography. The CRC optional protocols thus provide an example of the elevation and expansion of an international human rights law treaty obligation to "take measures" in a particular area, to a criminalization obligation, at least for those states choosing to become party to the optional protocol.

Interestingly, however, criminalization itself was not at the forefront of the rationale behind the development of a protocol in each case. The preliminary draft optional protocol on children in armed conflict of 1993 did not include

27 United Nations, Economic and Social Council, 1983. UN Doc. E/RES/1983/38.

28 United Nations, Economic and Social Council, 1984. UN Doc. E/CN.4/1984/72, paras 11 to 36.

criminalization. Rather, the primary concern of the preliminary draft protocol was to raise the age of recruitment of children into the armed forces from 15 years, as contained in CRC Article 38, to 18 years.[29] The draft focused on recruitment to state armed forces and did not refer to non-state armed groups. The preliminary draft addressed recruitment age by simply stating that states parties shall "refrain" from recruiting any person under 18 years without specifying any enforcement or implementation method.[30] Comments submitted on the preliminary draft optional protocol proposed that states parties should be under an obligation to make it a "criminal offence" knowingly to recruit persons under the age of 18 years.[31] Whilst the proposal was not accepted, by 1998 the draft of the protocol included a new specific obligation to take all "appropriate measures" to prevent recruitment of persons under the age of 18 years by non-governmental armed groups involved in hostilities. Shortly thereafter, in July 1998, the Rome Statute of the International Criminal Court was adopted, including its stipulation that conscripting or enlisting children under the age of 15 years or using them to participate actively in hostilities constituted a war crime in both international and non-international armed conflicts.

The fact that children may be recruited, including forcibly, for use in armed conflict by non-state actors, as highlighted by the Rome Statute, constituted a key consideration in the inclusion of criminalization in a revised draft protocol prepared by the United States in December 1999.[32] That draft provided that states parties should ensure that recruitment of persons below age 18 by dissident armed forces or other organized armed groups for use in armed conflict was punishable as a criminal offence under national laws. The draft adopted the following year provided that states parties should prohibit and criminalize the recruitment of use in hostilities of persons under the age of 18 years by armed groups that are distinct from the armed forces of a state.[33] This language was included, in almost identical form, by the General Assembly in its resolution of 16 March 2001 adopting OP-CRC-AC.

Whereas criminalization was not an original aim of OP-CRC-AC, the 1993 draft optional protocol concerning the elimination of sexual exploitation and trafficking in children (OP-CRC-SC) already focused heavily on use of criminal law. The 1993 draft declared that crimes of sexual exploitation of or trafficking in children represented crimes against humanity and required states parties to ensure that national legislation extended to crimes of sexual exploitation of or

29 See United Nations, Commission on Human Rights, 1994c. UN Doc. E/CN.4/1994/WG.13/2.

30 United Nations, Committee on the Rights of the Child, 1993. UN Doc. CRC/C/16, Annex p.60.

31 United Nations, Commission on Human Rights, 1994d. UN Doc. E/CN.4/1994/WG.13/2/Add.1, p.10, para 5.

32 United Nations, Commission on Human Rights, 1999b. UN Doc. E/CN.4/2000/WG.13/2/Add.1, para 16.

33 *Ibid.*, Annex, Article 4.

trafficking in children.[34] The extensive use of criminal law in the draft protocol drew from a number of precedents, including the 1949 Convention for the Suppression of the Traffic in Persons and of the Exploitation of the Prostitution of Others, the 1992 Programme of Action for the Prevention of the Sale of Children, Child Prostitution and Child Pornography and for the Elimination of the Exploitation of Child Labour, as well as national criminal laws. In this respect, it is clear that one of the original aims of a proposed optional protocol on sexual exploitation of children was to reinforce the criminalization of the sale of children, child prostitution, and child pornography.

From this starting point, discussions on the preparation of the draft protocol centred more on the scope and formulation of criminalization than on whether criminalization represented an appropriate obligation for inclusion in the instrument. Accordingly, sessions of the Working Group tasked with drafting the protocol developed definitions of the acts, in addition to considering whether child sex tourism should also form part of the protocol criminalization obligation as a separate offence.[35] Definitional issues considered by the Group included whether criminalization of the sale of children should be limited to sale for the purposes of coercing or inducing the child into child prostitution or child pornography, or could be for any form of sexual, economic, or criminal exploitation. This discussion was driven in large part by pragmatic considerations such as the exact mandate of the Working Group, the wording of CRC Article 35, and the existence of other international instruments that addressed non-sexual forms of exploitation, including commercial inter-country adoption and non-sexual forms of exploitative child labour.[36] This clearly positivist approach to formulation of international human rights law criminalization requirements was also reflected in the approach of the Working Group to specify activities that should constitute an offence in relation to sale of children, child prostitution, and child pornography. The observer for New Zealand, for example, at the fifth session of the Working Group stated that it was important that the optional protocol should be clear on exactly what states parties would be required to criminalize and proposed that the protocol specify activities to be penalized, such as facilitating, coercing, and inducing, in the substantive criminalization article, rather than within definitions.[37] This proposal was accepted and, as a result, the final protocol contains detailed wording that describes act elements related to the sale of children for specified purposes, to child prostitution, and to child pornography that states parties are obliged to ensure are fully covered under criminal or penal law.

34 United Nations, Commission on Human Rights 1994a. UN Doc. E/CN.4/1994/45/Add.1, Articles 1 and 2.

35 United Nations, Commission on Human Rights, 1996. UN Doc. E/CN.4/1996/101.

36 See, for example, United Nations, Commission on Human Rights, 1998a. UN Doc. E/CN.4/1998/103, paras 27 to 40.

37 United Nations, Commission on Human Rights, 1999a. UN Doc. E/CN.4/1999/74, para 21.

CPED Articles 4 and 25

The final treaty-based criminalization requirement contained in international human rights law is found in the 2006 CPED. Whereas CPED was agreed just over 10 years ago, the question of enforced disappearances had come to the fore in the mid 1960s and late 1970s, due to concern over situations in Guatemala and Chile.[38] In 1980, the United Nations General Assembly urged the Chilean authorities to investigate and clarify the fate of persons who had disappeared for political reasons and to institute "criminal proceedings" against those responsible for such disappearances.[39] Such General Assembly resolutions, along with decisions of the Inter-American Court of Human Rights, not only confirmed that enforced disappearance constituted a multiple human rights violation but also set the stage for an international obligation to characterize the act as an offence under national law and to carry out an effective criminal investigation. Notably, such bodies called for criminal investigation notwithstanding the fact that, and perhaps even especially because, such acts were often carried out by agents acting under cover of public authority.

Driven, in large part, by the situation in a number of countries in the Americas, drafting processes on a UN Declaration on the Protection of All Persons from Enforced Disappearances and an Inter-American Convention on Forced Disappearance of Persons commenced almost simultaneously, with the processes, at different moments, serving to reinforce each other. Incorporating provisions from the draft OAS Convention relating to disappearance "as a common crime," Article 4(1) of the Declaration on the Protection of All Persons from Enforced Disappearance adopted by General Assembly resolution 47/133 in February 1993 stated that all acts of enforced disappearance shall be "offences under criminal law," punishable by appropriate penalties which shall take into account their extreme seriousness. A proposal for an international convention on the prevention and punishment of enforced disappearances was subsequently made in August 1995. By 1998, a draft convention had been transmitted to the Commission on Human Rights. The draft proposed that states parties undertake to adopt the necessary legislative measures to define the forced disappearance of persons as an "independent offence" and to impose an appropriate punishment commensurate with its extreme gravity.[40] By 2002, broad consensus existed that enforced disappearance should be subject to criminal law measures, although member states remained somewhat divided on whether this meant that specific criminalization was required. Some delegations considered that states should not be required to characterize enforced disappearance as an independent offence in their domestic criminal law, but merely to prosecute the perpetrators of acts of enforced disappearance.[41]

38 See United Nations, Commission on Human Rights, 2002. UN Doc. E/CN.4/2002/71.

39 United Nations, General Assembly, 1980. UN Doc. A/RES/35/188.

40 United Nations, Commission on Human Rights, 1998b. UN Doc. E/CN.4/Sub.2/1998/19, Annex, Article 5.

41 United Nations, Commission on Human Rights, 2004. UN Doc. E/CN.4/2004/59, para 50.

Such an approach would have established an international obligation only to take some form of criminal law action, such as through existing kidnapping, homicide, illegal restraint, abduction, torture, or hostage taking offences, rather than to codify the specific elements of the act of forced disappearance as a separate offence. By contrast, states in favour of a separate offence argued that scattershot prosecutions should be avoided and that enforced disappearance must be made a criminal offence *in itself*, given its specific and complex nature, which was not merely a series of random acts.[42] Article 4 of the final agreed Convention stated that each state party shall take the necessary measures to ensure that enforced disappearance constitutes an offence under its criminal law. This is to be interpreted as requiring a specific criminal offence in law that contains the elements of the definition of enforced disappearance. In concluding observations, the Committee on Enforced Disappearances has stated, for example, that reference to a range of existing offences and regulations is not sufficient to meet the Article 4 obligation, as the offence of enforced disappearance is not a series of different crimes but rather a single complex offence. As such, the Committee considers that the definition of enforced disappearance as a separate offence best enables a state party to comply with the obligation under article 4.[43]

Lessons from human rights treaty-based criminalization

The processes leading to the formation of a direct human rights treaty obligation to create a criminal offence within ICERD, CAT, OP-CRC-AC, OP-CRC-SC, and CPED show a range of relationships between international human rights law and criminal law. At one end of this range is the proposition (prior to formulation of the human rights treaty criminalization obligation) that "the act is a human rights issue but not presently a crime." At the other end of the range is the proposition that "the act is widely recognized as a crime but is also a human rights issue."

The example of ICERD sits at one end of this range. At the time of drafting of the Convention, racial discrimination was clearly identified as a human rights issue, with the right to equality before the law and equal protection against discrimination entrenched in UDHR Article 7. Whilst some states had a criminal offence or aggravating circumstances in criminal law for racially motivated violence or incitement to such violence, the dissemination of ideas based on racial superiority and incitement to racial discrimination were not commonly criminalized.[44] The history of human rights and criminalization within ICERD is thus very much one of debate over whether the criminal law is an appropriate tool for protecting against the Convention condemnation of racial

42 United Nations, Commission on Human Rights, 2005b. UN Doc. E/CN.4/2005/66, para 28.

43 United Nations, Committee on Enforced Disappearances, 2014. UN Doc. CED/C/BEL/CO/1, para 11.

44 For a review of national approaches to racial hate speech, see Coliver, S. (ed.), 1992.

discrimination. State views in this respect ranged from the idea that criminal measures were required to create effective practical measures and a real rule of conduct, to the position that criminal law could never apply to ideological offences.[45] States most opposed to the use of criminal sanctions in the realm of non-discrimination even advanced the view that the international human rights system was premised on an awareness of responsibilities as free and equal citizens and not by fear of punishment – coming close to arguing that international human rights law should never be enforced through the use of criminal sanctions.[46]

From a dual nature of law perspective, the political, positivist negotiation process that gave rise to ICERD was clearly infused with moral discussion regarding the limits of state encroachment upon individual freedoms. Such discussion argued both for and against the use of criminalization from a moral perspective. Colombia, for example, noting that the Colombian constitution was based on the principles of Rousseau, argued that individualism has had to, and still had to, make concessions in the interest of the community, without stamping out the individual, without encroaching upon freedom, and whilst respecting the right to think and to express deliberate decisions in actions or words.[47] Indeed, for some states, the criminalization of dissemination of ideas based on racial superiority as a means to the elimination of racial discrimination breached Radbruch's threshold of extreme injustice for the outermost border of law and led to reservations against ICERD Article 4. On the other hand, those states that argued forcibly for criminalization also did so ostensibly from a moral perspective of the harm and suffering caused by specific global sociopolitical events – including national socialism, anti-Semitism, and colonialism. All of contemporary international human rights law is, in many ways, a response to the atrocities of the Second World War. However, the specific invocation of large-scale historic and ongoing harms and wrongs appeared to play a particular role in the inclusion of criminalization in the Declaration on the Elimination of All Forms of Racial Discrimination, as well as, subsequently, in ICERD.

Similar to ICERD, the criminalization requirement of OP-CRC-AC sits at the end of the range where – at the time of negotiation of the instrument – the act (of recruitment and use in hostilities of children) was recognized as a human rights concern but was not necessarily widely criminalized. In this case, the development of an international human rights law criminalization requirement was clearly influenced by international criminal law, which, in July 1998, included conscripting or enlisting children as a war crime in the new Rome Statute of the International Criminal Court.[48] The parallel focus on preventing

45 See, for example, United Nations, General Assembly, 1963. UN Doc. A/PV.1261, paras 119 and 134.

46 *Ibid.*, para 47.

47 United Nations, General Assembly, 1965. UN Doc. A/PV.1406, paras 68–69.

48 Prior to which, recruitment of children was prohibited by Additional Protocols I and II, but was not included within the grave breaches scheme of the Conventions, under which states are required to apply penal sanctions.

engagement of children in armed conflict in both the development of international human rights law and international criminal law in turn arose from increased recognition of the situation of child soldiers. The harm to such children was emphasized in the preamble to the preliminary draft optional protocol, which stated that involvement in hostilities of persons who have not attained the age of 18 years was "harmful" for them physically and psychologically and affected the full implementation of the rights of the child, including the right to life.[49] As with criminalization in ICERD, dual nature of law theory well captures both the practical, political motivations for criminalization of recruitment of children and the legal moral theory perspective. Whereas the inclusion of criminalization in OP-CRC-AC is undoubtedly due to the fact that key countries, such as the United States, were instrumental in advocating for it, at the same time, the OP-CRC-AC negotiation history captures something of moral legal theory. The recognition that involvement in hostilities is both harmful and a violation of the rights of the child, for instance, reflects almost precisely a proposition found in criminal theory: that the criminal law may legitimately proscribe those actions that harm an individual by violating his or her rights.

ICERD and OP-CRC-AC demonstrate the translation of a human rights issue into a criminalization requirement. At the other end of the range lies the situation where an act is already recognized as a crime, but is also a human rights concern. The criminalization of sale of children and child pornography by OP-CRC-SC falls within this category. Criminal law, including at the international level, has long, for example, included within its ambit sexual acts committed without consent, as well as acts of procuring for prostitution and exploiting the prostitution of another. The inclusion of protection from sexual exploitation, sexual abuse, and sale of the child in CRC Articles 34 and 35 in 1989 was, in many ways, the reflection of an area more traditionally covered by the criminal law, in the wording of an international human rights treaty. The extension of CRC, and subsequently OP-CRC-SC, to provide such protection reflects an expanded understanding of human rights, building upon notions of equality, dignity, and opportunity for full development of the human person within the particular sphere of the rights of the child. In this way, OP-CRC-SC clarifies and reinforces a global standard for an area largely already within the realm of the criminal law. As a human rights instrument, it emphasizes that sale of children, child prostitution, and child pornography are crimes and, at the same time, human rights violations. By providing common, core elements of the crimes, the Protocol aims to make clear exactly what states parties should criminalize. In addition to the moral message that these exact acts – as defined by the Protocol – are crimes and human rights violations, the Protocol has the practical effect of promoting harmonization of national laws. In the absence of a common approach to criminalization and criminal law definitions, sale of

49 United Nations, Commission on Human Rights, 1993. UN Doc. E/CN.4/1994/91, preamble.

children, child prostitution, and child pornography may be prosecuted under broader national laws on slavery, kidnapping, prostitution, obscenity, or pornography. The use of such diverse criminal laws can create challenges when it comes to international cooperation for the investigation and prosecution of crimes. By contrast, where criminal law provisions are equivalent, processes of international cooperation in criminal investigations, such as mutual legal assistance and extradition, are greatly facilitated.[50]

The significant focus of OP-CRC-SC on criminal law for protection against sale of children, child prostitution, and child pornography provides it with a structure that is more akin to the international suppression conventions than an international human rights treaty. Indeed, the difference in the relative focus on criminalization as between, for example, OP-CRC-SC and ICERD is quite notable. Criminalization in ICERD is not accorded a particularly distinct single article, is incorporated alongside other general obligations to adopt measures or to not permit, and is not accompanied by any general criminal law provisions. ICERD does not, for example, create any extensive criminal justice regime, such as the jurisdictional reach of the required criminal offence or by obliging states parties to arrest, extradite, or otherwise cooperate in respect of suspected offenders. By contrast, within OP-CRC-SC, the obligation to criminalize is contained in a distinct article, and the Protocol addresses associated general criminal law issues of attempt, liability of legal persons, jurisdiction, extradition, asset forfeiture, and international cooperation.[51]

This far more expansive treatment of criminal law issues within an international human rights instrument is due to a number of factors. In the first place, the fact that OP-CRC-SC clarifies and reinforces criminalization in an area largely already within the realm of the criminal law provides a starting point and space for a more detailed treatment of the exact offence elements and associated general criminal law issues. By contrast, and at the other end of the range, where the act is not widely already a crime, negotiations on the translation of a human rights issue into a criminalization requirement (such as in ICERD and OP-CRC-AC) have tended to focus more on whether the instrument should require criminalization *at all*, rather than the practical machinery of criminal law and procedure. In addition, in the case of OP-CRC-SC, the transnational element that may be present in acts of sale of children, child prostitution, and child pornography provides an additional impetus for the inclusion of general criminal law provisions on jurisdiction and international cooperation.

Around the middle of the range, the cases of CAT and CPED represent situations where the acts of torture and enforced disappearance were largely recognized as both crimes and human rights violations around the time of the instrument drafting process. In each case, the act was widely criminalized at the

50 On the principle of dual criminality in international cooperation in criminal matters, see United Nations Office on Drugs and Crime, 2012, p.48.

51 OP-CRC-AC Articles 3(2), 3(4), 4, 5, 6, and 7.

national level, but states agreed, due to the particular violation of rights represented by the act, that there was a need to provide for a criminalization obligation at the international level. In a manner similar to OP-CRC-SC, the broad existing consensus on criminalization provided an opportunity for CAT and CPED to also address matters of the general part of criminal law. Within CAT, for example, some six out of 16 substantive articles are dedicated to the criminalization obligation and associated criminal justice machinery. The Convention addresses the general criminal law issues of attempt; complicity; participation; penalties; jurisdictions; arrest; preliminary enquiry; notification to other states; standards of evidence; extradition; and mutual legal assistance.[52] For CPED, some 11 out of 25 substantive articles address criminalization of three distinct acts,[53] as well as providing for accomplice, participation, and superior liability; penalties; mitigating and aggravating circumstances; statutes of limitations; jurisdiction; arrest; preliminary enquiry; custody; notification to other states; extradition; and mutual legal assistance.[54]

What, then, does this range in international human rights treaty law-based criminalization tell us? Can any lessons for criminalization theory be identified from the five instances? The first point to note is that whilst human rights principles discussed in Chapter 4, such as the general security of person obligation and the general crime investigatory obligation, do show some consistency with treaty-based criminalization, such principles are not determinative of inclusion of a criminalization requirement in human rights treaty wording. The general security of person obligation amounts to a human rights obligation to develop a legal framework, including criminalization, for the prevention and suppression of, at least, violent acts such as threats to life, serious assault, kidnapping, and rape, which represent the most direct affront to rights to life, liberty, and property, and to freedom from cruel, inhuman, or degrading treatment. Four of the five instances of treaty-based criminalization (torture; enforced disappearance; involvement of children in armed conflict; and sale of children, child prostitution, and child pornography) fall broadly within this category. However, a number of key rights on which the general security of person obligation is based – including the right to life (ICCPR Article 6); the right not to be held in slavery (ICCPR Article 8); and the right not to be subjected to cruel, inhuman, or degrading treatment (ICCPR Article 7) – do not include criminalization requirements within treaty wording itself. Rather, the obligation to protect facets of these rights through the criminal law has been developed later through international soft law.

Similarly, the general crime investigatory obligation of international human rights law shows some consistency with treaty-based criminalization but is by no means determinative. Under the general crime investigatory obligation,

52 CAT Articles 4 to 9.
53 CPED Articles 4 and 25.
54 CPED Articles 4 to 11, 13, 14, and 25.

the question whether punishment in the sense of criminal prosecution is required depends on the affected right and on the seriousness of the particular violation. Under this principle, whilst serious or grave human rights violations may require prosecution or punishment, less serious violations could adequately be addressed by non-criminal matters. Whereas violation of those rights that carry a treaty-based criminalization requirement could be argued to always constitute a serious or grave violation, it is clear that many rights where violation is considered serious do not require criminal offences on treaty wording alone.

Overall, dual nature of law theory provides at least a limited explanation for the place of criminalization within international human rights treaties. A moral argument for use of the criminal law, such as the seriousness of a violation due to its fundamental challenge to equality or freedom and security, is often invoked by states arguing for a treaty-based criminalization requirement. The introduction of this argument in the first place, however, is highly dependent upon the particular circumstances of the negotiation of each instrument, including the extent to which an act is already widely covered by national criminal laws, as well as the sociopolitical realist interests of influential states. Identifying exactly why a criminalization requirement is agreed by states in one context, and not another though, remains challenging. During the negotiation of the Convention on the Rights of Persons with Disabilities, for example, initial proposals for elements of the Convention included a requirement for states to characterize violence within and outside the home, as well as sexual abuse committed against persons with disabilities, as offences under national law and to adopt the measures needed to penalize them.[55] Whereas Article 16 (Freedom from exploitation, violence and abuse) of the final Convention requires states parties to "put in place effective legislation and policies … to ensure that instances of exploitation, violence and abuse against persons with disabilities are identified, investigated and, *where appropriate, prosecuted*," the Convention does not include a strict criminalization requirement.[56] This is despite the fact that it addresses issues, such as non-discrimination, freedom from torture, liberty, and security of person, and freedom from exploitation, violence, and abuse, that have attracted criminalization provisions in other human rights treaties. Reports of the Ad Hoc Committee established to consider proposals for a convention on the rights of persons with disabilities reveal almost no discussion at all about the use of criminal sanctions. Discussion around the draft article on freedom from violence and abuse, for example, focused on terms such as "legal remedies" and "judicial involvement," as opposed to use of the criminal law.[57] This may

55 United Nations, Ad Hoc Committee on a Comprehensive and Integral International Convention on Protection and Promotion of the Rights and Dignity of Persons with Disabilities, 2003. UN Doc. A/AC.265/2003/CRP/13. Proposal by Venezuela.

56 Extract from CRPD reprinted with the permission of the United Nations.

57 United Nations, 2004. Online resource.

have been, in part, due to a presumption that violence and abuse were already sufficiently covered by national criminal laws. On the other hand, the particular vulnerabilities of persons with disabilities raise a number of issues, such as forced interventions, economic exploitation, forced segregation, neglect in care, and mental abuse, all of which may be subject to varied treatment within national legal systems.

Summary

The nine core United Nations human rights treaties contain just five requirements for criminalization within treaty wording. These are found in ICERD, CAT, OP-CRC-AC, OP-CRC-SC, and CPED. The drafting history of these obligations reveals a range of relationships between international human rights law and criminal law. At the two ends of this range are two types of human rights treaty-based criminalization: the creation of a new international criminalization requirement for the protection of a human rights issue on the one hand, and the clarification and operationalization of existing offences within the human rights sphere on the other hand.

Whereas international human rights instruments have not traditionally been directly concerned with the proper extent of the criminal law, a congruence of global trends, advocacy by an influential country, and an argument that draws from legal theory can be sufficient for an international human rights treaty to break with this traditional approach and to directly require criminalization. In particular, a recent trend has emerged to address existing parts of the criminal law within the human rights context, resulting in reinforcement of a global standard for criminalization in a particular area, along with transnational enforcement mechanisms not dissimilar to the suppression conventions. At the same time, however, inclusion of criminalization is not necessarily driven by a clear principled approach and is dependent on both the political realities of international negotiations and the nature and extent of existing criminal laws.

6 Criminalization in human rights cases

The five direct criminalization obligations contained in the core international human rights treaties represent only a small part of the international human rights law and criminalization picture. The far larger part is composed of the collective decisions of international human rights courts and tribunals. These provide the soft law interpretative standards that delineate the meaning and application of treaty-based rights to the question of criminalization. At the regional level, the ECtHR, in particular, offers one of the more extensive sources of human rights criminalization jurisprudence. Judgments of the ECtHR do not strictly bind non-parties to the particular case. However, as noted by the Court in *Pretty*, judgments issued in individual cases nonetheless establish precedents, albeit to a greater or lesser extent.[1] The combined jurisprudence of the ECtHR on a particular issue can therefore be taken as an authoritative expression of international human rights standards within the regional European system.

Whereas ECtHR case law contains a significant number of cases related to the content and use of the criminal law, it is easy to see, on one level, why the perception sometimes prevails that international human rights law has little to say about the substantive criminal law. A quantitative analysis of ECtHR decisions, for example, indicates that the European Court encounters human rights objections to criminal procedure far more often than it does regarding substantive criminal law. Of over 21,000 ECtHR English language judgments, around half involve alleged violations of the right to fair trial, of which over 2,000 cases carry a keyword of "criminal proceedings."[2] By contrast, less than 100 judgments in total contain the word "criminalization," of which the majority refer only to the concept in passing. The difference in numbers is striking, if somewhat misleading. International human rights courts and tribunals do not often engage in *in abstracto* reasoning regarding criminal law in general, and multiple routes exist towards consideration of the human rights compatibility of criminal law provisions. As such, the ECtHR is not often inclined to use terms

1 *Pretty v. United Kingdom*, ECHR, para 75.
2 Results from search of http://hudoc.echr.coe.int/.

such as "criminalization." Rather, the *in concreto* nature of international human rights jurisprudence means that judgments more often concern individual convictions, or at least threatened convictions, than they do criminalization *per se*. At the same time, not all challenges to convictions involve questions of criminalization. Of the over 3,000 ECtHR judgments that concern criminal convictions, many arise from alleged criminal procedure failings and have nothing to say about the criminal law itself.

As a result, identifying the complete jurisprudence of an international human rights tribunal, such as the ECtHR, on criminalization is challenging. Relevant ECtHR decisions are largely dispersed. They often cut across different ECHR articles and factual circumstances. The discussion in this chapter draws from identification and review of almost 80 ECtHR judgments or decisions that concern the compatibility of the criminal law with the provisions of the ECHR. The cases reviewed are listed at the end of this book. The case group does not exhaustively identify all ECtHR cases relevant to criminalization, but is rather a representative cross-section of cases that exemplify the approach and principles of the Court to matters of the criminal law. A significant issue here is the identification of when a case "addresses" the question of criminalization. As discussed in Chapter 4, issues of the compatibility of national criminal law with international human rights law can arise through a number of routes. These include cases that invoke a direct negative or positive criminalization obligation, as well as cases that concern the specific crime prevention obligation and general crime investigatory obligation.

Direct negative and positive criminalization cases

In the most direct human rights criminalization cases, the applicant submits that a specific criminal law is incompatible with the rights and freedoms of the human rights instrument (the negative criminalization obligation) or that the positive obligations of the instrument require that a specific act should be a criminal offence (the positive criminalization obligation). In the first of these possibilities, the case is typically brought by an applicant who could find himself or herself subject to the criminal law. Thus, for example, in the ECHR case of *Norris v. Ireland*, the applicant complained that under the law in force in Ireland he was liable to prosecution on account of his homosexual conduct. In *A, B and C v. Ireland*, the applicants complained about the prohibition of abortion in Ireland on health and well-being grounds. In *Friend, the Countryside Alliance and Others v. United Kingdom*, the applicants argued that the creation of criminal offences for hunting a wild mammal with a dog constituted a violation of a number of their Convention rights. In *Pretty v. United Kingdom*, the applicant submitted that the blanket nature of the criminal law on assisted suicide interfered with a number of her rights under the Convention, and in *S.A.S. v. France*, the applicant argued that the criminal prohibition in law of wearing clothing designed to conceal the face constituted a violation of her Convention rights.

In none of these cases was the applicant convicted of a criminal offence and complained rather about the potential application of the criminal law to his or her circumstances. In such cases, the Court recognizes that a law may breach the rights of an individual in the absence of a specific instance of enforcement. The applicant can thus claim to be a "victim" if he or she is required either to modify his or her conduct or risk being prosecuted, or if he or she is a member of a certain category of persons who risk being directly affected by the legislation.[3] These cases represent the closest that the ECtHR comes to direct consideration of the compatibility of national criminal law with the European Convention under a negative criminalization obligation. It is apparent, however, that the consideration of the Court nonetheless is still, at least formally, through the lens of the circumstances of the particular applicant. The ECtHR has recalled on a number of occasions that its jurisdiction is confined to examining the application of a national law in a specific case and that it cannot consider in the abstract the compatibility of a law with the Convention.[4] Thus, in *A, B and C*, the Court made reference to the specific situation of the applicants as regards their access to relevant information on abortion and the psychological and physical impact of travelling abroad for an abortion.[5] In *Friend*, the Court noted that there was no evidence that the applicants would, for example, lose their homes as a result of the hunting ban, and in *Pretty*, the Court recognized the devastating effects of the applicant's degenerative disease and her particular physical and mental suffering.[6] Nonetheless, at the same time, it is clear that the Court does treat such applicants, to a large extent, as representative of a "class of persons" affected by the criminal law. In *S.A.S.*, for instance, the reasoning of the Court was almost exclusively focused on the impact on the situation "of women" who, "like the applicant," had chosen to wear the full-face veil for reasons related to their beliefs.[7] Similarly, in *A, B and C*, whilst the Court was cognizant of the different situations of the three applicants, the judgment also tended towards *in abstracto* consideration of the compatibility of Irish law on abortion with the Convention, rather than an analysis of the alleged specific violations experienced by the applicants.[8]

This class of cases represents a strong source of human rights reasoning on the proper extent of the criminal law. The direct nature of the application to the Court results in a relatively clear direction from the ECtHR as to the acceptability of criminalization from a human rights perspective. In all of *A, B and C*,

3 *S.A.S. v. France*, ECHR, para 57.

4 See *Acmanne and others v. Belgium*, ECHR. See also *Salabiaku v. France*, ECHR, para 30; and *Wingrove v. United Kingdom*, ECHR, para 50.

5 *A, B and C v. Ireland*, ECHR, para 239.

6 *Friend, the Countryside Alliance and Others v. United Kingdom*, ECHR, para 45, and *Pretty v. United Kingdom*, ECHR, paras 64 and 65.

7 *S.A.S. v. France*, ECHR, para 146.

8 *A, B and C v. Ireland*, ECHR, concurring opinion of Judge Lopez Guerra, joined by Judge Casadevall, para 4.

Friend, *Pretty*, and *S.A.S.*, for example, the Court found no violation of Convention rights as regards the impugned criminal law. Whereas these decisions are binding strictly only on the state party to the particular dispute, such cases do create a certain manner of precedent that the impugned acts *can* be a criminal offence. By contrast, in *Norris*, in line with its decision in *Dudgeon*, the Court found a violation of the Convention in respect of the effect of the impugned legislation on the applicant, effectively ruling that the act of buggery should *not* be a criminal offence.

Alongside cases in which the applicant submits that an act should *not* be a criminal offence, the ECtHR has also considered a significant number of cases in which it is argued that a specific act *should* be a criminal offence according to a Convention positive criminalization obligation. Such cases are typically brought by an individual who has been the victim of the impugned act, but has been unable to secure national prosecution of the perpetrator. In *Siliadin v. France*, for example, the applicant argued that French criminal law did not contain specific offences of slavery, servitude, or forced labour.[9] In *Söderman v. Sweden*, the applicant contended that the failure to criminalize the act of covert or illicit filming amounted to a violation of Article 8 (Right to respect for private and family life) of the Convention.[10] In *X and Y v. The Netherlands*, the applicant submitted that the lack of a criminal law provision covering sexual acts committed against a mentally handicapped person constituted a violation of Article 8 of the Convention, and in *Vo v. France*, the applicant complained of the absence of criminal legislation to prevent and punish the taking of her unborn child's life as unintentional homicide in breach of Article 2 of the Convention.[11] In each of these cases, the Court considered, reasonably directly, whether criminal law provisions were required under positive obligations of the Convention to prevent and effectively punish perpetrators of the impugned act. In *Siliadin*, for example, the Court applied reasoning under the general crime investigatory obligation to find that the substantive right under Article 4 of the Convention not to be held in slavery or servitude, combined with the requirement under Article 1 to secure to everyone Convention rights and freedoms, resulted in an obligation to enact criminal law legislation to protect against slavery and servitude.[12] In *Vo*, the Court, in line with reasoning from *Calvelli and Ciglio v. Italy*, considered whether the procedural positive obligation of Article 2 (Right to life) extended to a requirement for criminal law measures in the specific case of the unborn child.[13] As with the direct negative criminalization obligation cases, the "direct positive" class provides reasonably clear guidance as to conduct which should

9 *Siliadin v. France*, ECHR, para 98.
10 *Söderman v. Sweden*, ECHR, para 63.
11 *X and Y v. The Netherlands*, ECHR, paras 14–17, and *Vo v. France*, ECHR, para 46.
12 *Siliadin v. France*, ECHR, paras 143–148.
13 *Vo v. France*, ECHR, para 90.

be criminalized by states parties to the European Convention. Of the examples given, the Court found a positive criminalization requirement in each case, with the exception of *Vo.*

Conviction cases

As well as the clear question asked of the Court in direct positive and negative criminalization cases, ECtHR jurisprudence also contains cases which pertain to criminalization in a more indirect sense. In particular, the Court sees a large number of cases brought by applicants who have been convicted of a criminal offence under national law. A number of ECHR cases challenge, for example, criminal convictions for publications considered contrary to accepted public standards, such as on the grounds of obscenity. Thus, for instance, *Handyside v. United Kingdom* concerned a challenge under ECHR Article 10 (Freedom of expression) to a conviction under the United Kingdom Obscene Publications Act 1959 for publication for gain of a book providing advice on drugs, sex, and pornography. *Müller v. Switzerland* considered a conviction under Article 204 of the Swiss Criminal Code on obscene items for publication of graphic paintings in an exhibition, and *Perrin v. United Kingdom* examined a conviction also under the United Kingdom Obscene Publications Act 1959 for publishing an obscene article on a website. Within the domain of expression and publication, the ECtHR has also had opportunity to examine the compatibility with the Convention of criminal convictions for defamation, for example in *Lindon, Otchakovsky-Laurens and July v. France*, in which the applicants submitted that their convictions for defamation on account of a literary novel based on real-life events were contrary to the right to freedom of expression. ECHR Article 10 was also invoked in, amongst others, *Gough v. United Kingdom*, concerning a challenge to multiple convictions for breach of the peace as a result of public nudity; *Mondragon v. Spain*, as regards a conviction for insulting the king; *Stoll v. Switzerland*, in respect of a conviction for publishing secret official deliberations; *Palusinski v. Poland*, regarding a conviction for incitement to drug use as a result of the publication of a "guide" to narcotics; *Perìnçek v. Switzerland*, concerning a conviction for denial of genocide; and *Neij v Sweden*, regarding a criminal conviction for copyright infringement through computer file sharing.

ECHR conviction cases are not limited, however, to those involving freedom of expression. The Court has also had occasion to consider convictions for a wide range of acts, including in *Acmanne v. Belgium*, in which the applicants challenged the compatibility of their conviction for refusing to let their children undergo methods of tuberculosis screening, with ECHR Article 8 (Right to respect for private and family life). In *X v. United Kingdom*, the applicant, a practicing Sikh, complained that his conviction for failing to wear a crash helmet when riding his motor cycle was incompatible with the Article 9 right to freedom of religion. In *Stübing v. Germany*, the applicant alleged that his criminal conviction for incest violated his Article 8 right to private and family life. In *Bayatyan v. Armenia*, the Court considered the compatibility of the applicant's conviction for refusal to serve in the army with Article 9 (Right to freedom of thought, conscience and religion). In *Kokkinakis v. Greece*, the applicant argued that his conviction for proselytism violated ECHR Article 9, and in *Laskey, Jaggard and Brown v. United Kingdom*, the applicants submitted that their criminal convictions for assault and causing bodily harm in the course of a consensual sado-masochistic encounter were incompatible with ECHR Article 8.

Whilst conviction-based cases of the ECtHR are more numerous than direct challenges to the existence or absence of criminal law, they are frequently more challenging to interpret from a criminalization perspective. This is because human rights challenges to criminal convictions are "one step removed" from direct consideration of the criminal law *per se*. The extent and certainty of the criminalization conclusion therefore vary, depending upon whether the Court finds a violation or not of the Convention, as well as the way in which the Court frames and examines the issue. A particular challenge is to discern whether the conclusions of the Court in conviction cases relate to the specific act carried out or to the national law offence itself. In some cases, the Court frames its analysis around the specific act and considers whether the act can legitimately be made subject to *any* criminal sanction. In other instances, the Court places a greater focus on the conviction that occurred and the offence in law. In the latter instance, it can further sometimes be difficult to conclude whether the underlying offence is, in principle, compatible with Convention rights or whether it was merely applied in a way, in that instance, which violated the Convention. Determining an exact criminalization conclusion can also be especially complicated in the case of broad offences in criminal law – such as breach of the peace or insult. Convictions for such crimes may concern conduct that constitutes only a small subset of a much larger range of acts punishable in principle by the national law offence.

The finding of the Court as to the existence (or not) of a violation also has an impact on the nature and extent of criminalization conclusions. Where the Court finds no violation, it can usually be inferred that either the specific conduct, and/or the offence in law itself *can* legitimately be a criminal offence as regards the standards of the Convention. At least where the conviction is substantively challenged on the basis of a non-procedure-related right, such as the right to life, the right to respect for private and family life, the right to freedom of thought, conscience and religion, or the right to freedom of expression. The extent and certainty of this conclusion depend greatly, however, on the manner in which the court considers the application, as well as the nature and breadth of both the specific conduct and the national offence.

In the case of *Gough*, concerning multiple convictions for public nudity, for example, the Court focused heavily on the acceptability of a criminal conviction for the particular conduct, with reference to the number and nature of the specific acts performed, as well as to the intent of the applicant. As a result, the judgment is probably best read as confirming the compatibility of criminalization of "public nudity" with the Convention (specifically, Article 10 of the Convention), rather than criminalization of "breach of the peace," for which the applicant was actually convicted. The limitation of criminalization conclusions to the particular facts of a case is a common theme in conviction-based cases. In *Vejdeland and Others v. Sweden*, concerning the conviction of the applicants for distributing leaflets containing statements offensive to homosexuals, for instance, the Court focused almost exclusively on the circumstances and nature of the specific conduct, alongside the (mere) fact of conviction, as opposed to analysing the content of the "ethnic agitation" offence used in national law.[14] In finding no violation, the Court made a few general statements about the criminalization of hate speech on the basis of sexual orientation.[15] However, these were not sufficiently precise to enable any conclusion beyond that of the acceptability of a criminal conviction for the conduct in the particular case *vis-à-vis* the Convention rights invoked.

Only in a limited number of conviction-based cases where the European Court finds no violation does the Court examine the legal offence itself in detail. In *Stoll*, for example, in which the applicant challenged his conviction for publishing secret official deliberations, the Court considered whether the purely formal notion of secrecy underlying Article 293 of the Swiss Criminal Code was compatible with the requirements of the Convention. In this respect, the Court found that the Code was compatible with ECHR Article 10, insofar as it offered sufficient opportunity for national courts to weigh up the interests at stake and to consider whether a "confidential" classification of a particular document was justified. In reaching this finding, the Court was also informed by a comparative study of legislation concerning state secrets, which found that the disclosure of certain types of classified information appeared to be punishable in all Council of Europe countries, albeit with a wide variety of approaches adopted.[16] *Stoll* thus provides an example of a conviction-based case where it can be concluded with greater certainty that criminalization of the act, disclosing official state secrets, as set out in national law is broadly compatible with Convention rights, or at least with the right to freedom of expression under ECHR Article 10.

Interpreting the criminalization implications in conviction cases where the European Court finds a violation of substantive rights requires similar care. In a few cases it is clear from the reasoning of the Court that the violation stems directly from the offence in national law, no matter how it is applied. In *Mondragon*, for example, concerning a conviction for insulting the king, the violation of ECHR Article 10 was based, to a large extent, on the fact that the specific offence in the criminal code afforded the head of state a greater degree of protection than other persons, protected by the ordinary law on insults or institutions such as the Government and Parliament. The Court went on to note that a special law on insults would not, as a rule, be in keeping with the Spirit of the Convention.[17] The Court

14 *Vejdeland and Others v. Sweden*, ECHR, paras 50–60.

15 The Court noted that discrimination based on sexual orientation is as serious as discrimination based on race, origin, or colour. *Ibid.*, para 55.

16 *Stoll v. Switzerland*, ECHR, paras 44, 138, and 139.

17 *Otegi Mondragon v. Spain*, ECHR, para 25.

also found similarly in *Colombani v. France*, in which the applicant challenged his conviction for insulting a foreign head of state. In that case, the Court held that it was the special protection afforded to foreign heads of state by the national law that undermined freedom of expression.[18] A small number of other cases, such as *Şükran Aydin and Others v. Turkey*, in which the applicants challenged their conviction for speaking Kurdish during an election campaign, also consider directly the underlying criminal framework. In that case, the Court held that a regulatory framework consisting of a total prohibition on the use of unofficial languages, coupled with criminal sanctions, could not be held to be compatible with the essential values of a democratic society, including freedom of expression as guaranteed by Article 10 of the Convention.[19] Such cases, whilst formally further removed from direct consideration of the criminal law by the Court, enable criminalization conclusions to be drawn about the offence *per se*, almost at the same level as direct negative criminalization cases such as *Norris, A, B and C, Friend, the Countryside Alliance and Others*, and *S.A.S.*

More often, however, as with conviction cases in which no violation is found, the conclusion from violation conviction cases must usually be limited to the particular conduct and circumstances at hand. In *Erdoğdu v. Turkey*, for example, the applicant argued that his conviction for "undermining the territorial integrity of Turkey" as a result of an article published in a periodical of which he was the editor violated Articles 9 (Freedom of thought, conscience and religion) and 10 (Freedom of expression) of the Convention. In finding a violation of Article 10, the Court focused its analysis solely on the opinions expressed in the article. The Court did not examine the components of the national law offence, but simply took the criminal conviction as the factual element constituting an interference with Article 10. As a result, the strict reading of the decision extends only to the use of (any) criminal law to punish dissemination of the particular speech which resulted in the conviction, as opposed to the human rights compatibility of the offence in Turkish law of acts "undermining territorial integrity."[20]

The importance of delineating a Convention violation pertaining to the particular act, as opposed to the underlying offence in law, is also well illustrated by a number of cases that concern criminal convictions for defamation. In *Dąbrowski v. Poland*, for example, the applicant challenged his criminal conviction for defamation under the penal code arising from a series of newspaper articles containing allegations about a deputy mayor. The Court found a violation of Article 10 (Freedom of expression) and held that the conviction amounted to a kind of censorship likely to deter journalists from contributing to public discussion of issues affecting the life of the community.[21] The judgment is silent,

18 *Colombani and Others v. France*, ECHR, para 69.
19 *Şükran Aydin and Others v. Turkey*, ECHR, para 55.
20 *Erdoğdu v. Turkey*, ECHR, para 9.
21 *Dąbrowski v. Poland*, ECHR, para 37.

however, on whether the existence *per se* of a criminal offence of defamation is compatible with the Convention and focuses solely on the restriction of rights in the applicant's context. It is only through examination of a larger number of ECtHR defamation cases that a picture of general acceptance by the European Court of the criminalization of defamation emerges. In, amongst others, *Lindon v. France* and *Armellini v. Austria*, for example, the Court found no violation of Article 10 in the case of criminal convictions for defamation. Defamation thus represents an act where a body of case law is required in order to draw criminalization conclusions – taking into account the silence of the ECtHR on the underlying offence in violation defamation conviction cases, its general statements in non-violation cases, as well as the relative consistency of definition in national laws, and congruence between the act in individual cases and the offence in law.

Within the area of ECtHR conviction-based cases, lastly, a small number of cases based on Articles 6 (Right to a fair trial) and 7 (No punishment without law) can allow criminalization conclusions to be drawn. Articles 6 and 7 may also be invoked in conviction cases to argue, for example, that an offence in law violated the presumption of innocence, that the state failed to sufficiently particularize the offence, or that the act did not in fact constitute a criminal offence at the time when the act was committed. As these points largely go to the construction of an offence, as opposed to its substantive content, such challenges do not necessarily provide much insight into what may or may not legitimately be criminalized. Nonetheless, in a small number of cases, it is implicit or explicit in the Court's judgment that the underlying act itself indeed can, or should, be a criminal offence. In *S.W. v. United Kingdom*, for example, the applicant complained under Article 7 that his conviction for rape upon his wife did not constitute a criminal offence at the relevant time. Despite the largely procedural nature of the challenge to the conviction, the Court opined on the substance of the offence. Showing clearly that it was of the view that the offence of rape should not be subject to any form of marital immunity, the Court stated that the abandonment of the unacceptable idea of a husband being immune against prosecution for rape of his wife is in conformity with the fundamental objectives of the Convention.[22] Other Article 6 or 7 cases are not as explicit, but nonetheless reveal some recognition by the Court of the general acceptability of the substance of the offence. In *Ashlarba v. Georgia*, for example, the Court, in finding no violation of Article 7, highlighted that the criminalization of being a member of the "thieves underworld" was part of a wider legislative package, the aim of which was to intensify the fight against organized crime.[23]

Article 6 and 7 cases also consolidate the important principle that restrictions on criminalization for contracting states to the European Convention only arise insofar as a particular Convention right is engaged and violated. First formulated

22 *S.W. v. United Kingdom*, ECHR, para 44.
23 *Ashlarba v. Georgia*, ECHR, para 39.

in *Engel*, the Court has expressed this principle as leaving states free to designate as a criminal offence an act or omission not constituting the normal exercise of one of the rights that the Convention protects.[24] The formulation is referred to in a number of Article 6 conviction cases, including *Salabiaku v. France*, concerning a criminal conviction for smuggling prohibited goods, *H.M.A. v Spain*, concerning a conviction for an environmentally damaging discharge, and *Hansen v. Denmark*, involving a criminal conviction for infringing rules regarding rest periods during carriage of goods. In each of these cases, the Court recalled that the principle implied that the state was free, accordingly, to define the constituent elements of the resulting offence.[25] Whereas the Court did not explicitly state in these cases that the conviction or underlying offence did not engage any other (substantive) Convention rights, an argument does exist that the formulation evidences a broad position of the Court that the substance of the offence does not, on the face of it, raise other Convention issues in these cases. It is also notable in this respect that the European Court does not consider itself bound by the manner in which an application is formulated. In *Dallas v. United Kingdom*, for example, the Court asserted that it was free to choose the characterization to be given in law to the facts of the case, before proceeding to decide under which Convention article the application should be examined.[26]

Investigatory and procedural obligation cases

Finally, in addition to direct criminalization cases and conviction cases, ECtHR jurisprudence also includes cases that touch on criminalization through the general crime investigatory obligation to have in place effective machinery for investigating complaints of human rights violations, combined with the duty to ensure that there is a thorough and effective investigation capable of leading to the identification and punishment of those responsible. These cases are typically brought by applicants who have been the victim of a particular act but are not satisfied with the response of the state. A number of such cases (including *Siliadin, Söderman, X and Y*, and *Vo*) have already been encountered in the form of direct positive criminalization cases, wherever the applicant argues specifically that a certain offence should have existed in national law. In addition, however, criminalization conclusions may also be drawn from a wider range of cases that address the general crime investigatory obligation. At the core of this category of cases are ECtHR judgments such as *Osman v. United Kingdom*, *Beganović v. Croatia*, and *M.C. v. Bulgaria*, which confirm the requirement for criminal law provisions to punish and deter acts of intentional taking of life, serious

24 *Engel and Others v. The Netherlands*, ECHR, para 81.

25 *Salabiaku v. France*, ECHR, para 27; *H.M.A. v. Spain*, ECHR, p.123; and *Hansen v. Denmark*, ECHR, p.6.

26 *Dallas v. United Kingdom*, ECHR, para. 58.

violence, and rape, respectively. In each of these cases, the criminalization requirement arises from the nature of positive obligations under substantive articles of the Convention, taken alone and in conjunction with Article 13 (Right to an effective remedy). In *Beganović*, for example, the Court found that the severity of a physical attack by a group of individuals against another individual, involving kicking and hitting, constituted ill-treatment for the purposes of Article 3 (Prohibition of torture) and required the implementation of adequate criminal law mechanisms.[27]

In some instances, ECtHR judgments that rely on investigatory or procedural obligations can provide a high degree of granularity concerning the specific elements of a criminal offence. Thus, for example, in the case of acts leading to loss of life, judgments such as *Osman v. United Kingdom*, *Calvelli and Ciglio v. Italy*, *Šilih v. Slovenia, and Öneryildiz v. Turkey* define homicide criminalization obligations through application of the procedural obligation of Article 2 (Right to life) to set up an effective judicial system in order to hold those responsible accountable.[28] The cases clarify that if an infringement of the right to life or to personal integrity is not caused intentionally, then the procedural obligation of Article 2 to set up an effective judicial system does not necessarily require the provision of a criminal law remedy in every case. In the specific case of death due to medical negligence, considered in *Calvelli* and *Šilih*, the Court held that the Article 2 procedural obligation could be satisfied if the legal system afforded victims a remedy in the civil courts, either alone or in conjunction with a remedy in the criminal courts, enabling any responsibility of the doctors concerned to be established and any appropriate civil redress, such as an order for damages and/or for the publication of the decision, to be obtained.[29] In other words, under the European human rights system, criminalization of acts such as gross negligence manslaughter (in English law) or negligent manslaughter (in German law) is not necessarily required, at least when it comes to medical negligence.

On the other hand, *Öneryildiz*, which concerned a landslide and explosion at a waste disposal site, demonstrates that where it is established that negligence goes beyond an error of judgment or carelessness and authorities, fully realizing the likely consequences, fail to take measures that are necessary to avert the risks inherent in the dangerous activity, then a failure to charge those responsible with a criminal offence may amount to a violation of Article 2.[30] In this case, the fact that the ECtHR made such statements within a "principles" section of the judgment lends weight to the establishment of a European human rights

27 *Beganović v Croatia*, ECHR, para 69.

28 Under the procedural limb of Article 2, states parties to the ECHR have positive obligations of a procedural aspect, including the duty to investigate deaths that may have occurred in breach of the Convention. See *McCann and Others v. United Kingdom*, ECHR, 1995.

29 *Šilih v. Slovenia*, ECHR, para 194.

30 *Öneryildiz v. Turkey*, ECHR, para 93.

position on criminalization and acts leading to death. Similarly, cases such as *M.C.* provide a relatively detailed view on the elements of the crime of rape. *M.C.*, for example, clarifies that positive obligations under Articles 3 and 8 of the Convention must be seen as requiring the penalization and effective prosecution of any non-consensual sexual act, including in the absence of physical resistance by the victim.[31] Further cases, such as *Angelova v. Bulgaria*, show that positive procedural obligations under Articles 2 and 3 of the Convention do not require separate criminalization of racially motivated murder or serious bodily injury, at least where there exists the possibility within criminal law to impose a more severe sentence depending upon, amongst other reasons, the motive of the offender.

Criminalization cases – acts and rights

Whilst reasonably extensive, the criminalization jurisprudence of an international human rights court or tribunal such as the ECtHR does not cover all, or even any substantial proportion, of the range of possible criminal acts. In order to properly describe an international human rights law perspective on the criminal law, those acts that are found in human rights cases must be systematically characterized.

Describing which criminal acts are examined by international human rights case law, and which are not, has been significantly aided by the finalization, in 2015, of the *International Classification of Crimes for Statistical Purposes* (ICCS).[32] The ICCS is the first common framework to group all kinds of criminal offences into categories that can be used for producing crime statistics. The ICCS has its roots in work undertaken at the European level over ten years ago. In the context of the European Commission Action Plan to Measure Crime and Criminal Justice 2006–2010, a number of work streams, including the development of an EU-level Offence Classification System in 2009, as well as the European Commission's Group of Experts on the Policy Needs for Data on Crime and Criminal Justice 2006–2008, undertook key steps towards consolidation and harmonization of crime and criminal justice definitions and statistics.[33] This work was drawn upon by the United Nations system in its development of the ICCS, which was endorsed first by the Conference of European Statisticians in 2012 and finally in 2015 by the United Nations Statistical Commission.[34] The ICCS has subsequently been adopted and used for data collection by the statistical office of the European Union, as well as by the United Nations Office on Drugs and Crime through the United Nations Survey of Crime Trends and Operations of Criminal Justice Systems.

31 *M.C. v. Bulgaria*, ECHR, para 166.
32 United Nations Office on Drugs and Crime, 2015. Online resource.
33 Vermeulen, G., 2009; European Commission, 2006. Online resource.
34 United Nations, Statistical Commission, 2015. UN Doc. E/2015/24, p.16.

The ICCS aims to capture the universe of acts that are considered criminal in all national and international laws. As such, the ICCS adopts a positivist approach of including any act which is defined as a criminal offence and punishable by law under any national criminal legislation. In order to avoid merely reproducing legal language, however, the ICCS adopts an "event-based approach" based on behavioural descriptions of actions and contextual attributes, rather than strictly legal specifications derived from criminal laws. The unit of classification of the ICCS is thus the "act" that constitutes a criminal offence. This makes the ICCS ideal as a tool for describing and classifying a list of acts that form the basis of applications to the ECtHR and in respect of which criminalization questions arise.

The ICCS consists of a number of classification levels. The top level (level 1) consists of 11 act categories.[35] Each level 1 category is further divided to levels 2, 3, and 4, used to describe acts that constitute a subset of those coded to higher levels. Thus, for example, category 1 is used for "acts leading to death or intending to cause death." Both intentional homicide and non-intentional homicide sit at level 2 within category 1, coded 0101 and 0103, respectively. Under non-intentional homicide (0103), non-negligent manslaughter and negligent manslaughter sit at level 3 and are coded 01031 and 01032, respectively. Negligent manslaughter is further divided into vehicular homicide (010321) and non-vehicular homicide (010322) at level 4. Through this classification structure, the ICCS can be used as a common system by national law enforcement and criminal justice authorities for comparable recording of offences, formal charges against suspects, and convictions. In the same way, the ICCS also has utility for classifying existing records or references to criminal acts, such as those found in the judgments of international human rights courts and tribunals. This provides a powerful tool for bringing a clear criminal act structure to otherwise unstructured information on crimes that form the basis of international human rights challenges.

The table at the end of this book assigns ICCS level 1 and level 2 codes to a group of ECHR criminalization cases that well exemplify the range of criminal acts that the Court has encountered to date. The case group indicates that, amongst criminalization cases, the ECtHR most frequently considers "acts against public order, authority and provisions of the state" (ICCS category 08), "acts leading to harm or intending to cause harm to the person" (ICCS category 02), and "injurious acts of a sexual nature" (ICCS category 03). Other criminal acts that form the basis of a number of ECHR cases include "acts

35 ICCS Level 1 Categories: (01) Acts leading to death or intending to cause death; (02) Acts leading to harm or intending to cause harm to the person; (03) Injurious acts of a sexual nature; (04) Acts against property involving violence or threat against a person; (05) Acts against property only; (06) Acts involving controlled psychoactive substances or other drugs; (07) Acts involving fraud, deception or corruption; (08) Acts against public order, authority and provisions of the State; (09) Acts against public safety and state security; (10) Acts against the natural environment; and (11) Other criminal acts not elsewhere classified.

leading to death" (ICCS category 01) and "acts against public safety and state security" (ICCS category 09).

This ICCS lens suggests that two broad areas of criminalization commonly form the basis of human rights challenges to date before the ECtHR. The first of these concerns the criminalization of interpersonal acts committed physically against an individual, as well as where the state regulates aspects of expression or personal relationships. The second is a wide range of acts that may be considered as generally contrary to public authority or public safety and security.

The first (ICCS categories 01, 02, and 03) includes a number of ECHR cases involving acts leading to death or intending to cause death, such as the case of *Osman*, which concerns intentional taking of life, and *Antonov*, which considers causing death by dangerous driving. The cases of *Rowley*, *Pretty*, and *A, B and C* also look at the criminalization of corporate manslaughter, assisting suicide, and procuring miscarriage, respectively. ECHR cases such as *Beganović*, *K.A.*, *Laskey*, *Jaggard and Brown*, and *Opuz* further relate to the criminal act of assault, including in the context of chastisement of children and of sadomasochistic activities, as well as to acts of domestic violence. Sexual acts against the person are considered in cases such as *C.R.*, *M.C.*, *S.W.*, and *X and Y*, all of which concerned rape, as well as *Söderman* that examined the act of voyeurism. ECHR cases such as *M.K.*, *O'Keefe*, and *Stubbings* further concern sexual acts against children or child pornography, as in the case of *Karttunen*. The case of *Siliadin* examines the criminalization of servitude, whilst *Rantsev* concerns the offence of trafficking in persons. The cases of *Calvelli*, *Šilih*, and *Öneryildiz* involve bodily harm due to negligence in situations of persons under care. In the area of state regulation of aspects of expression or personal relationships, ECHR cases such as *Armellini*, *Bozhkov*, *Cumpana*, *Lindon*, *Rujak*, *Janowski*, and *Radio France* consider the criminalization of defamation and insult. A large number of cases also address criminalization of same-sex relations or other forms of sexual conduct, types of speech, and modes of insult. The ECtHR looked at criminalization of obscene publications, for example, in *Handyside*, *Müller*, and *Perrin*. The cases of *A.D.T.*, *Dudgeon*, *L. and V.*, and *Norris* examined criminal offences concerning same-sex relations and *Stübing*, the act of incest. In the area of regulated speech, *Í.A* and *Wingrove* considered criminalization of blasphemy, *Kokkinakis*, the act of proselytism, *Feret* and *Osmani*, incitement to racial hatred and discrimination, *Norwood*, religious hate speech, and *Vejdeland*, sexual-orientation hate speech. Cases involving insult against the state include *Akçam*, where the ECtHR considered an offence of denigrating the nation, and *Colombani* and *Mondragon*, which concerned a criminal offence of insulting a head of state.

Falling within acts contrary to public authority, safety, or security (ICCS categories 08 and 09), the wearing of clothing designed to conceal the face was examined by the ECtHR in *S.A.S.*, criminalization of a breach of building planning regulations in *Ehrmann*, contempt of court by *Dallas*, and the use of languages in election campaigns by *Şükran*. The case of *Hansen* involved criminal sanctions for breach of transport regulations, *Acmanne* examined a refusal to comply with compulsory health screening, and *Bayatyan* looked at the criminal law on conscientious objection. The case of *Stoll* concerned the criminalization of disclosing state secrets, *Ashlarba*, the membership of a criminal group, *Aydin*, the membership of a banned organization, and *X*, the failure to wear a motorcycle helmet. In addition, the ECtHR had cause to consider environmentally harmful emissions in *H.M.A.*, fox hunting in *Friend*, and denial of genocide in *Perìnçek*.

Remaining ECHR criminalization cases are distributed quite broadly across the other ICCS categories. A handful of cases, for example, consider criminalization of acts against property (ICCS category 06), acts involving psychoactive substances or other drugs (ICCS category 05), and acts involving fraud, deception, or corruption (ICCS category 07). These include the cases of *Blumberga*, which involved the act of burglary, *Neij*, which concerned copyright infringement through file sharing, *Salabiaku*, drug trafficking, *Palusinski*, incitement to use drugs, and *K.U.*, the act of malicious misrepresentation.

The distribution of acts coming before an international human rights court or tribunal in criminalization cases is a function of many factors. These include the nature of the act itself, the construction of any existing criminal law, and the manner in which it is applied to the set of facts in each individual case, as well as public and individual perceptions of the fairness and reasonableness of the law. Most importantly, however, the range of acts in international human rights criminalization cases is constrained and shaped by the nature and content of the substantive rights themselves. For the ECtHR, the focus of the Convention on civil and political rights means that the Court considers a large number of criminalization cases under Articles 8 (Right to respect for private and family life) and 10 (Freedom of expression) of the Convention. For cases listed at the end of this book, Article 8 is invoked in around 25 per cent of cases and Article 10 in almost 40 per cent. The remainder of cases invoke a range of ECHR articles, including Article 2 (Right to life), Article 3 (Prohibition of torture), and Article 9 (Freedom of thought, conscience and religion).

It is not perhaps so surprising that Articles 8 and 10 are the most frequently invoked in ECHR criminalization cases. The concept of private life under Article 8 is a broad concept that includes not only the "inner circle" in which the individual lives his own personal life as he chooses but also the right to establish and develop relationships with other persons and the outside world. As a result, activities or measures concerning private life have been found by the European Court to include, amongst others, interception of private communications; the collection and use of personal data; invasions of physical and moral integrity such as corporal punishment; compulsory medical treatment; and compulsory safety measures. When it comes to criminalization, the particular scope of Article 8 means that a significant proportion of ECHR criminalization cases concern the criminalization of acts related to the establishment of relationships with other human beings as well as issues of identity and personal development. Specific criminal acts for which ECHR Article 8 is engaged include procuring miscarriage (*A, B and C*); refusing compulsory health screening (*Acmanne*); assault in the context of sadomasochistic activities (*K.A.* and *Laskey*); sexual offences against children (*M.K.*, *O'Keefe*, and *Stubbings*); same-sex relations (*A.D.T.*, *Dudgeon*, and *Norris*); incest (*Stübing*); voyeurism (*Söderman*); rape (*G*, *M.C.* and *X and Y*); assisting suicide (*Pretty*); wearing of clothing designed to conceal the face (*S.A.S.*); and publication of photographs of an individual without consent (*Egeland*). Many of these acts involve sexual acts or other acts that are closely connected to the body of the individual, highlighting the intersection between the focus of Article 8 on relationships and the identity of the individual, and the use of the criminal law by the state to regulate behaviour within this area. The right to private and family life of ECHR Article 8 is not, however, a "catch-all" right that can be applied to any act that is the subject of the criminal law. The ECHR case of *Friend* (criminalization of hunting a wild mammal with a dog), for example, demonstrates that acts constituting broader social or cultural activities and relationships are much less likely to engage Article 8. In *Friend*, the European Court noted that, whilst there is a zone of interaction of a person with others, even in a public context, which may fall within the scope of "private life," hunting is, by its very nature, a public activity that is too far removed from personal autonomy and interpersonal relations to engage Article 8.[36]

As well as acts engaging ECHR Article 8, a large number of ECHR criminalization cases invoke Article 10 (freedom of expression). The majority of these acts fall under ICCS categories 2 (harm to the person) and 8 (acts involving public order and state authority). Acts in ICCS category 2 typically involve insult to a specific individual and include the acts of defamation (*Armellini*, *Bozhkov*, *Lindon*, and *Radio France*), insult (*Cumpana*, *Rujak*, and *Janowski*), and invasion of privacy (*Egeland*). Article 10 cases falling in ICCS category 8 involve expression directed more generally, including insulting or denigrating the state or head of state (*Akçam*, *Colombani*, and *Mondragon*), blasphemy (*Í.A* and *Wingrove*), obscene publications (*Handyside*, *Müller*, and *Perrin*), hate speech (*Feret*, *Norwood*, *Osmani*, and *Vejdeland*), and outraging public decency or breach of the peace (*S and G* and *Gough*). The significant number of ECHR cases involving freedom of expression (ECHR Article 10), and acts involving public order or state authority (ICCS category 8), well demonstrates the particular sensitivities around use of the criminal law to regulate expression that may be considered contrary to a common standard and/or is not directed against an identifiable individual.

Finally, in addition to cases under ECHR Article 8 and Article 10, criminalization cases can also be seen under ECHR Articles 2 (Right to life), 3 (Prohibition of torture), and 4 (Prohibition of slavery). As would be expected, the majority of cases under Article 2 fall in ICCS category 1 (acts leading to death). These include *Antonov* (causing death by dangerous driving), *Osman* (intentional taking of life), *Pretty* (assisting suicide), *Öneryildiz* (negligence in dangerous activities), and *Rowley* (corporate manslaughter). ECHR Article 3 and 4 cases predominantly

36 *Friend, the Countryside Alliance and Others v. United Kingdom*, ECHR, p.16.

fall within ICCS category 2 (harm to the person) and include *Beganović* (assault), *A* (reasonable chastisement), *Rantsev* (trafficking in persons), and *Siliadin* (servitude).

Criminalization cases – outcomes

As discussed earlier in this chapter, interpreting ECtHR criminalization cases is not straightforward. The criminalization conclusions that can be drawn from findings of the Court on violation or no violation of ECHR articles depend heavily upon the way in which the issue is framed before the Court. Careful language is needed in order to correctly capture the extent of the Court's conclusions. In the case of direct negative criminalization cases that represent a challenge to a specific criminal law, the finding of a violation can usually be interpreted as authority that the act *should not* be a criminal offence. A finding of no violation in such cases indicates that the impugned act *can* be a criminal offence. In direct positive criminalization cases, a violation of the state's positive obligation to protect against a particular act implies that the particular act *should be* a criminal offence. Conversely, where there is no violation of the positive human rights obligation, it can be concluded that the particular act *need not* be a criminal offence. In conviction cases, in which an applicant challenges the human rights compatibility of a criminal conviction, where no violation of Convention rights is found, it can usually be inferred that either the specific conduct, and/or the offence in law *can* be a criminal offence. Conviction cases in which the Court finds a violation arising from the nature of the criminal law itself, on the other hand, can be used, with caution, to argue that the impugned act *should not be* a criminal offence. Finally, in general crime investigatory cases, the finding of a violation usually means that the act *should be* a criminal offence, whereas the finding of no violation implies that the act *need not* be a criminal offence.

The list of ECHR cases at the end of this book, all of which allow reasonably clear criminalization conclusions to be drawn, is classified according to these four categories of "should be," "can be," "need not be," and "should not be" a criminal offence. For this group of cases, Figure 6.1 provides a visualisation of the distribution of criminalization outcomes across the judgments. For ease of visualization, outcomes of "can be" and "need not be" a criminal offence have been combined into a single "can be an offence" category.

For the broadly representative case group, Figure 6.1 reveals that the decision of the ECtHR on violation or no violation of Convention rights in criminalization cases (some 60 per cent of cases reviewed) most commonly means that the impugned act *can* be a criminal offence. In such cases, the judgment of the Court suggests that states are not obliged to make the act in question a criminal offence, but neither are states in violation of the ECHR if the act is criminalized. In other words, for a very large range of acts, the ECtHR is widely permissive of criminalization. Such cases are broadly distributed across the ICCS categories and include acts such as assisting suicide (*Pretty*),

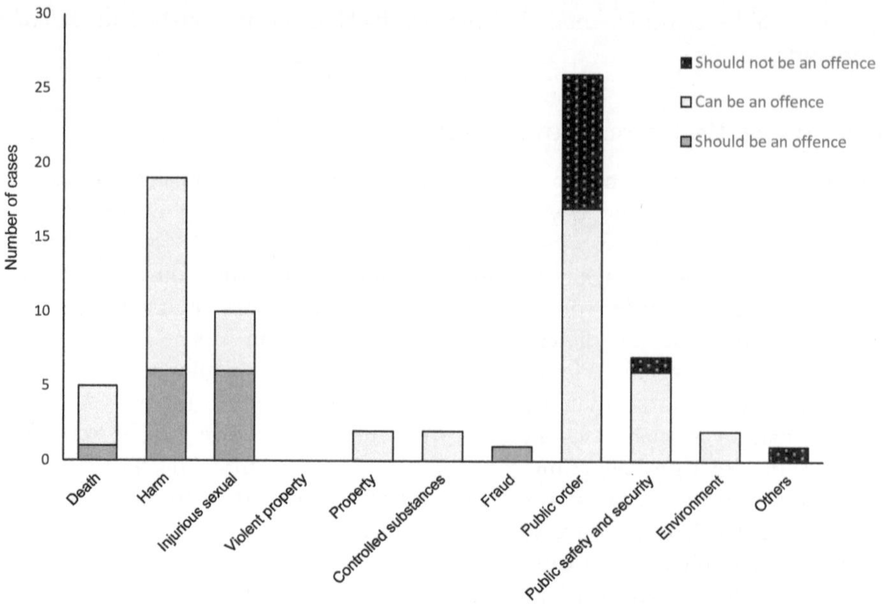

Figure 6.1 ECHR Criminalization Cases by Outcome and ICCS Level 1

copyright infringement (*Neij*), possession and distribution of obscene publications (*Handyside*, *Müller*, and *Perrin*), breach of public order (*Kudrevičius*), and hunting a wild mammal with a dog (*Friend*). All of which, the ECtHR holds, can be a criminal offence.

Figure 6.1 also shows the fewer number of acts which decisions of the ECtHR suggest should, or should not, be a criminal offence. Perhaps unsurprisingly, cases where the decision of the Court suggests that an act *should* be a criminal offence are all found in ICCS categories 1 (acts leading to death), 2 (harm to the person), 3 (injurious sexual acts), and 4 (fraud). These acts include intentional taking of life (*Osman*); rape (*M.C.*, *C.R.*, *S.W.*, and *X and Y*); assault (*Beganović* and *A*); sexual offences against children (*Stubbings*); trafficking in persons (*Rantsev*); slavery (*Siliadin*); domestic violence (*Opuz*); filming for voyeurism (*Söderman*); and malicious misrepresentation involving child welfare (*K.U.*). These cases fall under a range of ECHR articles, including Article 2 (Right to life) (*Opuz* and *Osman*), Article 3 (Prohibition of torture) (*Beganović*, *M.C.*, and *A*), Article 4 (Prohibition of slavery) (*Rantsev* and *Siliadin*), and Article 8 (Right to private life) (*Söderman*, *Stubbings*, *M.C.*, and *X and Y*).

Perhaps most strikingly, however, almost all of the acts which the ECtHR suggests that *should not* be a criminal offence are to be found in ICCS category 8 (acts against public order and the state). These include insulting a head of state (*Colombani* and *Mondragon*); denigrating the nation (*Akçam*); proselytism

(*Kokkinakis*); use of languages in election campaigns (*Şükran*); and consensual same-sex relations (*A.D.T.*, Dudgeon, *L. and V.*, and *Norris*). Two notable acts that the Court suggests should not be an offence that fall outside of ICCS category 8 are conscientious objection (*Bayatyan*, ICCS category 9 (acts against public safety and state security)) and wide denial of genocide (*Perinçek*, ICCS category 11 (other acts)). These cases fall primarily under ECHR Article 8 (Right to private life) (*A.D.T.*, *Dudgeon*, *L. and V.* and *Norris*), Article 9 (Freedom of thought, conscience and religion) (*Bayatyan* and *Kokkinakis*), and Article 10 (Freedom of expression) (*Akçam*, *Colombani*, *Mondragon*, *Perinçek*, and *Şükran*).

Comparison of the outcomes of ECtHR criminalization cases with the findings of United Nations human rights treaty bodies demonstrates a wider resonance of the position of the ECtHR on matters of criminalization within international human rights law as a whole. Just as judgments of the European Court form an important feature of ECHR compliance for all states parties, so United Nations treaty body concluding observations have a special status as regards interpretation of the treaty and the treaty obligations of each state party.[37] United Nations treaty body concluding observations differ from judgments of the European Court in that they are not legally binding on states parties and are developed following a periodic process of state party reporting and dialogue with the relevant treaty monitoring Committee. In addition, the majority of treaty bodies are also able to accept individual communications alleging violation of a convention right. Committee decisions in individual cases represent an authoritative interpretation of the treaty, containing non-legally binding recommendations to the state party.

In the same way as ECHR criminalization cases fall across multiple ECHR articles, so references to use of the criminal law in the United Nations human rights system arise under a range of substantive rights. In the United Nations system, these are found across the nine core international human rights treaties and their protocols. Hence statements on criminalization exist in the work of multiple treaty bodies. In light of the nature of concluding observations, such statements are not often accompanied by the depth of reasoning found in ECtHR judgments. Rather, treaty bodies may, for example, simply recommend "decriminalization" of a particular act, express "concern" that a specific act is included in or excluded from the criminal law, or urge a state party to ensure the criminalization of an act. By contrast, individual communications considered by treaty bodies are structured more similarly to ECtHR cases, with criminalization conclusions dependent upon the particular legal challenge, treaty articles invoked, and a finding of violation or no violation.

As might be expected, many criminalization references made by treaty bodies concern the five specific human rights treaty-based obligations to include a particular act within the criminal law. Thus, for example, the Committee on the Rights of the Child has called on states parties to OP-CRC-AC to explicitly prohibit by law and criminalize the use of children in hostilities, and states parties to OP-CRC-SC to take necessary measures to ensure that possession of

37 See O'Flaherty, M., 2006, p.34.

child pornography is fully covered under criminal law.[38] The Committee on the Elimination of Racial Discrimination has urged a state party to expedite the passing of legislation to criminalize the promotion of racial hatred and racial discrimination and the dissemination of racist material and ideology.[39] And the Human Rights Committee has called on a state party to consider amending the criminal code in order to criminalize torture.[40] In addition, treaty bodies sometimes refer to criminalization obligations in wider international treaty law, including criminalization obligations in respect of trafficking in persons, and the manufacturing and trafficking of small arms and light weapons, in accordance with the Trafficking and Firearms Protocols supplementing the United Nations Convention against Transnational Organized Crime, as well as criminalization of acts of a racist and xenophobic nature committed through computer systems, under the Additional Protocol to the Council of Europe Convention on Cybercrime.[41]

A number of these international treaty criminalization obligations, such as trafficking in persons, slavery, and sexual offences against children that are reinforced by treaty body concluding observations, correspond to acts which ECtHR cases also suggest *should be* a criminal offence. This confirms consensus at the international level regarding criminalization of such acts, in line with the human rights general security of person obligation to prosecute and punish acts that represent a particular affront to the right to life, personal liberty, and security. In the same vein, whereas rape is not specifically criminalized within the core international human rights treaties, both treaty body concluding observations and decisions of the ECtHR agree that all forms of rape, including marital rape, should be a criminal offence.[42] Similarly, both treaty body concluding observations and ECHR cases confirm that acts of domestic violence should also be criminalized.[43] Within this broad area, treaty body concluding observations

38 United Nations, Committee on the Rights of the Child, 2010b. UN Doc. CRC/C/OPAC/SLE/CO/1, para 24; United Nations, Committee on the Rights of the Child, 2007. UN Doc. CRC/C/OPSC/CRI/CO/1, para 15.

39 United Nations, Committee on the Elimination of Racial Discrimination, 2009. UN Doc. CERD/C/POL/CO/19, para 9.

40 United Nations, Human Rights Committee, 2009b. UN Doc. CCPR/C/RUS/CO/6, para 15.

41 United Nations, Committee on the Rights of the Child, 2011. UN Doc. CRC/C/OPAC/BLR/CO/1, para 21; United Nations, Committee on the Elimination of Racial Discrimination, 2005. UN Doc. CERD/C/LUX/CO/13, para 14.

42 Note that rape can constitute a crime against humanity and a war crime under Articles 7(1)(g), 8(2)(b)(xxii), and 8(2)(e)(vi) of the Rome Statute. Rape also forms part of the definition of violence against women in the Inter-American Convention on the Prevention, Punishment and Eradication of Violence against Women, in respect of which states parties must include in their domestic penal legislation such provisions as may be needed to prevent, punish, and eradicate violence against women. In international human rights law jurisprudence, see United Nations, Committee against Torture, 2011a. UN Doc. CAT/C/MUS/CO/3, para 16; *M. C. v. Bulgaria*, ECHR; *R. v. United Kingdom*, ECHR; *X and Y v. The Netherlands*, ECHR.

43 See United Nations, Committee on Economic, Social and Cultural Rights, 2011. UN Doc. E/C.12/DEU/CO/5, para 23; United Nations, Committee against Torture, 2011b. UN Doc. CAT/C/KWT/CO/2, para 23; *Opuz v. Turkey*, ECHR.

further indicate that a number of specific acts that have not, to date, been the subject of ECtHR criminalization cases, including female genital mutilation, making accusations against children of witchcraft, and sexual harassment in the workplace, *should* be criminal offences.[44] Interestingly, because of the nature of the particular challenge, whereas the ECHR case of *Stübing* holds that incest *can* be a criminal offence, the Committee on the Elimination of Discrimination against Women recommends that incest *should* be a criminal offence.[45]

One significant difference between the ECtHR and the recommendations of human rights treaty bodies is in the area of incitement to racial hatred and discrimination. In light of ICERD Article 4, human rights treaty bodies frequently recommend that acts of incitement to racial hatred *should be* a criminal offence, albeit tempered by the view of CERD General Comment 35 that criminalization of forms of racist expression should be reserved for serious cases.[46] By contrast, in the European system, due largely to the fact that the text of the ECHR does not contain any specific prohibition on racial hatred or discrimination, and that the Article 14 prohibition on discrimination is not free standing, such cases most commonly arise as conviction cases. In such cases, an individual challenges his or her conviction arising from acts of incitement to hatred or discrimination, most usually under Article 10. Whereas the Court may find a violation, depending upon the particular speech or expression in the case at hand, the ECtHR has not found that the type of act itself should not be criminalized. As a result, hate speech cases in the ECHR fall within the category of *can be* a criminal offence, as opposed to *should be* an offence. The lack of a positive obligation to criminalize or punish hate speech within the ECHR system has been noted by commentators.[47] Further, whereas the ECtHR has found that the separate criminalization of racially motivated violent offences is not necessarily required if other means may be employed to punish perpetrators who have racist motives, human rights treaty bodies instead tend to emphasize the importance of a distinct offence of racially motivated violence and/or the application of racially motivated aggravating circumstances.[48] Finally, in the same way as for racial hatred, human rights treaty bodies have recommended that incitement to hatred

44 United Nations, Human Rights Committee, 2006. UN Doc. CCPR/C/CAF/CO/2, para 11; United Nations, Committee on the Rights of the Child, 2009. UN Doc. CRC/C/COD/CO/2; United Nations, Committee on Economic, Social and Cultural Rights, 2005. UN Doc. E/C.12/1/Add.107, para 110; United Nations, Human Rights Committee, 2008a. UN Doc. CCPR/C/JPN/CO/5, para 13.

45 United Nations, Committee on the Elimination of Discrimination against Women, 2002. UN Doc. A/57/38 (SUPP), para 334.

46 See, for example, United Nations, Committee on the Elimination of Racial Discrimination, 2014. UN Doc. CERD/C/CMR/CO/19–21, para 7.

47 Oxford Human Rights Hub, 2015. Online resource.

48 See *Angelova and Iliev v. Bulgaria*, ECHR, as compared with United Nations, Committee on the Elimination of Racial Discrimination, 2015. UN Doc CERD/C/GTM/CO/14–15, para 19.

or violence based on sexual orientation *should be* a criminal offence, whereas the European Court has found only that this *can be* a criminal offence.[49]

As regards acts which the ECHR finds *should not* be criminal offence, there is reasonable agreement with the recommendations of treaty bodies. Thus, for example, in the same way as the ECtHR, treaty bodies have recommended that sexual relations between consenting adults of the same sex be decriminalized, expressed concern about the existence of crimes such as injuring the honour and dignity of the President, and called for the decriminalization of proselytism.[50] On the other hand, treaty bodies have also recommended that a number of acts should not be offences where the ECHR allows that they *can* be criminalized. The approach of the European Court, for example, is generally to allow that defamation can be a criminal offence, although it emphasizes that a prison sentence could be imposed only in exceptional circumstances.[51] By contrast, treaty bodies tend to go a step further and hold that states should consider decriminalizing defamation, or at least restrict the application of the criminal law to the most serious cases, with imprisonment never being an appropriate punishment.[52] One reason for this difference may be that the ECtHR takes into account a European common consensus which tends towards criminalization of defamation, together with the attendant margin of appreciation.[53] Treaty bodies, in comparison, direct concluding observations at a state party, having in mind the situation within the country in general. In this regard, recommendations in respect of defamation and criminalization are often made within the context of application of such laws to human rights defenders, journalists, or social activists.[54] These differences in focus and approach could explain the preference of human rights treaty bodies for decriminalization of defamation.

Two other acts where differences are discernible between the ECtHR and United Nations treaty bodies are blasphemy and abortion. In both cases, the ECtHR has found that the act can be a criminal offence.[55] By contrast, treaty bodies have

49 See United Nations, Human Rights Committee, 2014a. Doc. CCPR/C/LVA/CO/3, para 19; United Nations, Committee against Torture, 2010. UN Doc. CAT/C/MDA/CO/2, para 27; *Vejdeland and Others v. Sweden*, ECHR.

50 See United Nations, Human Rights Committee, 2014c. UN Doc. CCPR/C/KWT/CO/2, para 30; *A.D.T. v. United Kingdom*, ECHR; United Nations, Human Rights Committee, 2005. UN Doc. CCPR/CO/84/TJK, para 22; *Colombani and Others v. France*, ECHR; United Nations, Human Rights Committee, 2012. UN Doc. CCPR/C/ARM/CO/2, para 24; and *Kokkinakis v. Greece*, ECHR.

51 See *Cumpana and Mazare v. Romania*, ECHR.

52 See, for example, United Nations, Human Rights Committee, 2013c. UN Doc. CCPR/C/PRY/CO/3, para 25, and United Nations, Human Rights Committee, 2011b. UN Doc. CCPR/C/GC/34, para 47.

53 See International Press Institute, 2015.

54 See, for example, United Nations, Human Rights Committee, 2015b. UN Doc. CCPR/C/HRV/CO/3, para 23; United Nations, Human Rights Committee, 2013b. UN Doc. CCPR/C/CHN-MAC/CO/1, para 15; United Nations, Human Rights Committee, 2009b. UN Doc. CCPR/C/RUS/CO/6, para 24.

55 See *Wingrove v. United Kingdom*, ECHR, and *A, B and C v. Ireland*, ECHR.

expressed concern that blasphemy is criminalized and called for the repeal of provisions criminalizing abortion.[56] The United Nations Human Rights Committee, in its General Comment 34, is clear, for example, that prohibitions of displays of lack of respect for a religion or other belief system, including blasphemy laws, are incompatible with the Covenant.[57] The European Court, in the cases of *Wingrove* and *İA*, on the other hand, has reasoned that such an offence is compatible with the European Convention due to a high threshold of profanation embodied in the definition of the offence of blasphemy, the fact that the criminalized act must also constitute an abusive attack, and due to the margin of appreciation in this area.[58]

One explanation for the difference could derive from the fact that, as with racial hatred, the ICCPR contains a specific requirement for the prohibition by law of religious hatred that constitutes incitement to discrimination under Article 20(2). Whilst this prohibition does not strictly demand criminalization, the Human Rights Committee postulates that the flip side of the high-threshold offence flowing from Article 20(2) is that "low-threshold" displays of lack of respect for a religion are incompatible with the Covenant.[59] No equivalent standard exists in the wording of the European Convention, with the result that blasphemy cases fall as conviction-type cases under Article 10. As regards abortion, one possible reason for the differences in approach may relate to the fact that the leading European case, *A, B and C*, concerned a criminal prohibition on abortion for health and well-being reasons, but with a right to lawfully travel abroad for an abortion and access to information and medical care in the respondent country. By contrast, treaty body recommendations have most usually been directed to countries where such options are not so readily available.[60] Finally, human rights treaty bodies recommend that a number of other acts not considered by the ECHR to date should not be made subject to criminal sanctions. These include vagrancy, truancy, wandering and child "status offences," imitating the opposite sex, adultery, apostasy, and trespassing on land.[61]

56 United Nations, Human Rights Committee, 2014b. UN Doc. CCPR/C/IRL/CO/4, para 22, and United Nations, Human Rights Committee, 2003. UN Doc. CCPR/CO/79/LKA, para 12.

57 United Nations, Human Rights Committee, 2011b. UN Doc. CCPR/C/GC/34, para 48.

58 See *İ.A. v. Turkey*, ECHR, para 29, and *Wingrove v. United Kingdom*, ECHR, para 61.

59 Temperman, J., 2015.

60 See, for example, United Nations, Committee on Economic, Social and Cultural Rights, 2012. UN Doc. E/C.12/PER/CO/2–4, para 21; United Nations, Human Rights Committee, 2004b. UN Doc. CCPR/CO/82/MAR, para 29; United Nations, Committee against Torture, 2011c. UN Doc. CAT/C/PRY/CO/4–6, para 22.

61 United Nations, Human Rights Committee, 2009a. UN Doc. CCPR/C/RWA/CO/3, para 16; United Nations, Committee on the Rights of the Child, 2010a. UN Doc. CRC/C/NGA/CO/3–4, para 85; United Nations, Human Rights Committee, 2014c. UN Doc. CCPR/C/KWT/CO/2, para 30; United Nations, Human Rights Committee, 2015a. UN Doc. CCPR/C/CIV/CO/1, para 11; United Nations, Human Rights Committee, 2007. UN Doc. CCPR/C/SDN/CO/3, para 26; United Nations, Human Rights Committee, 2008b. UN Doc. CCPR/C/IRL/CO/3, para 23.

The scan of ECtHR criminalization findings, and its comparison with human rights treaty body recommendations, highlights that there are some common points of agreement across international human rights mechanisms on the proper use and extent of the criminal law. At the same time, however, criminalization conclusions are, in practice, heavily dependent upon the parameters of underlying human rights treaties, as well as the procedural and structural framework within which criminalization issues come to be considered. Different human rights frameworks and differences between individual complaints and country-wide recommendations are seen to contribute to variations in criminalization conclusions as between human rights mechanisms. For the ECtHR in particular, the range of acts which should or should not be a criminal offence is comparatively restricted. Cases where the ECtHR suggests that an act *should* be a criminal offence often fall within ICCS categories 1 (acts leading to death), 2 (harm to the person), 3 (injurious sexual acts), and 4 (fraud). The framing of such cases varies from conviction cases, in which the ECtHR confirms that the impugned act should be criminalized, to direct positive and investigatory and procedural obligation cases, in which the Court finds a positive criminalization obligation, either directly or via the general crime investigatory obligation. As discussed further in the next chapter, such acts tend to involve acts directed against the person that engage fundamental aspects of human rights, including dignity and personal integrity. Similarly, cases where the Court finds that an act should not be a criminal offence are limited in number and fall predominantly with ICCS category 8 (acts against public order and the state). Such cases are most usually direct negative or conviction cases in which the Court invokes a negative criminalization obligation. Most commonly, however, the ECtHR finds that an act *can* be a criminal offence. This broad swathe of permissiveness is not seen so clearly in the recommendations of treaty bodies, which – due to the nature of concluding observations – tend to emphasize Committee views on the requirements of human rights treaties, in terms of demanding criminalization or restricting criminalization. Being directed at country situations in general, as opposed to the solution of an individual complaint, treaty body recommendations are also less nuanced than decisions of the European Court. As in the case of blasphemy and abortion, this sometimes results in a clearer, stronger view on the acceptability, or not, of criminalization. The wide range of United Nations human rights instruments, including the five instance of treaty-based criminalization requirement, further means that treaty bodies tend to encounter and pronounce upon a broader range of acts than found in the jurisprudence of the ECtHR. The majority of ECHR criminalization cases fall under just two articles of the Convention: Article 8 (Right to respect for private and family life) and Article 10 (Freedom of expression). The nature of the substantive rights protected by the ECHR, in turn, shapes the range of acts that may be challenged, with large numbers of ECHR criminalization cases involving acts under ICCS categories 2 (acts leading to harm or intending to cause harm to the person), 3 (injurious acts of a sexual nature), or 8 (acts against public order, authority and provisions of the state). Despite these limitations and differences between human rights systems, international human rights law is clear that acts such as trafficking in persons, slavery, sexual offences against children, rape, homicide, and domestic violence must be criminal offences. It is also clear that sexual relations between consenting adults, acts such as injuring the honour and dignity of state authorities, and proselytism should not be criminalized.

Summary

Criminalization cases from the ECtHR and United Nations human rights treaty jurisprudence show that an international human rights tribunal addresses issues of criminalization through multiple routes, including direct negative and positive criminalization cases, conviction-based cases, and investigatory and procedural obligation cases. To date, the majority of ECHR cases that involve questions of criminalization concern acts leading to harm to the person, injurious acts of a sexual nature, or acts against public order, as coded by the ICCS. These cases are most often examined by the Court under ECHR Articles 8 (Right to respect for private and family life) and 10 (Freedom of expression). Identifying the "outcome" of criminalization cases is not always straightforward, particularly in the case of conviction cases. ECHR case law suggests, however, that the ECtHR most usually holds that an impugned act *can* be a criminal offence. In respect of some acts related to causing death, harm or injurious sexual acts, the ECtHR confirms that certain acts *should* be criminal offences. The Court holds that an act *should not* be a criminal offence in a small number cases, mostly involving acts against public order or public safety. Comparison of criminalization outcomes from the ECtHR with findings of United Nations human rights treaty bodies shows reasonable alignment, albeit with some differences that arise from the different procedural and structural frameworks of the two human rights systems within which criminalization issues come to be considered.

7 Reasoning in criminalization cases

A first question when it comes to identifying the reasoning behind the decisions of an international human rights court, such as the ECtHR, is whether the court consistently invokes recognizable legal, moral, or philosophical theories in its application of convention rights. That is, whether the court or tribunal is known to be guided in its decisions by a particular moral legal theory. As the open-textured language and the structure of human rights instruments leave human rights courts and tribunals significant opportunities for choice in interpretation, the question bears upon the issue of a wider theory of interpretation of human rights.[1] In turn, the way in which human rights courts approach this interpretation is tied, in many ways, to the heritage of international human rights law.

At the time of the preparation of the Universal Declaration of Human Rights (UDHR) in 1946, work did not commence in a jurisprudential or philosophical vacuum. Rather, a certain heritage in philosophical rights-based thought and national constitutional rights can be clearly identified. Commentators such as Stephen Marks argue that the UDHR has solid roots in the French Declaration through the natural law concept that the individual has rights against the state, through the rule of law requirement that legal rules should dictate the behaviour of all within the state's jurisdiction, and through the social contract that orders society for the common good. Marks asserts that the drafters of the UDHR frequently acknowledged and drew upon these roots, making each of these ideas part of an incomplete revolution of modernity.[2] In the same vein, James Griffin claims that from roots deep in Greek and Roman antiquity through to Thomas Aquinas, Hugo Grotius, and John Locke, legal philosophical, religious, and political writers have all formulated and expressed various conceptions of inherent or natural rights.[3] Locke's Second Treatise of Government (1690), for example, refers to a right of freedom of person and liberty of acting according to one's own will, which Locke holds is grounded in the capacity of reason.[4] Whilst the nature and extent of natural rights in the Second Treatise are

1 Letsas, G., 2007, p.3.
2 Marks, S.P., 1998, p.511.
3 Griffin, J., 2008, pp.9–14.
4 Locke, J., 1980 (originally published 1690), pp.26 and 79.

somewhat amorphous, its influence on the development of American political thought, in particular during the late 18th century during the drafting of the US Bill of Rights, is not widely challenged. A certain amount of cross-fertilization of philosophical ideas between the United States and France, along with a diverse set of ideas and natural law tenets from the Enlightenment, likely similarly influenced the French Declarations of the Rights of Man and of the Citizen of 1789 and 1793.[5]

As such, it is not perhaps unreasonable to postulate a direct, or at least indirect, line between political and moral philosophies, both from antiquity and the Enlightenment, and through the codification of modern international human rights law. To these influences, Marks also highlights the influence on international human rights law of Socialism, with its focus on economic and social rights, as well as non-Western sources, including Chinese, Japanese, Indian, African, and Islamic civilizations. Other writers, such as Jack Donnelly, heavily dispute the proposition that conceptions of individual rights can be identified in the history of such cultures and argue that human rights are purely an artefact of modern Western civilization.[6] Overall, the exact origin and interplay of such influences on contemporary human rights law remain a matter of continued debate in human rights literature.

If the question of influences on the development of modern international human rights law is unresolved, then the closely linked issue of the underlying theoretical foundations of human rights law is perhaps even more controversial. Michael Freeman contends that the identifiable existence or not of a defensible theoretical foundation for international human rights law is more than simply an academic question. He claims that the problem for human rights is that it needs what some of its philosophical friends claim is impossible: a meta-ethical foundation which can "trump" claims of cultural relativism.[7] In other words – so the argument goes – whilst international human rights law carries theoretical legal weight, this is likely to be insufficient, particularly in the absence of practical enforceability, to counter relativist objections to the universality of human rights if unaccompanied by a solid theoretical foundation that goes above and beyond the multilateral negotiations that gave rise to the international human rights standard. The point is well made, and few would seriously dispute the value, in principle, of a sound theoretical basis to human rights – were one to be identified. Views diverge, however, on the question of whether such a task is possible in the first place. At one extreme lies the position that whilst certain historic influences may be identified, the quest for secure philosophical foundations of human rights practice is philosophically doomed to fail and is practically useless. Under this position, international human rights law standards are simply positive law political compromises arrived at in an attempt to achieve as near as possible cross-cultural consensus. At the other extreme lies the commitment to a single unifying theory of rights that is claimed to offer the necessary foundational rigour.

5 Ludwikowski, R.R., 1990.
6 Donnelly, J., 1982; Donnelly, J., 2007.
7 Freeman, M., 1994, p.501.

As regards the ECHR, on the one hand, it has been argued that largely liberal principles underpin its substantive rights. George Letsas, for example, holds that legality and liberalism are objective values of political morality that shape and guide the interpretation of the ECHR.[8] Under this view, ECHR rights should give effect to the right of individuals to choose and pursue their own conception of the good life, and protect them from moralistic and paternalistic restrictions. As Letsas himself admits, however, the ECtHR also shows strands of case law that may be challenging to justify under liberal principles. These include where the ECtHR has recourse to consensus as an interpretive principle, in the form of the "European consensus" standard that looks to the existence or non-existence of common ground in the law and practice of Council of Europe member states. This may have the result of opening the door to non-liberal moralistic preferences of the majority or authorize the use of state coercion in an unprincipled and arbitrary manner. As such, it is likely an oversimplification to suggest that the concepts and reasoning of the ECtHR are guided solely by liberal principles. Rather, diverse influences on the development of international human rights law frequently provide a place for human rights courts to adopt approaches such as moralism and overall welfare interests. The fact that the contours of individual rights are commonly described not solely by the effect on the individual himself or herself but also by the nature and extent of the corresponding state obligation provides significant latitude for the Court to invoke such principles. As a result, no single moral legal theory is determinative of ECtHR reasoning.

The lack of a single moral legal theory underpinning international human rights law is one reason why distilling a conceptual framework from the jurisprudence of an international human rights court or tribunal is far from straightforward. Another reason, however, is that the conceptual framework of international human rights law is itself an evolving socio-juridical system. Whereas international human rights law provides a core treaty-based structure of rights, such as respect for private and family life, and freedoms of thought, conscience, and religion, the balance and reasoning that takes place within the structure of these substantive rights is itself determined, in the main, by judges who seek to apply the rights within individual *in concreto* cases. In the case of the ECtHR, for example, sections in Court judgments labelled "general principles" set out elements of the right based on its collective interpretation in case law, often over many decades. These may include mention of high-level principles, such as pluralism, tolerance, fair treatment, broadmindedness, and proportionality, that guide application of the right. As the focus is on describing key reference points for the right from individual cases, however, little guidance is given as to an overall structure for the application of such principles in practice. As a result, existing ECHR "principles" are quite different to a full moral-legal system that starts from a clean conceptual approach.

In addition, the framework provided for judicial reasoning by treaty-based rights differs substantially as between individual rights. ECHR Articles 3 (Prohibition of torture) and 4 (Prohibition of slavery), for example, simply state that "no one shall"

8 Letsas, G., 2007, p.5.

be subjected to torture or to inhuman or degrading treatment or punishment. Other articles, such as Articles 8 (Private and family life), 9 (Thought, conscience and religion), 10 (Freedom of expression), and 11 (Freedom of assembly), contain more extensive structures for guiding their application, through the inclusion of grounds of justification for restrictions on the right. Whether an ECHR article is extensive or minimalistic, the Court must follow established legal approaches to the determination of a violation, as developed in its case law. In the case of rights without restriction clauses, the Court must determine whether the state provided practical and effective protection of the rights guaranteed. In the case of rights with restriction clauses, the Court must identify whether any interference is proportionate to the legitimate aim pursued, having regard to a fair balance between the competing interests at stake and the margin of appreciation enjoyed by the state. These processes themselves form part of the "reasoning" of the ECtHR and can control the extent to which the Court is free to invoke different concepts and principles. Rights with restriction clauses, for example, can oblige the Court to consider aspects such as "social needs" for restrictions on individual rights, as well as needs for protection of "morals."

Taking these considerations into account, the ECHR case table at the end of this book identifies and classifies underlying grounds of reasoning employed in ECHR criminalization cases. In this sense, the "reasoning" of the ECtHR means a consideration, principle, or argument that is decisive, or at least highly influential, with respect to the decision of the Court as regards the question of criminalization – in particular, having in mind liberal and other moral principles that have influenced international human rights law. The review of cases suggests that whilst the ECtHR employs a very wide range of reasoning and concepts in criminalization cases, six main grounds of reasoning stand out: societal interests; offense; autonomy; harm; community consensus; and human dignity. Each of these six concepts features in reasoning in around 20 per cent, or more, of cases reviewed, with societal interests invoked in reasoning in over one-third of cases.

Societal interests

The most common ground of reasoning employed by the ECtHR in criminalization cases is that of societal interests. The language of the ECHR explicitly allows for restrictions on a number of rights in pursuit of a range of interests, many of which can be considered as "societal" interests. These include national security, public safety, economic well-being of the country, the prevention of disorder or crime, public order, health or morals, and territorial integrity.[9] In the criminalization case table at the end of this book, reasoning was classified to the "societal interests" category wherever the Court used an argument related to the interests of society, the community, or groups of persons at large, as opposed to of specific individuals, to support criminalization findings. "Interests" in this sense is a wide term. Interests considered by the Court in the context of criminalization include health (*Acmanne*,

9 See ECHR Articles 8, 9, 10, and 11.

Pretty, and *Laskey*), the administration of justice (*Dallas*), the quality of the environment and cultural heritage (*Ehrmann*), societal order and peaceful community relations (*Feret*, *Gough*, *Kudrevičius*, *Norwood*, *Osmani*, and *Şükran Aydin*), and family structures (*Stübing*). Cases involving such interests fall almost exclusively under ECHR Articles 8 (Private and family life), 9 (Thought, conscience and religion), 10 (Freedom of expression), and 11 (Freedom of assembly), in light of their specific restriction clauses. In many cases, societal interests reasoning is seen to support a finding by the Court that the act in question *can* be a criminal offence. In a small number of cases, however, the ECtHR considers a societal interest that might count in favour of criminalization, but reasons that the act should nonetheless *not* be a criminal offence (*A.D.T*, *Bayatyan*, *Colombani*, and *Şükran Aydin*).

The societal interest probably most often invoked in criminalization reasoning of the ECtHR is the interest of public order. Whilst the Court frequently refers to the prevention of disorder and the protection of public order as a legitimate aim of restrictions on rights, it does not often explore the concept in depth, at least in criminalization cases. In *Gough* (nudity in public), for example, the Court, in finding that the act could be a criminal offence, merely noted that the issue of public nudity raised moral and "public-order" considerations.[10] In *Norwood* (religious hate speech), the Court, in finding that a conviction for displaying a sign which was threatening, abusive, or insulting and likely to cause harassment, alarm, or distress was compatible with Convention rights, emphasized that such acts were incompatible with the values guaranteed by the Convention, notably, "social peace."[11] In *Aydin* (supporting a banned organization), the Court observed that the applicant's conviction for contravening a ban imposed on an association's activity was designed to protect public order and safety.[12]

By contrast, in *Bayatyan* (conscientious objection to military service), the Court acknowledged the government's argument that evasion of service may result in serious consequences for "public order" if the authorities were to allow every religious organization to interpret and comply with the law in force as their respective religious beliefs provided.[13] However, the Court did not find this convincing, especially taking into account that at the time of the applicant's conviction for evading military service, the authorities had already pledged to introduce alternative civilian service. The conviction and the criminal law therefore gave rise to a violation of ECHR Article 9. Similarly, in *Şükran* (election campaigns), the Court noted that the government asserted that the offence of using any language other than Turkish in campaigning for election was necessary for the prevention of disorder. The Court, however, found that such a ban did not meet a pressing social need and was not proportionate to any such aim. The interference with the right to freedom of expression arising from the criminal law therefore gave rise to a violation of ECHR Article 10.

10 *Gough v. United Kingdom*, ECHR, para 172.
11 *Norwood v. United Kingdom*, ECHR, p.4.
12 *Aydin v. Germany*, ECHR, para 58.
13 *Bayatyan v. Armenia*, ECHR, para 84.

A second societal interest commonly used in reasoning of the Court is that of public health. This arises mostly within the context of Article 8 (Right to private life), as a societal interest to be taken into account in the restriction of acts that may fall within this sphere. In *Acmanne* (compulsory health screening), for example, the Court held that the criminal conviction of an individual for refusing to undergo compulsory methods of tuberculosis screening was proportionate to the aim pursued and necessary to protect *health* in a democratic society.[14] In *Laskey* (assault in the context of sadomasochistic activities), the Court found that public health considerations were at stake, as the activities involved a significant degree of injury or wounding which could not be characterized as trifling or transient. The Court determined that the interference with the applicants' right to private life was necessary in a democratic society for the protection of health within the meaning of ECHR Article 8, paragraph 2. It is notable that the concept of health in *Laskey*, as well as invoking issues of public health, also concerns the specific health of the applicants themselves, in a sense related to autonomy and paternalism. These aspects of the case are discussed below. Overall, at least in cases that involve the societal interest of public health, the Court appears to give reasonable weight to public health reasoning in support of criminalization. In *A. D.T.* (same-sex relations), for instance, the Court noted the *absence* of any public-health considerations, as part of its reasoning for finding that legislation criminalizing homosexual acts between men in private constituted a violation of ECHR Article 8.[15]

A further societal interest recognized by the Court is that of social harmony. The Court refers to this concept in a number of different contexts, with the underlying idea that legitimate restrictions on rights may be necessary in order to ensure that individuals are able to live together effectively in society. In *Ehrmann* (building planning regulations), for example, the Court, in finding that a conviction for executing building work without the required notices and authorizations did not breach ECHR Article 10, stated that the planning regulations fulfilled the function of regulating conduct in matters of land use and contributed to creating the conditions for the harmonization of "social life."[16] The Court recognized that there was also an important link with the protection of the rights of others, in particular, the owners of neighbouring constructions. At the same time, however, it emphasized the role of national authorities in determining what is in the general interest of the community and noted that the measures ensured the protection of the common good and respect for the collective intent as expressed in planning choices.

Similarly, in *S.A.S.* (wearing of clothing designed to conceal the face), the Court found that a criminal offence of face concealment in public could be justified in so far as it sought to guarantee the conditions of "living together."[17] The concept of social harmony does not, however, protect all aspects of all ways

14 *Acmanne and others v. Belgium*, ECHR, p.257.
15 *A.D.T. v. United Kingdom*, ECHR, para 38.
16 *Ehrmann v. France*, ECHR, p.12.
17 *S.A.S. v. France*, ECHR, para 142.

of life or interests that a group, society, or community may have. In *Friend* (hunting a wild mammal with a dog), for example, the Court, in finding that the criminal prohibition was legitimate, noted that it was of relevance that the wider "public or social dimensions" to a traditional hunt had also been preserved in drag or trail hunting, even though the hunt would not culminate in the killing of a wild mammal by hounds.[18] As such, social harmony-based reasoning does not protect every detail of established public and social dimensions and interactions from criminalization.

Overall, analysis of ECHR criminalization cases shows that the ECtHR quite frequently employs the concept of societal interests in support of criminalization. Due to the structure of the European Convention, where this is the case, the societal interest argument for criminalization is used by the Court to justify the infringement of individual human rights. Some of these interests are societal coordination-type interests, where rules, such as planning regulations, public health rules, or clothing conventions, exist in order to facilitate the co-existence of persons who will encounter each other in day-to-day life or need to share resources. Others more directly concern the prevention of conflict and the infliction of harm or offense on indeterminate others or groups of persons, such as in the case of rules on hate speech and banned organizations. In the Court's view, not all societal interests can be enforced by the criminal law, however. In particular, where the restriction or performance of the societal requirement can be achieved in alternate ways, then the Court is less likely to find that criminal law may be used to enforce the societal interest over and above an individual Convention right.

Autonomy

Whilst the ECtHR has a certain deference for societal interests, at the same time it also places a high value on the concept of individual autonomy.

The Court most often associates the concept of autonomy with ECHR Article 8 (Right to private life). In *Pretty* (assisting suicide), the Court stated that it considered that the notion of personal autonomy is an important principle underlying the interpretation of Article 8 guarantees. The Court links the concept of autonomy with the ideas of identity, choice, and self-determination.[19] Within this context, respect for personal autonomy may operate to prevent criminalization, if a particular criminal law disproportionately infringes upon the exercise of individual autonomy. In practice, and somewhat surprisingly, given the strong liberal heritage of international human rights law, there are comparatively few cases where the Court relies on autonomy-based reasoning as a shield against overly intrusive criminalization of acts involving only one individual or consenting individuals. The clearest example is likely *Dudgeon* (same-sex

18 *Friend, the Countryside Alliance and Others v. United Kingdom*, ECHR, para 50.

19 See, for example, *Aksu v. Turkey*, ECHR, para 58; *Odièvre v. France*, ECHR; and *Parrillo v. Italy*, ECHR, Dissenting opinion of Judge Sajó, para 1.

relations), where the Court, in finding that criminal laws on buggery were incompatible with ECHR Article 8, held that societal and moral arguments advanced by the government could not warrant the application of penal sanctions when consenting adults alone were involved.[20]

Such determinations involve the Court weighing the concept of personal autonomy against societal interests and the rights of others. In *Pretty*, for example, the Court noted that it was necessary to weigh considerations of public health and safety against the countervailing principle of personal autonomy.[21] In that instance the Court held – largely from reasoning based on vulnerability (discussed further below) – that the concept of personal autonomy did not override the need to protect persons who may be weak and vulnerable from acts intended to assist in ending life. As a result, a blanket criminal law on assisted suicide was held not to violate ECHR Article 8. The Court also recognized that the personal autonomy of the individual was at stake in *Laskey* (assault in the context of sadomasochistic activities) due to the consensual nature of the activities. On examining the proportionality of the infringement, the Court similarly found, however, that the criminal prohibition was necessary for the protection of health.[22] In *Gough* (nudity in public), whilst the applicant submitted that restrictions pertaining to a person's mode of personal presentation were a function of personal identity and an exercise of personal autonomy, the Court held that the convictions were not disproportionate to the legitimate aim of the prevention of disorder.[23]

Autonomy also features in the reasoning of the Court as a wider consideration, including as a factor deserving of protection from the acts of others. In *Siliadin* (servitude), for example, the Court, in finding that national criminal law did not provide effective protection against the forced servitude experienced by the applicant, noted that the applicant had been clearly deprived of her personal autonomy.[24] In *Rantsev* (trafficking in persons), the Court, in finding that trafficking in persons fell within the scope of ECHR Article 4 (Prohibition of slavery and forced labour) and was properly subject to the criminal law, highlighted that trafficking threatens the fundamental freedoms of its victims and treats human beings as commodities to be bought and sold.[25] In *Kokkinakis* (proselytism), the Court used the concept of restriction of choice to distinguish between bearing Christian witness and "improper proselytism." In its reasoning for holding that the former should not be a criminal offence, it identified improper proselytism with reference to, amongst other factors, exerting improper pressure on people in distress or in need, including even through the use of violence or brainwashing.[26]

20 *Dudgeon v. United Kingdom*, ECHR, para 60.
21 *Pretty v. United Kingdom*, ECHR, para 73.
22 *Laskey, Jaggard and Brown v. United Kingdom*, ECHR, paras 44 and 50.
23 *Gough v. United Kingdom*, ECHR, para 184.
24 *Siliadin v. France*, ECHR, para 122.
25 *Rantsev v. Cyprus and Russia*, ECHR, paras 281–282.
26 *Kokkinakis v. Greece*, ECHR, para 48.

Overall, the ECtHR considers that the serious restriction of the autonomy of one individual by another is a ground that can support criminalization, in order to protect the freedom of choice and self-determination of individuals. In general, ECHR Article 8 also protects the autonomy of a single individual, or group of consenting individuals, in respect of restrictions imposed by the state on acts which do not directly involve others. Autonomy is, however, balanced by the Court with other interests, such as societal interests, and in a number of cases has been found by the ECtHR to be legitimately limited by the criminal law pursuant to such interests.

Harm and offense

In addition to reasoning based on societal interests and autonomy, the ECtHR also draws on the concepts of harm and offense in reaching criminalization findings. As noted earlier in this book, harm and offense themselves form key pillars of criminalization theory: John Stuart Mill famously holding, in the late 19th century, that the only purpose for which power can be rightfully exercised is to prevent "harm" to others.

For the ECtHR, harm to others is equally a reason in support of criminalization. In *Laskey* (assault in the context of sadomasochistic activities), for example, the Court held that the state was unquestionably entitled to seek to regulate activities which involved the infliction of "physical harm" through the operation of the criminal law.[27] In *Beganović* (assault), the Court stated that the main purpose of imposing criminal sanctions was to restrain and deter the offender from causing further "harm."[28] In *Dudgeon* (same-sex relations), the Court repeated the words of the United Kingdom's Wolfenden Report that the overall function served by the criminal law was to preserve public order and decency and to protect the citizen from what was offensive or "injurious."[29] Thus, whilst for the European Court, the prevention of harm is not the only purpose for which the criminal law may be used, it is certainly a reason in support of criminalization, and in some cases, a main justification for criminalization.

In ECHR criminalization cases, harm-based reasoning is found across a range of ECHR articles and *International Classification of Crimes for Statistical Purposes* (ICCS) acts. In *G* (rape), for example, the Court considered a criminal offence of rape which did not allow for any defence based either on an accused's mistaken belief about a child's age or on apparent consent by a child. In holding that the offence was compatible with the Convention, the Court highlighted that the consequences of penetrative sex for a child of 12 or under may be very "harmful."[30] In *Öneryildiz* (negligence in dangerous activities), the Court noted that in determining the responsibility of the state under ECHR Article 2, the "harmfulness" of the activity in question was one factor that must be taken into

27 *Laskey, Jaggard and Brown v. United Kingdom*, para 43.
28 *Beganović v Croatia*, ECHR, para 85.
29 *Dudgeon v. United Kingdom*, para 49.
30 *G. v. United Kingdom*, para 39.

account.[31] In *Opuz* (domestic violence), the Court stated that a failure to take reasonable measures which could have had a real prospect of altering the outcome or mitigating the harm was sufficient to engage the responsibility of the state.[32] In *Perinçek* (denial of genocide), the Court considered the capacity of the statements made to lead, directly or indirectly, to harmful consequences.[33]

The manner in which the ECtHR employs harm-based reasoning suggests that the Court has a wide understanding of the concept. The primary sense in which it recognizes the concept is as bodily harm to specific others, including through the consideration of ill-treatment and its minimum level of severity under ECHR Article 3 (Prohibition of torture). Cases such as *Opuz* (domestic violence), *A* (reasonable chastisement), and *Beganović* (assault), for instance, involve bodily harm to specific others. The Court also recognizes non-bodily harm to indeterminate others. In *Perinçek* (denial of genocide), the Court's reference to the harmful consequences of statements, for example, appears to be in the context of assessing the impact on populations in general. In addition, the Court seems to acknowledge the possibility of harm to self. In *Palusinski* (incitement to use drugs), for instance, the applicant submitted that nobody had sustained any "harm" after reading his book on narcotic drugs. In finding that the conviction was compatible with ECHR Article 10, the Court accepted the point but emphasized that the book contained very little, if any, information on the "negative consequences" of the use of such substances.[34]

Perhaps unsurprisingly, the ECtHR does not elaborate a definition of harm for the purposes of reasoning under the Convention. Rather, the Court appears to use the term in a relatively non-specific way, including drawing upon the harm principle from legal philosophy in its broadest sense. Whilst the prevention of harm is mostly employed by the Court as a direct reason in support of criminalization, in *Pretty* (assisting suicide), the Court linked the concept of harm with the balance between societal interests and individual autonomy. In that case, the Court, in holding that the offence of assisting suicide could apply in the case of terminally ill individuals, noted that the more serious the harm involved, the more heavily will weigh in the balance considerations of public health and safety against the countervailing principle of personal autonomy.[35] In other words, where one individual may cause serious harm to another, even with consent, the greater the likelihood that any consideration of personal autonomy will be overridden by the public interest in the general prevention of such act.

In addition to the concept of harm, the ECtHR also recognizes the criminalization concept of *offense*. As noted earlier in this book, in legal theory, offense to others is proposed as a basis for criminalization that is distinct from harm. Joel Feinberg, for

31 *Öneryildiz v. Turkey*, ECHR, para 73.
32 *Opuz v. Turkey*, ECHR, para 136.
33 *Perinçek v. Switzerland*, ECHR, para 207.
34 *Palusinski v. Poland*, ECHR, p.10.
35 *Pretty v. United Kingdom*, ECHR, para 74.

instance, argues that wrongfully causing universally disliked mental states is a separate and distinct legitimizing principle for criminalization. As might be expected, almost all criminalization cases in which the Court invokes the concept of offense fall under ECHR Article 10 (Freedom of expression). Most commonly, the concept is invoked in the sense of offense experienced directly by specific individuals, such as in the case of defamation, insult, hate speech, or public nudity. The Court's starting position is that offensive speech or acts are, in principle, acceptable, in so far as freedom of expression is applicable not only to information or ideas that are favourably received but also to those that offend, shock, or disturb.[36] The ECtHR may, however, permit criminalization of offensive speech or acts in some circumstances. It employs a number of lines of reasoning in this regard.

Under one approach, offensive speech or acts may not benefit from the protection of Article 10 in the first place. In *Rujak* (insult), for example, the Court affirmed that certain classes of speech, such as lewd and obscene speech, have no essential role in the expression of ideas, such that an offensive statement may fall outside the protection of freedom of expression where the sole intent of the statement is to insult.[37] In finding that a criminal conviction for tarnishing the reputation of Croatia was acceptable, the Court held that the statement mostly concerned vulgar and "offensive" language that fell outside the protection of Article 10 of the Convention because it amounted to wanton denigration and its sole intent was to insult. This line of reasoning suggests that statements intended to insult can be criminalized, since they do not amount to imparting information or ideas, as protected by Article 10. Under another approach, Article 10 may be applicable to the speech or act in question, but criminalization is accepted by the Court as a necessary restriction due to a pressing social need. This scheme requires consideration of the conduct or speech in question within the social context. In *İ.A.* (blasphemy), for example, the Court found that Article 10 was applicable in the case of a criminal conviction for blasphemy and insult to religious beliefs, arising from the publication of a book on theological issues. It held, however, that the book contained not only comments that offended or shocked but also an abusive attack on the Prophet of Islam. Reasoning that believers may legitimately feel themselves to be the subject of unwarranted and offensive attacks, the Court found that criminalization was intended to provide protection against offensive attacks on matters regarded as sacred by Muslims and reasonably met a pressing social need.[38] Other cases in which the Court found Article 10 to be applicable, but criminalization to be compatible with the Convention, include *Müller* (obscene publications). In that case, the Court held that a conviction for obscene publications liable grossly to "offend" the sense of sexual propriety of persons of ordinary sensitivity did not violate Article 10.[39]

36 See, for example, *Karataş v. Turkey*, ECHR, para 48.
37 *Rujak v. Croatia*, ECHR, para 29.
38 *İ.A. v. Turkey*, ECHR, para 30.
39 *Müller and Others v. Switzerland*, ECHR, para 36.

Similarly, in *Janowski* (insult), the Court held that a conviction for calling municipal guards "oafs" and "dumb" in public constituted a proportionate interference with Article 10 on the basis that the guards' actions did not warrant resort to offensive and abusive verbal attacks.[40] *Janowski* appears, however, to be on the margin of criminalization based on the concept of offense. In a dissenting opinion, Judges Bratza and Rozakis comment that the offense in law allowed no discretion to the domestic court other than to convict wherever insults were addressed to a civil servant carrying out his official duties. Bratza and Rozakis note, in particular, that using two insulting words which evidently reflected the applicant's sense of frustration could not be used to justify his prosecution. They also highlight that the words of insult were not in any way calculated to disturb public order. As a result, in their view, the wide application of the criminal offence of insulting a civil servant could not be said to respond to a pressing social need, nor be proportionate to any legitimate aim served.

Whilst the ECtHR often uses reasoning related to offense to find that criminalization is acceptable, in a small number of cases, the Court finds the act should not be a criminal offence. In *Mondragon* (insulting a head of state), for example, the Court held that a conviction for falsely accusing or insulting the king was incompatible with ECHR Article 10. The Court criticized the fact that the criminal offence afforded the head of state a greater degree of protection than other persons, who were only protected by the ordinary law on insults. The Court also emphasized that the comments in question, which concerned the king's responsibility as head of state, did not concern the king's private life or his personal honour. Nor did they amount to a gratuitous personal attack against him and were unconnected to the innermost core of individual dignity.[41] As such, the case highlights that the criminal law related to offense must generally provide equal protection to all, as well as avoid prohibiting speech that is not intended to insult, undermine dignity, or attack honour.

Finally, reasoning related to offense was considered by the Court, and rejected, in the case of *Dudgeon* (same-sex relations). Unlike other cases, where offense is invoked in a direct experiential sense, in *Dudgeon*, the Court acknowledged the possible existence of a "mere knowledge" form of offense, whereby the practice of a particular act could be argued to offend the moral ethos of the community. The Court effectively rejected this argument for criminalization, holding that although members of the public who regarded homosexuality as immoral may be shocked, offended, or disturbed by the commission by others of private homosexual acts, this could not on its own warrant the application of penal sanctions when consenting adults alone were involved.[42]

Overall, reasoning related to offense is an important, and common, line of criminalization argumentation for the ECtHR. Offense is invoked in respect of

40 *Janowski v. Poland*, ECHR, paras 34 and 35.
41 *Otegi Mondragon v. Spain*, ECHR, paras 55 and 57.
42 *Dudgeon v. United Kingdom*, ECHR, para 60.

a wide range of acts including same-sex relations, nudity in public, obscene publications, insult, defamation, and blasphemy. All of these acts have in common, however, that they engage, or could be argued to engage, ECHR Article 10 on freedom of expression. In general, the Court readily recognizes causing experiential offense to another as a ground of criminalization. The boundary at which such criminalization is acceptable for the Court is hard to define. However, insults within the context of a heated argument, or statements whose sole intent is not to insult or undermine dignity, and which still impart information or ideas, are likely to be excluded from criminalization under offense-based reasoning.

Community consensus

In addition to societal interests, autonomy, harm and offense, a further principle considered by the Court is that of community consensus. This concept reflects the idea that societies and communities may hold certain common values or principles to be important and potentially deserving of protection by the criminal law. The wording of the European Convention introduces the possibility of such reasoning through inclusion of the protection of morals as a ground for restrictions on rights under ECHR Articles 8 (Right to private life), 9 (Freedom of religion), 10 (Freedom of expression), and 11 (Freedom of association). For the ECtHR, an appeal to morals may not necessarily be based on a critical morality reasoned from specific principles, but can include a generally accepted norm in any particular, democratic, society. In addition to the inclusion of community morals within ECHR restriction clauses, the European Court's approach to determining the size of the margin of appreciation also relies on a form of community consensus reasoning, in the form of the Court's concept of a European consensus.

In ECtHR criminalization cases, the concept of community consensus around a certain norm or moral standard is most often considered in the context of ECHR Articles 8 (Right to private life), and 10 (Freedom of expression). One of the most direct considerations of community consensus reasoning is found in the case of *S.A.S.* (wearing of clothing designed to conceal the face). In that case, the Court first observed that there was no European consensus against a ban. Within the resultant wide margin of appreciation, the Court then gave precedence to a perceived French community consensus. It observed that whether one should be permitted to wear the full-face veil in public places constituted a choice of society. The Court went on to observe that individuals who were present in places open to all may not wish to see practices or attitudes developing there which would fundamentally call into question the possibility of open interpersonal relationships, which, by virtue of an established "consensus," formed an indispensable element of community life within the society in question.[43] Under such a consensus, the Court accepted that the barrier raised against others by a veil concealing the face was perceived as breaching the right

43 *S.A.S. v. France*, ECHR, paras 120 and 122.

of others to live in a space of socialization which made living together easier. As a result, the Court held that the criminal offence did not violate the Convention.

Further cases where the ECtHR has allowed for criminalization with reference to a notion of community consensus include *Stübing* (incest) and *Laskey* (assault in the context of sadomasochistic activities). In *Stübing*, the Court noted that there was no consensus amongst member states as to whether the consensual commitment of sexual acts between adult siblings should be criminally sanctioned. The Court did, however, identify a broad consensus that sexual relationships between siblings were neither accepted by the legal order nor by society as a whole. Taking into account the broad margin of appreciation, the Court concluded that a conviction for incest was compatible with the Convention.[44] In *Laskey* (assault in the context of sadomasochistic activities), Judge Pettiti, in concurring that criminal restrictions were justified, famously noted that the protection of private life did not mean the protection of baseness or the promotion of criminal "immoralism."[45]

In other cases, the ECtHR considered arguments for criminalization based on a community consensus of morality, but determined that the concept did not present sufficient grounds for a legitimate restriction on individual rights. In *Dudgeon* (same-sex relations), for example, the Court noted that the criminal offence of "gross indecency" between males was originally passed in order to enforce the then prevailing conception of sexual morality. The Court accepted that a large number of members of the community held the view that a change in the law would be seriously damaging to the moral fabric of society and accepted that this was a matter which may be legitimately taken into account by the national authorities. The Court highlighted, however, that this could not, of itself, be decisive as to the necessity for the interference with private life. In finding a violation of ECHR Article 8, the Court reasoned that the concern that any relaxation in the law would tend to erode existing moral standards could not, without more, warrant interfering with private life to such an extent. In so doing, the Court had regard to the fact that similar measures were not considered necessary in other member states of the Council of Europe.[46]

The community consensus line of reasoning employed by the Court recognizes a role for the prevailing social position in determining the extent to which criminal law restrictions can be placed on individual rights. The Court explicitly recognizes this through its position that it must have regard to changing conditions in contracting states and respond to any emerging consensus as to the standards to be achieved.[47] The consensus to be taken into account includes both that at European level and within the particular state in question. *Dudgeon* (same-sex relations) shows that where a European consensus can be identified, and differs from the local consensus, the Court may give precedence to the European consensus. Where no clear European consensus can be identified, however, the Court may, as in *S.A.S.* (wearing of clothing

44 *Stübing v. Germany*, ECHR, para 27.
45 *Laskey, Jaggard and Brown v. United Kingdom*, ECHR, concurring opinion of Judge Petitti.
46 *Dudgeon v. United Kingdom*, ECHR, para 61.
47 *Bayatyan v. Armenia*, ECHR, para 102.

designed to conceal the face), allow more weight for the local consensus. Community consensus reasoning, at least in the form of a local consensus, is found most often in respect of acts that could cause offense, according to a standard of public morality or tolerance. Relevant ECtHR cases include, for example, *Akçam* (denigrating the nation), *Handyside* and *Müller* (obscene publications), *Wingrove* (blasphemy), and *Gough* (nudity in public). The concept does not often come to the fore, however, where acts clearly engage other grounds of reasoning, such as harm or serious restriction of autonomy. This likely reflects the fact that these two principles themselves present good grounds for restriction of rights and, in many ways, carry an inherent consensus of wrongfulness.

As such, community consensus reasoning is utilized most often by the ECtHR in the context of criminalization where an act is generally condemned by society, but may not so clearly cause harm to others or restrict autonomy. There is, in this sense, an overlap between community consensus and societal interests. Community consensus reasoning is often wider, however, than clear societal interests in common goods, such as public order or public health. This is because the interest to which the consensus most usually attaches, that of "morals," is not easily subject to clear definition, or demonstration, as to why an individual act has wider societal implications. In this regard, a "public element" to the act is generally required in order for a community consensus to be persuasive towards criminalization. *S.A.S.*, *Gough*, and obscenity cases such as *Handyside* and *Müller*, for example, all concerned public acts. By contrast, the invocation of community consensus reasoning in respect of the private acts in *Dudgeon* was rejected by the Court.

Human dignity

The concept of human dignity plays a central, if somewhat complex, role in human rights discourse. In the first place, human dignity forms a part of the moral and philosophical heritage of international human rights law. The concept of *dignitas hominis*, for example, largely meaning "status," was present in classical Roman thought, in addition to a second broader concept of dignity, particularly developed by Cicero, where *dignitas* referred also to the dignity of persons as human beings not dependent on any particular status. The idea of *dignitas* subsequently became linked with Church doctrine and the distinguishing feature of Man as being made in the image of God and endowed with gifts of reason. In the Enlightenment, the dignity of Man came to be developed philosophically and used by Kant through his formulation that to treat people with dignity is to treat them as autonomous individuals able to choose their destiny.

Christopher McCrudden argues that, in modern times, dignity was introduced into the contemporary international discourse at the time of the drafting of the United Nations Charter and the UDHR, in particular by the prominent French Catholic philosopher, Jacques Maritain.[48] Maritain brought with him the

48 McCrudden, C., 2008, p.662.

theology of Thomas Aquinas and a conception of dignity that valued reason and autonomy, but also emphasized Man's place in society, in a more communitarian sense. McCrudden identifies that, drawing on the inclusion of dignity in the Preamble to the United Nations Charter, human dignity was added by René Cassin to the draft UDHR as a vital attempt to articulate the basis on which human rights could be said to exist. Both the International Covenant on Civil and Political Rights (ICCPR) and International Covenant on Economic, Social and Cultural Rights (ICESCR) reflect this foundational role of dignity through their formulation that rights derive from the inherent dignity of the human person. Whilst dignity provides a foundational aspect of human rights, it is also brought specifically into particular human rights and occurs in Articles 22 (Right to social security) and 23 (Right to work) of the UDHR, as well as ICESCR Article 13 (Right to education) and ICCPR Article 10 (Persons deprived of liberty). International human rights case law also shows that dignity is particularly associated with issues of bodily integrity, equality, and self-determination.[49] In this regard, a basic minimum content of the meaning of human dignity can be understood as the concept that each human being possesses an intrinsic worth that should be respected, with some forms of conduct being inconsistent with respect for that intrinsic worth.

The ECHR itself does not contain the term "dignity." However, the ECtHR invokes the term in a number of criminalization cases. Reasoning based on human dignity appears in ECHR criminalization cases in two main forms. The first is in the sense of attacks on the honour, standing, or reputation of an individual. The second is as regards the objectification, or demeaning and debasement of an individual. In the first sense, in the case of *Colombani* (insulting a head of state), the ECtHR noted that the rationale behind the criminal offence of insulting a foreign head of state was to protect from certain forms of attack on honour or "dignity." In so far as such reasoning constituted a form of *dignitas hominis*, or dignity by virtue of status, however, the Court rejected the concept as a ground for criminalization. The Court observed that the offence shielded heads of state from criticism solely on account of their function or status, irrespective of whether the criticism was warranted. In the Court's view, this amounted to conferring a special privilege. As a result, the Court held that the offence of insulting a foreign head of state was liable to inhibit freedom of expression without meeting any pressing social need capable of justifying such a restriction.[50] Reasoning based on human dignity in the sense of an attack on the honour or reputation of an individual is also found in some European Court defamation cases. In *Lindon* (defamation), for example, Judge Loucaides, in concurring that a conviction for defamation in respect of a political novel did not violate ECHR Article 10, highlighted the connection between untrue defamatory statements and protecting the dignity of individuals.[51] Similarly, in *Radio France* (defamation), the

49 See, for example, *Manuel Wackenheim v. France*, UNHRC.

50 *Colombani and Others v. France*, ECHR, para 69.

51 *Lindon, Otchakovsky-Laurens and July v. France*, ECHR., concurring opinion of Judge Loucaides, p.42.

Court, also holding that a conviction for defamation was compatible with ECHR Article 10, considered that the reasons given by the domestic court for its ruling that the applicant's honour and dignity had been damaged were relevant and sufficient.[52] Insofar as the European Court is more prepared to recognize reasoning based on human dignity for the crime of defamation, than for insulting the king, this is likely due to a conception of dignity for defamation that applies to the honour of all, as opposed to the selective *dignitas hominis*, based on status or rank.

In addition to human dignity associated with honour, dignity is also employed by the ECtHR in the sense of the objectification, or demeaning and debasement of an individual. In the case of *Rantsev* (trafficking in persons), for example, the Court highlighted that trafficking in persons, by its very nature and aim of exploitation, treated human beings as commodities to be bought and sold. Noting that slavery involved the exercise of a genuine right of ownership and reduction of status to an object, the Court concluded that trafficking in persons fell within the scope of ECHR Article 4 (prohibition of slavery). Drawing from the idea of commodification and objectification, the Court went on to state that trafficking threatened the "human dignity" of its victims. It held, as a result, that Article 4 required member states to adopt criminal law measures to punish traffickers.[53]

As well as commodification or objectification, the ECtHR further associates the concept of human dignity with the demeaning or debasement of an individual. In *C. R.* and *S.W.* (marital rape), for example, the Court referred to the essentially debasing character of rape and highlighted that the abandonment of the idea that a husband should be immune for rape of his wife was in conformity with the fundamental objectives of the Convention, the very essence of which was respect for "human dignity." In line with this reasoning, the Court held that the inclusion of marital rape within the criminal offence of rape was compatible with the Convention.[54] Debasement is also recognized as connected with human dignity in *Pretty* (assisting suicide). In that case, the Court noted that treatment which humiliated or debased an individual, diminishing his or her human dignity, may be characterized as degrading and fall within the prohibition of ECHR Article 3 (Prohibition of torture).[55]

The limits of human dignity as an argument in ECtHR criminalization cases, however, are seen in the case of *S.A.S.* (wearing of clothing designed to conceal the face). In support of criminalization, the Government argued that women who wore clothing that concealed their face in public were "effaced." The Government submitted that such effacement was necessarily dehumanizing and could not be regarded as consistent with human dignity. Following consideration of this argument, the Court determined that, however essential it might be, respect for human dignity could not legitimately justify a blanket ban on the wearing of the full-face veil in public places.[56]

52 *Radio France and Others v. France*, ECHR, para 32.
53 *Rantsev v. Cyprus and Russia*, ECHR, paras 282–284.
54 *S.W. v. United Kingdom*, ECHR, para 44.
55 *Pretty v. United Kingdom*, ECHR, para 52.
56 *S.A.S. v. France*, ECHR, para 120.

As discussed above, the Court preferred, rather, to justify the criminal measures with reference to an established community consensus around the possibility of open interpersonal relationships as an indispensable element of community life within the particular society.

Whilst *S.A.S.* suggests that human dignity in the sense of debasement may not be invoked as a reason for overriding individual autonomy, the case of *Laskey* (assault in the context of sadomasochistic activities) tends in the opposite direction. Concurring that a conviction for assault in the context of consensual sexual activities was compatible with the Convention, Judge Pettiti highlighted that the protection of private life meant the protection of a person's intimacy and "dignity." Judge Pettiti also considered that the state should be entitled to regulate, through operation of the criminal law, practices of sexual abuse that were "demeaning," even if they did not involve the infliction of physical harm.[57] Whilst, as discussed above, the levels of bodily harm involved, and the resultant public health considerations, represented the main line of reasoning for criminalization employed in *Laskey*, it is notable that at least one member of the ECtHR grounded argumentation for the criminal offence in the concept of human dignity.

Overall, it is clear that the ECtHR accords a high value to human dignity within criminalization reasoning. In so far as human dignity is perceived as the essence of the ECHR, any non-consensual act directed by one person at another which clearly violates dignity presents at least some argument for protection through the criminal law. Review of ECHR criminalization case law suggests that acts which humiliate, debase, or objectify an individual may fall into this category. In practice, this has the result that the criminalization of acts such as insult, defamation, rape, servitude, and human trafficking is justified, at least in part, with reference to human dignity. In all of these instances, the victim himself or herself perceives and experiences an affront to their dignity. As such, human dignity-based reasoning tends to justify the prohibition of acts committed by one individual against another, rather than the prohibition of acts involving only one individual, or where the act is consented to. *S.A.S.*, for instance, provides a strong indication that the ECtHR does not see human dignity as an objective value to be imposed on individuals against their wishes, at least when it comes to use of the criminal law. Notwithstanding Judge Pettiti's concurring opinion in *Laskey*, it is likely that an experiential affront to dignity caused by one individual against another represents the Court's primary ground of dignity-based criminalization reasoning.

Other grounds of reasoning

In addition to five primary grounds of reasoning employed in ECtHR criminalization cases, a wide range of other concepts used by the Court can be grouped into three broad areas. The first group includes established concepts in criminal theory, such as *mens rea*, wrongfulness, causation, omissions, alternatives, deterrence, and

57 *Laskey, Jaggard and Brown v. United Kingdom*, ECHR, concurring opinion of Judge Petitti.

seriousness. The second is closely related to the structure of the ECHR and includes concepts such as the rights of others, essential aspects of private life, personal integrity, pluralism, and discrimination. The third reflects the Court's reasoning around paternalism and vulnerability.

Criminal theory concepts

As regards the first area of reasoning, related to established criminal theory, the ECtHR commonly recognizes the general criminal law concept of *mens rea*. Perhaps most clearly, in the context of ECHR Article 2 (Right to life), the cases of *Šilih* and *Calvelli* (medical negligence), *Rowley* (corporate manslaughter), and *Antonov* (causing death dangerous driving), for example, show that if an infringement of the right to life or to personal integrity is not caused "intentionally," then the positive obligation imposed by Article 2 to set up an effective judicial system does not necessarily require the provision of a criminal law remedy in every case.[58]

The Court also considers intent, in both a specific and general sense, in a number of other cases, including, amongst others, *Rujak* (insult), *Lindon* (defamation), and *H.M.A.* (environmentally harmful emissions). In *Rujak*, as discussed above under the concept of offense, the Court held that a criminal conviction relating to offensive statements was acceptable as expression where the "sole intent" was to insult fell outside the scope of ECHR Article 10 (Freedom of expression). Similarly, in *Lindon*, the Court, in holding that a criminal conviction for defamation did not violate the Convention, reasoned that the underlying "intention" was to stigmatize.[59] In *H.M.A.*, the Court, in holding that a conviction for environmentally harmful emissions was compatible with the Convention, noted that the applicant had "knowingly and wilfully" omitted to display the requisite care and diligence.[60] Such cases highlight that the ECtHR recognizes the importance of state of mind in criminalization reasoning, including gradations between specific intent and general will to realize the act, as well as with respect to negligence and knowledge of the act. The Court aligns itself with criminal law theory in being more prepared to accept criminalization for intentional as opposed to unintentional acts. In the case of acts leading to death, however, the Court is, rather surprisingly, more hesitant than some legal systems to require use of the criminal law for negligent acts, in the absence of aggravating circumstances.

As regards other criminal law theory concepts, it is notable that the ECtHR refers to principles such as wrongfulness or causation comparatively rarely in its reasoning. Examples where this does occur include *K.U.* (malicious misrepresentation) and *Stubbings* (sexual offences against children). In *K.U.*, the Court placed emphasis on the act as an especially abhorrent type of "wrongdoing," due to its particular impact on the victim.[61] In *Stubbings*, in finding that the

58 See, for example, *Brenda Rowley v. United Kingdom*, ECHR, p.9.
59 *Lindon, Otchakovsky-Laurens and July v. France*, ECHR, p.30.
60 *H.M.A. v. Spain*, ECHR, p.124.
61 *K.U. v. Finland*, ECHR, para 46.

acts should be an offence, the Court stated that sexual abuse is unquestionably an abhorrent type of wrongdoing.[62] With respect to causation, in *H.M.A.* (environmentally harmful emissions), the Court, in finding that the act could be an offence, highlighted the "causal relationship" between the circumstantial evidence and the consequences. *H.M.A.* is also clear that the Court is prepared to accept omissions within the context of causation. The Court noted, for example, that the applicant, by failing to carry out his supervisory tasks and duties and by failing to take steps to prevent the outflow pipe valves being opened, had "caused" a risk which he should have foreseen and avoided.[63] In so far as such reasoning is comparatively rare, it may be that the ECtHR rather takes for granted requirements of wrongfulness and causation within national criminal law systems and has not, to date, been faced with a case where either was seriously at issue. The seeming acceptance of these principles by the Court does suggest, however, that they are material to the human rights compatibility of criminal laws.

The ECtHR more frequently refers to the general criminal law concept of deterrence as a reason for criminalization. The effective deterrence of criminal law provisions is invoked by the Court, in particular, in the case of threats to life. Such cases include *Osman* (intentional taking of life) and *Öneryildiz* (negligence in dangerous activities). The well-known formulation in *Osman* highlights the importance of effective criminal law provisions to "deter" the commission of offences against the person. In *Öneryildiz*, the Court found that the duty to provide effective deterrence against threats to the right to life equally applied in the context of dangerous activities.[64] In the context of other acts against the person, the Court often emphasizes the importance of criminal law as deterrence in cases where fundamental values and essential aspects of private life are at stake, as well as in the case of serious breaches of personal integrity. In the case of *X and Y* (rape), for example, the Court emphasized that effective deterrence was indispensable where fundamental values and essential aspects of private life were at stake and that this could be achieved only by criminal law provisions.[65] Other cases involving breaches of personal integrity where the Court has emphasized deterrence also include *Stubbings* (sexual offences against children) and *A* (reasonable chastisement). In effect, the Court holds that acts involving essential aspects of private life or serious breaches of personal integrity cannot be prevented by other forms of deterrence, such as administrative or civil sanctions.

In this way, the ECtHR's handling of deterrence is linked with its consideration of alternatives to criminalization. Whilst the Court emphasizes the importance of deterrence in certain instances, overall the Court appears to take seriously the possibility of achieving behavioural change and deterrence through alternatives to the criminal law. The Court provides two key markers in particular for when alternatives may provide sufficient protection of Convention rights. The first of these is

62 *Stubbings and Others v. United Kingdom*, ECHR, para 64.
63 *H.M.A. v. Spain*, ECHR, pp.120–124.
64 *Öneryildiz v. Turkey*, ECHR, para 89.
65 *X and Y v. The Netherlands*, ECHR, para 27.

in the case of non-intentional acts. The second is in the case of less serious acts. As regards non-intentional acts, in the specific case of death due to medical negligence considered in *Calvelli* and *Šilih*, the Court reasoned that criminalization was not required if the legal system afforded victims a remedy in the civil courts, either alone or in conjunction with a remedy in the criminal courts, that enabled any responsibility to be established and any appropriate "civil redress," such as an order for damages, to be obtained.[66] Similarly, in *Rowley* (corporate manslaughter), the Court, in finding that there was no need for a specific criminal law concerning careless endangering of life of vulnerable disabled persons under care, highlighted the alternative of health and safety regulatory offences.[67] In *Vo* (causing death of an unborn), the Court, in holding that criminal laws on unintentional homicide were not required to extend to the unborn child, emphasized the alternatives of an action for damages in the administrative courts.[68]

In respect of less-serious acts, the Court is clear that it is more prepared to view alternatives to the criminal law as fulfilling Convention obligations in such circumstances. In the case of *Söderman* (voyeurism), for example, whilst the Court found that the particular act in question should be a criminal offence, it noted that in respect of "less serious" acts between individuals, the obligation of the state to maintain and apply in practice an adequate legal framework affording protection did not always require that a criminal law provision covering the specific act be in place. The legal framework could also consist of civil law remedies capable of affording sufficient protection.[69] Such comments accord with the Court's position under the general crime investigatory obligation that the obligation to investigate is less exacting with regard to less serious crimes, such as those involving property, than with regard to more serious ones, such as violent crimes, and in particular those which would fall within the scope of Articles 2 and 3 of the Convention.[70] Along this line of reasoning, even in cases involving acts universally accepted as criminal, the Court, whilst not suggesting that the act should not be an offence, has still been prepared to consider the effectiveness of alternatives from the perspective of Convention rights. In *Blumberga* (burglary), for example, the Court, in the context of the right to property under the Protocol to the ECHR, noted that the possibility of bringing civil proceedings against the alleged perpetrators of a crime against property may provide the victims with a viable alternative means of securing the protection of his rights.[71]

Indeed, in some instances, a clear hesitation of the Court to resort to use of the criminal law can be detected, if respect for Convention rights can be achieved by other means. Judge Tulkens, for example, in the context of ensuring respect for private life under Article 8, emphasizes that recourse to the criminal law is not

66 *Šilih v. Slovenia*, ECHR, para 194.
67 *Brenda Rowley v. United Kingdom*, ECHR, pp.10–11.
68 *Vo v. France*, ECHR, para 94.
69 *Söderman v. Sweden*, ECHR, p.85.
70 *Blumberga* v. Latvia, ECHR, para 67.
71 *Ibid.*, para 68.

necessarily the only answer. In her concurring opinion in *M.C.* (rape), Tulkens noted that criminal proceedings should remain, both in theory and in practice, a last resort or subsidiary remedy and that their use called for a certain degree of "restraint." Tulkens also highlighted that the effectiveness of general deterrence based on the criminal law depended on various factors and that criminal law was not the only way of preventing undesirable behaviour.[72]

Despite this note of caution, where, conversely, an act is held to be sufficiently serious, alternatives may not be sufficient for protection of Convention rights, and seriousness forms part of the argument for criminalization. Indeed, seriousness appears to be used more often by the Court to argue that an act should or can be a criminal offence than where (lesser) seriousness is used to reason that an act should not be an offence. In *Wingrove* (blasphemy), for example, in finding that the act could be a criminal offence, the Court highlighted the "high degree" of profanation that must be attained, and that this, in itself, constituted a safeguard against arbitrariness.[73] In *Kudrevičius* (breach of public order), the Court, in finding that the act could be an offence, highlighted the "serious" disruptions caused by the applicants' conduct and noted that the almost complete obstruction of three major highways constituted conduct which, even though less serious than recourse to physical violence, could still be described as "reprehensible."[74] In *O'Keefe* (sexual acts against children), the Court reiterated the principle that ECHR Article 3 protects against conduct at a minimum level of seriousness and highlighted that criminal laws regarding sexual touching of, and intercourse with, minors were in place accordingly.[75]

It is in cases such as *O'Keefe* that the Court combines reasoning based on seriousness with that on deterrence to confirm a criminalization requirement. Seriousness as a ground of reasoning appears to be used in a slightly wider range of cases than deterrence. However, it is clear that both concepts are employed by the court at the top end of the criminalization spectrum, where justifications for criminal prohibition are strongest. At its core, and consistent with the human rights general crime investigatory obligation discussed in Chapter 4, seriousness and deterrence-based reasoning have the result that cases of violent intentional acts engaging ECHR Articles 2 (Right to life) and 3 (Prohibition of torture) and seriously breaching personal integrity, as well as those that involve essential aspects of private life under Article 8 (Right to private life), must be subject to the criminal law. Cases where the Court uses such reasoning fall, for instance, under ICCS categories 0101 (intentional homicide), 0201 (assault and threats), 0203 (slavery and exploitation), 0207 (dangerous acts), 0301 (sexual violence), and 0302 (sexual exploitation).

Overall, review of ECHR criminalization case law shows that a number of existing concepts in criminal theory, including *mens rea*, wrongfulness, causation, omissions, alternatives, deterrence, and seriousness, are relevant for the Court in determining

72 *M.C. v. Bulgaria*, ECHR, concurring opinion of Judge Tulkens, para 2.
73 *Wingrove v. United Kingdom*, ECHR, para 60.
74 *Kudrevičius and Others v. Lithuania*, ECHR, paras 174 and 177.
75 *O'Keefe v. United Kingdom*, ECHR, paras 16–21.

the acceptability of criminalization under the ECHR. This is not particularly surprising in light of commonalities in the structure of national criminal laws, as well as the degree of deference often given by the Court to the reasoning of national courts. Such criminal law concepts are, however, generally invoked significantly less often by the Court than reasoning related to societal interests, offense, autonomy, harm, community consensus, and human dignity. One reason for this may be that such criminal law concepts are less often relevant to determining the existence, or not, of a human rights violation in the context of criminalization than matters more closely related to the objective act element of the offence. Issues of harm, offense, and societal interests, for example, concern the nature of the act and the results or consequences. As such, they represent important areas of reasoning when it comes to determining the acceptability of criminalization of a particular act with the ECHR. In addition, concepts such as societal interests, autonomy, community consensus, and human dignity, represent core elements of the structure of the ECHR and thus form part of the general approach of the ECtHR to its analysis of issues before it.

ECHR structural principles

In a similar way, a number of grounds of reasoning that are closely related to the structure of the ECHR are apparent within ECtHR criminalization cases. These include the concepts of the rights of others, essential aspects of private life, personal integrity, pluralism, and discrimination.

In some ways, the "rights of others," whilst often referred to by the ECtHR in criminalization cases, do not necessarily represent a separable concept in itself. It is recorded as a ground of reasoning in the table of cases at the end of this book wherever the Court refers to the "protection of the rights of others" as a reason for restriction of rights under ECHR Articles 8, 9, 10, or 11. As such, the ground primarily recognizes the approach of the Court of balancing the rights of individuals affected by an act against the rights of those carrying out the act. *Perinçek* (denial of genocide), for instance, clearly recognizes a need, in some circumstances, to balance the Article 10 (Freedom of expression) rights of a person making a statement against the Article 8 (Right to private life) rights of persons who are the subject of a statement. In that case, the ECtHR considered the rights of the Armenians to respect for their identity constructed around the understanding that their community had suffered genocide, balanced against the right to freedom of expression under Article 10. In deciding upon the balance, and holding that a criminal conviction was not justified, the Court took into account a range of factors, including human dignity, harm, and seriousness.[76] As such, in many ways, the concept of the rights of others represents a methodological approach derived from the structure of the ECHR, rather than a substantive concept in itself.

By contrast, the concept of essential aspects of private life, also referred to previously in the context of deterrence, represents an independent ground of

76 *Perinçek v. Switzerland*, ECHR, para 280.

reasoning of the ECtHR that is used in a number of criminalization cases. The Court uses a number of different phrases for its reasoning in this area, including "purely private nature," "intimate aspects of private life," and "fundamental values and essential aspects of private life." Criminalization cases that include such reasoning concern acts such as consensual same-sex relations (*A.D.T.* and *Dudgeon*), rape (*G*, and *X and Y*), sexual offences against children (*Stubbings*), and voyeurism (*Söderman*). The Court's reasoning in this regard is that there is an innermost, or core, aspect of the right to private life that cannot generally be infringed upon and, in some cases, must be protected by the criminal law. Sexual conduct certainly falls within this sphere, as may other acts closely involving the body. As such, the European Court has found, for example, that sexual activities involving a number of persons in circumstances where it was unlikely that others would become aware of what was occurring were "genuinely private" and could not be restricted by the criminal law.[77]

Closely related to the concept of essential aspects of private life is the idea of personal integrity, which also centres around the body and is invoked in some ECHR criminalization cases. The Court often refers to this concept in the context of ECHR Article 3 (Prohibition of torture). In the concurring opinion of Judge Tulkens in *M.C.* (rape), for example, the Court highlighted that rape infringed the right to both physical and psychological personal integrity, as guaranteed by Article 3.[78] In *A* (reasonable chastisement), the Court emphasized that children and other vulnerable individuals, in particular, are entitled to protection against serious breaches of personal integrity – in that case, being beaten with a garden cane with considerable force.[79] Reasoning related to personal integrity is also found under Article 8, such as in the case of *Söderman* (voyeurism), where the Court held that covert filming of a naked child for sexual purposes violated the applicant's integrity.[80]

To some extent, as regards their role in criminalization reasoning, the ECtHR's notions of essential aspects of private life and personal integrity have overlaps with the broader concepts of autonomy and harm, respectively. As argued by Allridge and Brants, for example, with respect to private life and sexuality, the sexual is more than an intimate part of life, being rather a part of ourselves and how we decide to experience and develop that part of our existence.[81] In this vein, the case of *Gough* (same-sex relations) recognizes both that sexual acts concern a most "intimate aspect" of private life and that they engage individual freedom of choice in action.[82] Equally, acts involving violations of personal integrity often also cause harm to others. The case of *A* (reasonable

77 *A.D.T. v. United Kingdom*, ECHR, paras 37–38.
78 *M.C. v. Bulgaria*, ECHR, concurring opinion of Judge Tulkens, para 1.
79 *A v. United Kingdom*, ECHR, para 22.
80 *Söderman v. Sweden*, ECHR, para 117.
81 Alldridge, P., and Brants, C., 2001, p.119.
82 *Gough v. United Kingdom*, ECHR, para 52, and partially dissenting opinion of Judge Walsh, para 11, quoting Wolfenden Committee.

chastisement), for instance, highlights both the possibility of a breach of personal integrity under ECHR Article 8 and the achievement of a minimum level of severity of injury under Article 3. The concepts remain distinct, however, with notions of personal integrity often offering protection for an individual in the absence of harm in its strictest sense.

In addition to the concepts of intimate aspects of private life and personal integrity, a few ECHR criminalization cases also contain reasoning related to the core Convention concepts of pluralism and discrimination. In *Bayatyan* (conscientious objection), for example, the applicant, a Jehovah's Witness, was convicted for draft evasion following his conscientious objection to military service on the grounds of his religion. In holding that the conviction was incompatible with ECHR Article 9 (Freedom of thought, conscience and religion), the Court noted that the need to maintain true "religious pluralism" was vital to the survival of a democratic society.[83] Similarly, in *Kokkinakis* (proselytism), the Court, in holding that a conviction for proselytism was also incompatible with Article 9, emphasized that pluralism was indissociable from a democratic society.[84] Such reasoning suggests that the safeguarding of multiple principles within society, in so far as protected by the right to freedom of thought, conscience and religion, can present a shield against criminalization that may otherwise restrict such diversity.

Nonetheless, the case of *S.A.S.* (wearing of clothing designed to conceal the face) demonstrates that the ground of pluralism is comparatively weak and may be overridden by other considerations, such as community consensus. In *S.A.S*, the Court held that by prohibiting everyone from wearing clothing designed to conceal the face in public places, the respondent state had to a certain extent restricted the reach of pluralism, since the ban prevented certain women from expressing their personality and their beliefs by wearing the full-face veil in public.[85] The Court observed, however, that, on the other side of the argument, the principle of interaction between individuals was, in itself, essential for the expression of pluralism. In finding that the criminal prohibition did not violate ECHR Article 8 or 9, the Court placed higher value on the community consensus requirements of "living together" than on the protection of pluralism. *S.A. S.*, rather dangerously, suggests that the protection of pluralism as a constraint on criminalization could be subject to acceptance by the general community consensus and societal interests of the diverse practices and principles that constitute a pluralistic society in the first place. Upholding a community consensus against a particular practice or principle can thus weigh on the other side of the argument, as a reason in favour of criminalization.

Closely linked with the protection of pluralism is the protection of persons from discrimination in respect of the range of beliefs and principles that make

83 *Bayatyan v. Armenia*, ECHR, para 122.
84 *Kokkinakis v. Greece*, ECHR, para 31.
85 *S.A.S. v. France*, ECHR, para 153.

up a pluralistic society. Non-discrimination is enshrined in ECHR Article 14, which provides that the enjoyment of Convention rights shall be secured without discrimination on any ground. Whereas a number of ECHR criminalization cases contain argument submitted by the applicant under Article 14, it is only in comparatively few cases that the European Court gives consideration to issues of non-discrimination directly under Article 14. In *L. and V.* (same-sex relations), for instance, the applicants complained that the criminalization of homosexual acts of adult men with consenting adolescents between the ages of 14 and 18 was discriminatory, as heterosexual or lesbian relations between adults and adolescents in the same age bracket were not punishable. The Court highlighted that a difference in treatment would be discriminatory for the purposes of Article 14 if it had no objective and reasonable justification. In finding that criminalization was incompatible with Article 14, the Court noted that the national criminal code embodied a "predisposed bias" on the part of a heterosexual majority against a homosexual minority. The Court went on to hold that such negative attitudes could not, of themselves, be considered to amount to sufficient justification for the differential treatment.[86]

The case of *L. and V.* highlights the general concern of the ECtHR for equality in application of the criminal law. Similar reasoning can also be found in the Court's decisions under other substantive ECHR articles. Although a finding is not specifically reached under Article 14, non-discrimination is inherent, for example, to the Court's decision in cases such as *Colombani* and *Mondragon* (insulting a head of state). In *Colombani*, the Court held that conferring a "special legal status" on heads of state, shielding them from criticism solely on account of their function or status, could not be reconciled with modern practice and political conceptions.[87] Such cases support the position under Article 14 that the criminal law cannot treat persons differently if there is no legitimate aim achieved through proportionate means.

As well as a requirement for the criminal law to be non-discriminatory itself, the ECtHR also recognizes a role for criminalization in preventing acts of discrimination between individuals. As discussed in Chapter 5, such an aim has a long history in international human rights law, with the first contemporary direct human rights treaty-based requirement for criminalization, ICERD Article 4, aiming to provide effective practical measures in the fight against discrimination. ICERD Article 4 was controversial at the time, and it is only in recent years that the work of CERD and HRC has taken steps towards reconciling ICERD Article 4 and ICCPR Article 20 (Prohibition on advocacy of national, racial or religious hatred that constitutes incitement to discrimination, hostility or violence) around the criminalization of intentional, serious statements that constitute threats or incitement to racial or ethnic discrimination, hostility, or violence. ECHR criminalization cases similarly demonstrate the role of non-discrimination as reasoning in support of criminalization in

86 *L. and V. v. Austria*, ECHR, para 52.
87 *Colombani and Others v. France*, ECHR, para 68.

expression-related cases. In *Norwood* (religious hate speech), for example, the Court held that a conviction for racially aggravated causing of alarm or distress, arising from the display of a poster, was compatible with ECHR Article 10 (Freedom of expression). The Court emphasized that a general, vehement attack against a religious group was incompatible with tolerance, social peace, and "non-discrimination."[88] In *Vejdeland* (sexual-orientation hate speech), in confirming that a conviction in respect of the distribution of leaflets expressing contempt for homosexuals was compatible with ECHR Article 10, the Court stressed that discrimination based on sexual orientation was as serious as discrimination based on race, origin, or colour.[89]

ECHR criminalization cases also show, however, that discriminatory elements or motivations of a particular act may not necessarily demand separate criminalization. In *Angelova* (racially motivated homicide), for instance, the applicants complained that domestic legislation did not contain separate criminal offences for the acts of racially motivated murder or serious bodily injury. The Court held that this was not required, however, as other means could also be employed to attain the desired result of punishing perpetrators with racist motives. It was satisfied, in this respect, by the possibility in domestic legislation to impose a more severe sentence depending upon, amongst others, the motive of the offender, even though there was no direct reference to racist motives in the criminal law.[90]

Overall, ECHR criminalization case law suggests that the principles of pluralism and non-discrimination, in so far as they form part of the legal and philosophical heritage of international human rights law, do present relevant considerations for criminalization. The protection of pluralism, where beliefs and principles do not starkly contradict a community consensus or societal interest, can, for the ECtHR, present a possible constraint on criminalization. The criminal law is also constrained by a requirement not to be discriminatory without a legitimate aim achieved through proportionate means. At the same time, the prevention of discriminatory acts between individuals can, in some circumstances, provide a reason in support of criminalization. In this regard, discriminatory motives are especially relevant for the Court with respect to violent acts, as well as speech and expression. Reasoning related to pluralism and non-discrimination is often seen to be secondary, however, to other concepts, such as harm, offense, societal interests, and community consensus. Criminalization in *Norwood* (religious hate speech), for example, was supported by the Court, taking into account a number of principles, including offense, societal interests, and deterrence, as well as non-discrimination. In line with the general approach of criminal law, this suggests that "purely" discriminatory acts, such as discrimination in employment or the supply of goods and services, for example, may need to engage other principles, such as harm or offense to others, or to present a serious affront to a societal interest before an argument arises in favour of criminalization.

88 *Norwood v. United Kingdom*, ECHR, p.4.
89 *Vejdeland and Others v. Sweden*, ECHR, para 42.
90 *Angelova and Iliev v. Bulgaria*, ECHR, para 104.

Paternalism and vulnerability

A final ground of reasoning apparent in ECHR criminalization cases relates to paternalism and vulnerability. The ECtHR does not often address head-on the concept of paternalism in the context of criminalization, and such reasoning does not typically form part of its criminalization decisions. One of the very few criminalization cases that does appear to rely explicitly on paternalistic reasoning is *X* (failing to wear a motorcycle helmet). In that case, the Court held that criminalization of failure to wear a crash helmet was a "necessary safety measure" for motor cyclists.[91] The Court did not go beyond this statement by way of further reasoning. In general, however, in other contexts, comments by judges of the ECtHR tend to take a rather negative view of paternalism. Judge Tulkens, for example, asserts that paternalism runs counter to the case law of the ECtHR, as the Court has developed a real right to personal autonomy on the basis of Article 8.[92] Similarly, Judge Ziemele and others have argued that democracy is not helped by "well-intentioned paternalism."[93] In this sense, the minimal presence of reasoning based on paternalism in the ECHR criminalization cases examined is consistent with the view of George Letsas view that the European Convention and the Court are, on the whole, guided by liberalism as an objective value.

Whereas the ECtHR does not rely overtly on paternalist reasoning, as recognized by Letsas, its approach nonetheless contains significant elements that may not be expected under a purely liberal theory. In this regard, a number of ECHR criminalization cases suggest a strong influence in the Court's criminalization reasoning of the related concept of vulnerability. Vulnerability can be employed in a strictly non-paternalistic sense of the need to prevent harm or offense to others who are at particular risk. It may also, however, engage paternalistic considerations where used as an argument for the prevention of harm to self, or consented-to harm from others, by virtue of factors such as impairment of capacity or risk of undue influence by others.

The ECtHR employs the idea of vulnerability deserving protection as supporting criminalization in a number of cases. In *G* (strict liability rape), for example, the Court noted that the criminal law measures were intended to protect young and "vulnerable" children from premature sexual activity.[94] In *Perrin* (obscene material), the Court took into account the danger presented by the material in light of its accessibility to the young and vulnerable.[95] In *Pretty* (assisting suicide), the Court, in holding that assisting the suicide of terminally ill individuals could be a criminal offence, emphasized that many terminally ill individuals would be vulnerable and it was the vulnerability of

91 *X v. United Kingdom*, ECHR, p.235.

92 *Leyla Şahin v. Turkey*, ECHR, dissenting opinion of Judge Tulkens, para 12.

93 *Animal Defenders International v. United Kingdom*, ECHR, dissenting opinion of Judges Ziemele, Sajo, Kalaydjieva, Vucinic, and De Gaetano.

94 *G v. United Kingdom*, ECHR, para 36.

95 *Perrin v. United Kingdom*, ECHR, p.4.

the class that provided the rationale for the law in question.[96] In *Vejdeland* (sexual-orientation hate speech), Judges Yudkivska and Villiger, in their concurring opinions, highlighted that the leaflets containing the speech were disseminated amongst teenagers, who were vulnerable to different kinds of influence.[97] Such reasoning often covers the context where either a person is regarded as incapable of consenting to a particular act or where doubt exists as to whether he or she may be sufficiently capable or sufficiently free of external influences to consent. In this way, the concept of vulnerability presents a reason in favour of criminalization that is similar, in some respects, to that of "soft" paternalistic grounds. Soft paternalism holds that criminal legislation can prevent self-regarding harmful conduct, where that conduct is substantially non-voluntary or intervention is necessary to establish whether it is voluntary or not. More than this, however, the way in which the European Court employs vulnerability reasoning can tend towards general protection from exploitation, including in instances where the specific individual involved in the particular case at hand may, on the facts, have full capacity.

Links between grounds of reasoning

Amongst the range of concepts identified in ECHR criminalization cases, six key grounds of criminalization reasoning are especially prominent: harm, offense, autonomy, societal interests, community consensus, and human dignity. The criminalization case group included at the end of this book indicates a number of patterns regarding the distribution of these main grounds of reasoning, both with respect to the act in question and those grounds that are commonly found together.

In line with the wide understanding of the ECtHR of the concept of harm, reasoning based on harm is seen, for instance, across a number of different acts that are the subject of ECHR criminalization cases. Using the ICCS classification introduced in Chapter 6, these include in particular, as might be expected, cases that address the criminalization of acts leading to death (ICCS category 01), acts leading to harm to the person (ICCS category 02), and injurious acts of a sexual nature (ICCS category 03). The concept of harm also features, however, in cases involving acts against public order (ICCS category 08) and acts against public safety (ICCS category 09). Examples of such cases include review of the criminalization of membership of a criminal group (*Ashlarba*), compulsory health screening (*Acmanne*), failing to wear a motorcycle helmet (*X*), state secrets (*Stoll*), and same-sex relations (*Dudgeon*). Such cases demonstrate the broad range of contexts in which the Court considers arguments related to harm in its general sense of detrimental effects. In contrast to harm, ECtHR

96 *Pretty v. United Kingdom*, ECHR, para 74.
97 *Vejdeland and Others v. Sweden*, ECHR, concurring opinion of Judge Yudkivska joined by Judge Villiger, para 8.

reasoning related to offense appears almost exclusively in criminalization cases involving just two act categories: acts leading to harm to the person (ICCS category 02) and acts against public order (ICCS category 08). This is explained by the fact that acts of insult and defamation fall under ICCS category 0209, whilst acts such as nudity in public, blasphemy, hate speech, same-sex relations, and insulting the king fall within ICCS category 08, all of which engage ECHR Article 10 and offense-based reasoning.

ECtHR reasoning related to autonomy features in cases involving acts under ICCS categories 01, 02, and 03 (acts leading to death, harm to the person, and injurious acts of a sexual nature), as well as category 08 (acts against public order). This pattern reflects the particular relevance of individual autonomy to essential aspects of private life and personal integrity, as well as to freedom of expression. ECHR criminalization cases involving autonomy-based reasoning and coding to ICCS categories 01, 02, or 03, include, for example, *Pretty* (assisting suicide), *K.A.* and *Laskey* (assault in the context of sadomasochistic activities), *M.C.* (rape), *M.K.* (sexual offences against children), *Rantsev* (trafficking in persons), and *Siliadin* (servitude), all of which involve considerations of personal autonomy over the body. Under ICCS category 08 (acts against public order), the Court applies considerations of autonomy in respect of acts such as proselytism (*Kokkinakis*), same-sex relations (*Dudgeon*), obscene publications (*Perrin*), and blasphemy (*Wingrove*). Autonomy reasoning in such cases includes the consent (or lack of) of persons witnessing a form of public expression, as well as issues of sexual development and self-determination.

ECtHR reasoning based on societal interests is also most often seen in criminalization cases involving acts under ICCS category 08 (acts against public order). This may be expected, in so far as acts with a "public" dimension that fall under ICCS category 08 are likely, by definition, to engage considerations of societal interest. Acts within this category include contempt of court (*Dallas*), failure to comply with building planning regulations (*Ehrmann*), nudity in public (*Gough*), breach of public order (*Kudrevičius*), election campaigns (*Şükran*), and wearing of clothing designed to conceal the face (*S.A.S.*). In addition, reasoning based on societal interests is seen in ECHR criminalization cases involving acts under ICCS category 09 (acts against public safety and security). Such acts again have a public dimension and include refusing compulsory health screening (*Acmanne*), supporting a banned organization (*Aydin*), conscientious objection (*Bayatyan*), and publishing secret official deliberations (*Stoll*). A small number of cases with societal interests reasoning is also seen, however, in the case of acts leading to harm to the person (ICCS category 02). These represent acts where actions against an individual, such as medical negligence (*Calvelli*), invasion of privacy (*Egeland*), or assault in the context of sadomasochistic activities (*Laskey*), also engage broader issues of societal interest.

As might be expected, the distribution of community consensus reasoning by ICCS act is not dissimilar to that for societal interests. Community consensus reasoning is most often invoked by the ECtHR in cases involving acts under ICCS category 08 (acts against public order). These tend to be acts that have an actual or perceived public element, engaging conceptions of public morality and community values, such as same-sex relations (*Dudgeon, Norris, L. and V.*, and *A.D.T.*), obscene publications (*Handyside* and *Müller*), or wearing of clothing designed to conceal the face (*S.A.S.*).

Finally, in a manner similar to harm, reasoning related to human dignity is found in cases involving acts under ICCS categories 01, 02, and 03 (acts leading to death, harm to the person, and injurious acts of a sexual nature), as well as in respect of acts against public order (ICCS category 08). ECHR criminalization cases with dignity-based reasoning involving acts under categories ICCS 01, 02, and 03 include assault in the context of reasonable chastisement (*A*), rape (*C.R.* and *S.W.*), assisting suicide (*Pretty*), trafficking in persons (*Rantsev*), and servitude (*Siliadin*). A number of these cases exemplify dignity reasoning in its sense of commodification (*Rantsev*) or debasement (*C.R.* and *S.W.*). By contrast, where the case involves acts against public order (ICCS category 08), such as *Colombani* and *Mondragon* (insulting a head of state), then human dignity reasoning is often in its form of an attack on honour or standing.

For the group of ECHR criminalization case reviewed, it is notable that multiple grounds of reasoning are employed by the ECtHR in cases involving each act type at ICCS level 1. This fits with the fact that, for the group of ECHR criminalization cases, over 90 per cent have more than one ground of criminalization reasoning. Thus, for example, the Court applies reasoning based on all of harm, offense, autonomy, societal interests, community consensus, and human dignity to criminalization of acts leading to harm to a person (ICCS category 02). Similarly, cases involving acts against public order (ICCS category 08) contain reasoning from all five concepts. This reflects the fact that, from the perspective of the ECtHR, the criminalization of an individual act can engage a range of considerations. Indeed, for the group of ECHR criminalization cases listed at the end of this book, over half of the cases contain two or three different grounds of criminalization reasoning. Approximately one quarter contain four or five grounds. Under 10 per cent contain just one identified ground of criminalization reasoning. This means that criminalization outcomes decided by the Court can depend, to a significant extent, on the relationship between different reasoning grounds and the way in which the Court balances potentially competing considerations. As such, the ECtHR is seen to weigh, for example, the societal interest of public health and safety against the principle of personal autonomy, as well as to consider the balance between community consensus and other considerations such as human dignity and autonomy.

For the group of ECHR criminalization cases, where more than one ground of underlying reasoning is invoked, the most frequent pairings of criminalization reasoning are seen to be "autonomy with community consensus or societal interests," "harm with community consensus or societal interests," and "community consensus with societal interests." In addition, reasoning related to offense is often found together with community consensus or societal interests, as well as human dignity together with autonomy. In the wider grounds of reasoning, harm-based reasoning is also often seen together with reasoning based on vulnerability. This pattern confirms, in the first instance, the common balance faced by the Court in weighing the principle of personal autonomy against the interests and views of society. The Court undertakes this exercise in, amongst others, the criminalization cases of *Bayatyan* (conscientious objection),

Dudgeon (same-sex relations), *Egeland* (invasion of privacy), *Gough* (nudity in public), *İ.A* (blasphemy), *K.A.* and *Laskey* (sadomasochistic activities), *Pretty* (assisting suicide), *S and G* (outrage against public decency), *Stübing* (incest), and *Wingrove* (blasphemy). In all but two of these cases (*Bayatyan* and *Dudgeon*), the Court found that the balance weighed towards a community consensus or societal interest in favour of criminalization. This tends to suggest that the Court requires especially strong arguments to conclude that individual autonomy trumps an act criminalized by reason of societal or community consensus reasons, in particular where the act has a public element. In *Bayatyan*, the societal interest argument was severely weakened by the limited consequences of draft evasion, in light of the fact that alternative civilian service was to be introduced, which the applicant had agreed to undertake.[98] In *Dudgeon*, the only societal interest was public morality, which the Court held could not be used to justify a criminal law interference with a purely private act.[99]

Whereas autonomy and societal interests or community consensus tend to represent concepts to be weighed against each other, arguments related to harm or offense may often reinforce those of societal interests and community consensus. These grounds of reasoning are found together in criminalization cases such as *A, B and C* (procuring miscarriage), *Acmanne* (compulsory health screening), *Ashlarba* (membership of a criminal group), *Feret* (hate speech), *Handyside* (obscene publications), *Karttunen* (child pornography), *Laskey* (assault in the context of sadomasochistic activities), *Osmani* (hate speech), *Pretty* (assisting suicide), and *Stoll* (state secrets). Thus, in *Handyside*, for example, the European Court reasoned that the publication in question contained information that could have been interpreted as an encouragement to indulge in precocious activities "harmful" for children, as well as noting the effects on the "morals" of many of the children and adolescents who would read it.[100] In *Osmani*, the Court, in finding that a conviction for stirring up national, racial, and religious hatred was compatible with the Convention, highlighted the injury and damage caused following the applicant's speech, as well as the legitimate aims of protection of national security and public safety.[101] Use of reasoning related to both harm and societal interests or community consensus results in a strong argument for criminalization. In each of these cases, for example, the Court held that the act could be a criminal offence, based on such reasoning.

In so far as there is an overlap between societal interests and community consensus, a number of criminalization cases show reasoning in both of these areas. In this respect, "community consensus" can refer either to the European consensus to which the Court has reference in determining a margin of appreciation or to a national consensus, usually in the area of public morality. ECHR criminalization cases containing both societal interests and community consensus reasoning include *A.D.T.* (same-sex relations), *Bayatyan* (conscientious objection), *Egeland* (invasion of privacy),

98 *Bayatyan v. Armenia*, ECHR, para 124.
99 *Dudgeon v. United Kingdom*, ECHR, para 61.
100 *Handyside v. United Kingdom*, ECHR, p.19.
101 *Osmani v. Former Yugoslav Republic of Macedonia*, ECHR, pp.15 and 19.

Gough (public nudity), *Laskey* (assault in the context of sadomasochistic activities), *S.A.S.* (wearing of clothing designed to conceal the face), *Stoll* (state secrets), and *Stübing* (incest). In *Stoll*, for example, in finding that a conviction for publishing an ambassador's secret official communications was compatible with the Convention, the Court identified two societal interests, consisting of the interest of the public in being informed on topical issues and the interest of the authorities in effective diplomatic relations. In balancing these interests, the Court had reference to a consensus amongst member states of the Council of Europe on the need for appropriate criminal sanctions to prevent the disclosure of certain confidential items of information.[102] For those cases containing societal interest and community consensus reasoning, the Court most often finds that the act in question *can* be a criminal offence, suggesting, again, a high degree of deference by the Court to the overall needs and views of society.

As regards the ground of human dignity, this is often invoked in ECHR criminalization cases alongside reasoning based on autonomy. Autonomy and dignity arguments may align in the case of notions of dignity as objectifying an individual. However, dignity in the form of debasement or demeaning of individual may, in some circumstances, present on the other side of the argument to individual autonomy, where an individual consents to such treatment or does not view it as such. The cases of *Laskey* (assault in the context of sadomasochistic activities), *Pretty* (assisting suicide), *Rantsev* (human trafficking), and *Siliadin* (servitude) contain both dignity and autonomy grounds of reasoning. The two considerations tend to align in *Rantsev*, and *Siliadin*, in favour of criminalization, although present on opposite sides of the argument in *Laskey*, where human dignity implicitly supported criminalization over individual autonomy. In *Pretty*, dignity was argued both for and against criminalization, but did not ultimately form a significant part of the Court's criminalization reasoning.

In addition to the range of interactions and associations between the different grounds of ECtHR reasoning and the act forming the subject of a criminalization case, it is also possible to examine the relationship between ECtHR reasoning and criminalization case conclusions. For the group of ECHR criminalization cases listed at the end of this book, Figure 7.1 shows the relative number of times each of the six key grounds of reasoning is invoked in the group of cases, according to whether the ECtHR finds that the act *should not, can*, or *should* be a criminal offence. It should be noted that the fact that a ground is utilized in any particular case does not always mean that the ground is invoked in favour of the eventual outcome. Thus, for example, autonomy features as a ground of reasoning in *Pretty* (assisting suicide), even though the Court held, on vulnerability and societal interest grounds, that assisting suicide in the case of terminally ill persons *can* be a criminal offence, effectively overriding individual autonomy. Nonetheless, Figure 7.1 provides a broad picture as to which grounds of reasoning may tend to be associated with each criminalization outcome.

102 *Stoll v. Switzerland*, ECHR, para 155.

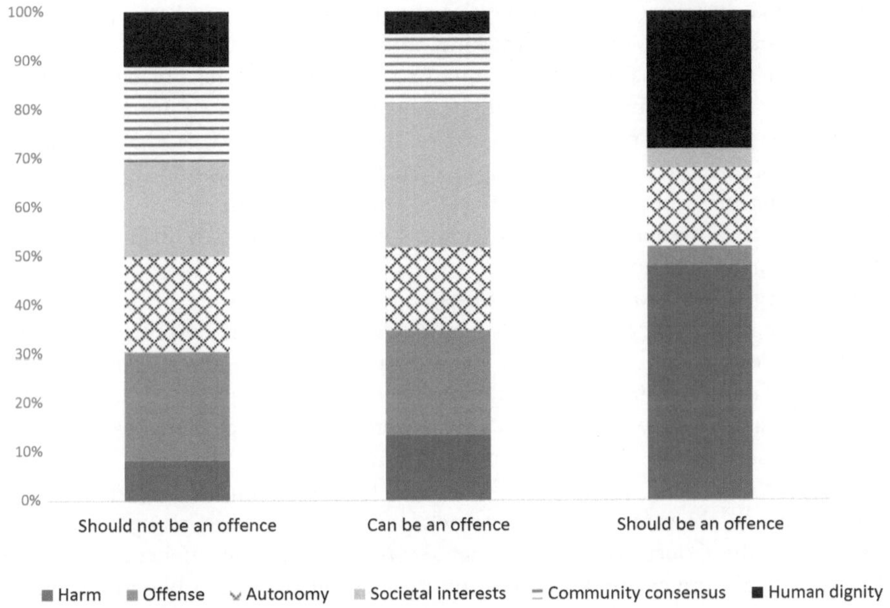

Figure 7.1 ECHR Criminalization Cases by Outcome and Underlying Reasoning

In the first instance, it is clear that harm is, for the Court, a strong reason in support of criminalization. For cases where the Court held that the act *should* be a criminal offence, harm reasoning constituted almost half of all identified grounds of reasoning. These mostly represent cases involving acts falling under ICCS categories 01, 02, and 03, such as assault, domestic violence, international taking of life, and sexual offences against children, where the Court found that criminalization was essential for the prevention of harm.[103] As might be expected, harm is also invoked in a number of cases where the Court holds that the act *can* be a criminal offence.[104] By contrast, it is comparatively rare for the Court to consider harm-based reasoning, but to find that an act should *not* be a criminal offence. The small number of cases mostly corresponds to harm arguments advanced in the context of same-sex relations.[105]

In the same way as for harm, reasoning based on human dignity appears comparatively most frequently in cases where the Court holds that an act *should* be an offence. Indeed, for such cases, almost 80 per cent of all identified grounds

103 See, for example, *A, Beganović, Opuz,* and *Stubbings*, ECHR.

104 See, for example, *A, B and C, Acmanne, Ashlarba, Feret, G, Handyside,* and *K.A. and A.D.*, ECHR.

105 See *Dudgeon* and *Norris*, ECHR.

of reasoning are made up by harm and human dignity. Acts in this category, which invoke human dignity, include assault in the context of reasonable chastisement, marital rape, human trafficking, and servitude,[106] with the Court reasoning that the criminal law was required to protect from the objectification or debasement of individuals. Interestingly, human dignity also shows as comparatively more frequent amongst cases where the Court finds that the act should *not* be an offence. This corresponds, in part, to dignity reasoning in its form of *dignitas hominis*, where the Court rejected the idea that a head of state should be entitled to a higher level of protection by the criminal law from insult and attacks on his or her honour.[107]

Reasoning related to societal interests appears comparatively most frequently in acts that the Court finds *can* be a criminal offence. This corresponds to the relatively broad deference given by the Court to societal interests and includes many acts falling within ICCS categories 08 (acts against public order) and 09 (acts against public safety and security), such as refusing compulsory health screening, supporting a banned organization, contempt of court, failure to comply with building planning regulations, nudity in public, and publishing state secrets.[108] Notably, however, societal interest reasoning rarely features in cases where the Court holds that an act *should* be a criminal offence, suggesting that the Court prefers to base clear positive criminalization obligations under Convention rights, on other grounds, such as harm and human dignity.

Related to this pattern, community consensus reasoning is not clearly invoked in any case in the group where the Court finds that an act *should* be a criminal offence. This may suggest that, whilst the Court clearly recognizes community consensus as a ground in support of criminalization, it does not see the views of a community as a reason, in itself, for positive criminalization obligations. Indeed, community consensus is invoked comparatively most frequently in cases where the Court holds that an act should *not* be a criminal offence. In these cases, involving acts such as same-sex relations, denigrating the nation, and use of languages in election campaigns, the Court considered a possible community consensus view, but held that this could not override other considerations, including autonomy.[109] This pattern may reflect the comparatively weak influence of community consensus as a ground in favour of criminalization compared to other grounds in the Court's criminalization reasoning.

Finally, individual autonomy is seen to show a reasonably consistent distribution across case criminalization outcomes. Interpreting this pattern is challenging, however, as the protection of autonomy may weigh either on the side of criminalization, in the case of protection from rape, human trafficking, or servitude, or against criminalization, as in the case of private same-sex relations,

106 See *C.R.*, *S.W.*, *Rantsev*, and *Siliadin*, ECHR.
107 See *Colombani* and *Mondragon*. ECHR.
108 See *Dallas, Ehrmann, Gough*, and *Stoll*, ECHR.
109 See *A.D.T., Dudgeon, L. and V., Norris, Akçam*, and *Şükran Aydin*, ECHR.

proselytism, or conscientious objection.[110] The consistent presence of autonomy-based reasoning in all three categories nonetheless confirms that autonomy is a relevant consideration both for restraining unjust criminalization and in requiring criminalization for the effective protection of human rights.

Overall, the use of underlying criminalization reasoning by the ECtHR suggests three broad patterns. Firstly, within the framework of ECHR rights, the Court employs a wide range of underlying concepts or grounds of reasoning in reaching criminalization outcomes. By frequency of use, six key grounds – harm, offense, autonomy, societal interests, community consensus, and human dignity – are identifiable. In addition, the Court utilizes a range of reasoning from criminal law theory, as well as concepts related to the structure of the ECHR itself, such as essential aspects of private life, personal integrity, pluralism, and discrimination. In general, the Court tends away from paternalistic reasoning, but does recognize the principle of vulnerability deserving protection. Secondly, it is notable that the key grounds of reasoning are used in multiple combinations in reaching any one criminalization finding. The Court commonly weighs the principle of personal autonomy against the interests and views of society, whereas arguments related to harm or offense may often reinforce those of societal interests and community consensus. Human dignity can be invoked in a number of senses, including in support of autonomy-based arguments, but also to protect honour or reputation. Thirdly, analysis suggests that the Court prefers to found positive criminalization obligations primarily on harm and dignity-based arguments, with some consideration also given to individual autonomy. By contrast, all six key grounds feature in cases where the Court finds that an act should not be, or can be, a criminal offence. In order for the Court to hold that an act should not be a criminal offence, however, there must usually be a key consideration pertaining to one or more of the grounds, such as a particularly weak societal interest in a purely private act.

Summary

This chapter examined the concepts and reasoning that underlie criminalization conclusions reached by the ECtHR in a group of almost 80 criminalization cases.

Whilst the identification of an underlying theory of interpretation of the ECHR is challenging, one approach suggests that the Convention is largely based on liberal concepts, although with significant deviations for the protection of community conceptions of morals. Review of underlying reasoning from ECHR criminalization cases broadly supports this theory. It also shows, however, that criminalization outcomes reached by the Court are based on a multiplicity of concepts, all of which are found in varying combinations. In any one case, some concepts reinforce each other, whilst others work on opposing sides of criminalization arguments. In line with a broadly liberal theory of

110 See *M.C. v. Bulgaria, Rantsev*, and *Siliadin*, as compared with *Dudgeon, Kokkinakis*, and *Bayatyan*. ECHR.

interpretation, the Court places value on the protection of individual autonomy, including in the face of possible paternalistic arguments. It is often prepared to defer, however, to arguments that criminal law is required for the protection of societal interests in health, safety, and security. In some cases, these extend to community conceptions of morality or commonly accepted behaviour, although a public element to the act is usually inherent to such cases.

The reasoning of the ECtHR is not limited to the balance between the demands of autonomy and community or society. The Court also frequently employs reasoning based on harm, offense, and human dignity, all of which offer grounds in support of criminalization. Human dignity, in particular, represents a complex ground of reasoning that is invoked by the Court in respect of acts which may humiliate, debase, or objectify an individual. Where the Court finds that human dignity and/or a risk of serious harm, in the broad sense of detrimental effects, are at stake, this represents a particularly strong argument for criminalization and can lead the Court to find that the act *should* be a criminal offence.

From a methodological perspective, analysis of a group of ECHR criminalization cases shows that it is possible to systematically identify and characterize underlying reasoning used by the ECtHR in determining the existence, or not, of a human rights violation and hence in reaching criminalization conclusions. The semi-quantitative nature of this approach, in particular, enables the identification of associations and patterns across *in concreto* cases that would not otherwise be easily apparent. This analytical power offers a route to development of legal data that can be used to enhance the consistency of international human rights law judgments, to a better understanding of patterns of judicial decision-making, and – as undertaken in the following chapters of this book – to enabling a comparison of international human rights jurisprudence with other legal fields.

8 Differences between criminal theory and an international human rights law approach

Does the criminalization jurisprudence of international human rights law merely reframe existing criminal theory within the terminology and structure of international rights? As shown in Chapter 7, the underlying reasoning of international human rights law criminalization cases certainly utilizes a number of concepts, such as harm, offense, and autonomy, that are also familiar to criminal law theorists. Both international human rights courts, such as the European Court of Human Rights (ECtHR), and criminal law theorists, such as Feinberg, have a primary concern for the rights of the individual in criminalization reasoning, largely rejecting utilitarian theories. The two systems also tend to draw, although to differing degrees, from both consequentialist and deontological ethics. At the same time, however, international human rights law criminalization jurisprudence shows at least four major methodological departures from criminal theory. This chapter argues that these are significant enough to create a unique approach for international human rights law to questions of criminalization. In so doing, international human rights law draws from, but does not simply reproduce or reframe, existing criminal theory.

Vertical and horizontal rights

Comparison between the approach of international human rights law to matters of criminalization and criminal theory is particularly pertinent in light of the role of rights within each field. A key difference in the structure of these rights, however, lies in the "vertical" and "horizontal" nature of each.

International human rights law, and its application to criminalization, is best viewed from the perspective of state obligations, in line with the position of states as the primary subjects of international law. Under this scheme, international human rights law weighs the legitimacy of a criminal law by its compatibility with the contours of the (positive and negative) state obligations for each separate human right invoked. The analysis is "vertical" with respect to the individual–state relationship, in so far as the state may restrict the freedoms of the individual to an extent determined by its own higher international law obligations. In the case of the ECtHR, for rights that can be subject to restrictions, the contours of the state's human rights obligations derive from the identification of a legitimate aim for limiting the right and the proportionality of the restriction within the margin of appreciation. As such, a right violation – and the resultant legitimacy of criminalization – is dependent not only on the effect of the act in question on the individuals involved but also on the state higher "norms of behaviour." This approach has some symmetry. The vertical matter of criminal responsibility as between the individual and the state is itself assessed with reference to the vertical construct of the international human rights law obligations of the state and the corresponding rights of the individual.

Strands of criminal theory also invoke notions of rights and correspondent duties. In the Anglo-American tradition, for example, Joel Feinberg relies on welfare interest rights as the basis for wrongful harm to others as a good reason in support of criminalization. As described in Chapter 3, however, Feinberg's rights violations do not depend on a vertical relationship between the individual and the state. Rather, Feinberg's welfare interest rights are conceived as individual "horizontal" claim rights that are more akin to the Hohfeldian notion of a perfectly correlative right–duty relationship. Violations of claim rights do not depend upon the contours of state obligations but solely upon the interference by one individual in the right, or claim, of another, being a claim that is acknowledged by all to be a valid claim against persons in general. Under this scheme, Feinberg's criminalization theory weighs the legitimacy of a criminal law by whether it causes harm or offense and, at the same time, violates the welfare interest rights of a specific individual. The vertical power–liability issue of criminalization as between the individual and the state is thus assessed with reference to the horizontal right–duty relationship between individuals.

The vertical versus horizontal conception of rights employed by the ECtHR and Feinberg, respectively, represents one of the greatest conceptual differences between the two systems as regards criminalization analysis. This, in turn, has significant implications for criminalization outcomes. In so far as there are presently no universal, independent, commonly agreed grounds for the correct operation of the criminal law, all views on the "correctness" of criminalization are highly dependent on the analytical approach taken. Understanding rights as vertical, as between the individual and the state, for instance, sets up one particular frame of criminalization analysis that allows certain considerations to be taken into account in deciding the correctness, or not, of criminalization. These considerations may well be, and in fact often are, different to those that can be taken into account under a horizontal notion of rights. The ECtHR's vertical conception of rights, for instance, enables the Court to take account of wider considerations than the largely consequentialist effect on individuals prioritized by Feinberg's horizontal scheme. This is the case, both as regards acts that involve identifiable individuals (such as a perpetrator and specific victim) and as regards acts "against society" where no specific victim is identifiable. These differences in theoretical approach produce different criminalization conclusions in some circumstances.

The impact of the difference between vertical and horizontal conceptions of rights is seen, for example, in the way in which international human rights law and criminal theorists apply the notion of autonomy to questions of criminalization. Both international human rights law and criminal theorists place high value on respect for autonomy. The protection of autonomy, for Feinberg, grounds his whole starting point for criminalization theory. He asserts that there is a standing presumption against all proposals to criminalize conduct that is derived simply from the interest all persons have in liberty.[1] Whilst the protection of autonomy is foundational to Feinberg's criminalization theory, in practice it is considered at a second stage of his scheme, after the gateway of harm. The extent to which a criminal prohibition limits the options open to an individual is one factor to be weighed on the scales once the gateway of harm presents a reason in favour of criminalization. The strength of the presumption against restriction of liberty varies not only with the type of interest in liberty but also with the degree to which that interest is actually invaded by the proposed legislation. Using an analogy of connected and disjoined railroad tracks linked by switches, Feinberg suggests that the closing of multiple, or fecund, options open to an individual "further up the line" is more restrictive of liberty than the closing of more limited options. The more fecund the option closed, the more harm is done to the general interest in liberty.[2]

For the ECtHR, on the other hand, liberty, or autonomy, is primarily a principle underlying the interpretation of the right to respect for private and family life (ECHR Article 8), as well as the prohibition of slavery and forced labour (ECHR Article 4). Autonomy is not therefore automatically a consideration in each case, but tends to be invoked where notions of identity, choice, or self-determination are particularly at stake. Across ECHR criminalization cases, autonomy-based reasoning features most strongly in cases involving acts especially close to the private sphere or personal identity, such as those concerning sexual relations and assisted suicide. Where autonomy is engaged as a consideration, it often features at the first stage of the European Court's reasoning, as germane to the existence of an infringement of the right. Where the right is subject to restrictions, the interest in autonomy can be outweighed, however, at a second stage of the Court's reasoning, by limitations such as societal interests or the rights of others, as in the cases of *Pretty* (assisting suicide) and *Laskey* (assault in the context of sadomasochistic activities).

Whereas the same notion, the protection of autonomy, is valued by both Feinberg and the ECtHR, the variations in its formulation, context, and, critically, description with reference to vertical or horizontal rights mean that Feinberg and the ECtHR can come to different conclusions regarding the criminalization of certain acts. In the case of assisted suicide, for example, the fact that the ECtHR could weigh autonomy against public health and safety in the case of *Pretty* was due to the place of autonomy within a "vertical" scheme of analysis for the right to private life. Whether criminalization of assisted suicide resulted in a violation of the private life of the applicant was assessed (vertically) by the Court against the contours of the state's obligation to respect and protect that right. Feinberg, by contrast, conducts his inquiry with reference to whether the individual experienced a violation of his or her "horizontal" claim rights. This means that the autonomy of the individual in choosing his or her own death is *not* weighed against societal considerations in the same way as by the

1 Feinberg, *Harm to Others*, p.206.
2 Feinberg, *Harm to Others*, pp.207–208.

ECtHR. If voluntariness can be established as a matter in each individual case of assisted suicide – as opposed to a risk in general – then under Feinberg's scheme, there is no violation of welfare interest rights and hence no argument in support of criminalization in the first place.[3] As such, Feinberg's basic position is that when a person *is* capable of making his own voluntary choices in self-regarding affairs, those choices should govern even in and, he argues, perhaps especially in matters of life and death.[4] This position is also largely adopted by other criminal theorists, such as Simester and von Hirsch, subject to various safeguards in their discussion on killing on request in *Crimes, Harms and Wrongs*.[5] Variations in an understanding and place of autonomy within their respective schemes, related to underlying structures of rights, thus lead the ECtHR and criminal law theorists to reach different conclusions on the criminalization of assisted suicide.

The analysis further illustrates a key difference between the vertical ECtHR scheme and Feinberg's horizontal welfare interest rights: that of the place of consent on the part of the victim. The ECtHR vertical analysis allows wider considerations to be weighed against the individual's consent to an act against himself or herself when determining the existence of a rights violation and the legitimacy of criminalization. In the Court's vertical analysis in *Laskey* (assault in the context of sadomasochistic activities), for example, the ECtHR held that a criminal conviction for assault did not violate Article 8 as a result of the wider consideration of the protection of health, notwithstanding the applicants' consent to the acts. Under Feinberg's horizontal welfare interest rights, on the other hand, consent on the part of the victim is largely determinative and generally not subject to other considerations that may impact on the existence, or not, of a welfare rights violation.[6] Thus, in *Harmless Wrongdoing*, in a discussion on the place of consent in the crimes of murder, mayhem, and battery, Feinberg broadly maintains that a liberal would permit the consent defence out of respect for personal autonomy, subject to appropriately stringent standards of voluntariness.[7]

Whilst Feinberg most usually prioritizes this type of horizontal claim right analysis, he does explore the relationship with wider societal interests in a few instances. In the case of duelling, for example, Feinberg's default horizontal scheme would suggest that no welfare rights violation arises due to the mutual consent of duelling parties and hence no justification for criminalization. In that case, Feinberg concedes, however, that

> there is a social interest in preserving civility and restraint in interpersonal relations, in maintaining personal security and freedom from anxiety generally, and

3 *Ibid.*
4 Feinberg, *Harm to Self*, p.367.
5 Simester, A.P., and von Hirsch, A., 2011, pp.168–183.
6 Feinberg, *Harm to Others*, p.115.
7 Feinberg, *Harmless Wrongdoing*, p.170.

> in keeping physical injuries to a minimum.... The liberal cannot be charged with inconsistency if he supports rules that keep these public harms in check.[8]

In supporting the criminalization of duelling, Feinberg thus adopts an approach much more akin to that of the European Court. He recognizes the validity of other considerations in the criminalization equation – if not strictly at the level of determination of a welfare interest rights violation, then at least as a separate or parallel consideration in the criminalization analysis. Such an approach is, however, quite an anomaly for Feinberg, and there is a sense in which Feinberg departs significantly from his scheme in order to justify criminalization of an act widely recognized as a criminal offence in practice.

Within Feinberg's general approach, other interpersonal acts that illustrate the effect of the ECtHR's vertical conception of rights, as opposed to Feinberg's horizontal welfare interest rights, include the criminalization of incest. In the ECtHR case of *Stübing* (incest), in assessing whether a conviction for incest constituted a violation of Article 8 (Right to private and family life), the Court took into account a "common conviction" that incest should be subject to criminal liability, as well as considerations that sexual relationships between siblings could seriously damage "family structures" and, as a consequence, "society as a whole."[9] This vertical assessment led the ECtHR to conclude that the criminal conviction was compatible with the right to private and family life. By contrast, Feinberg suggests that a contraceptively protected, privately performed, and genuinely consensual act of incest cannot amount to (Feinbergian) harm,[10] presumably due either to a lack of setback of interests, and/or to a lack of horizontal welfare interest rights violation as between the individuals involved. Whilst Feinberg does not set out his position explicitly, as with the case of duelling, he hints that if incest is to be a crime, then this must be for considerations other than a claim rights violation constituting harm to others.

The differences between the ECtHR's vertical scheme and Feinberg's horizontal scheme are also seen in the case of non-interpersonal crimes. In *Acmanne* (compulsory health screening), for example, the vertical scheme of the ECtHR enabled the Court to directly weigh the infringement of liberty arising from the criminal law, against the possible setback to the public interest in public and individual health, in determining the existence of a violation of ECHR Article 8 (Right to private and family life). By contrast, for public harms such as the public health risk introduced by a refusal to screen or vaccinate, Feinberg cannot identify the clear violation of another individual's claim right (such as to physical health and vigour) required by his horizontal scheme for criminalization. This leaves Feinberg with a, less analytical, reliance on the wrongfulness of such an act by virtue of a shared convergent interest in a regulatory rule designed to prevent setbacks of the public interest. Similarly, in

8 Feinberg, *Harmless Wrongdoing*, p.172. Reproduced with permission of the Licensor through PLSclear.

9 *Stübing v. Germany*, ECHR, paras 63–66.

10 Feinberg, *Harmless Wrongdoing*, p.21.

Ehrmann (building planning regulations), the ECtHR was able to weigh the restriction of expression arising from a criminal conviction for breach of planning regulations, against the public interest in the quality of the environment, the harmonization of social life, and the protection of cultural heritage, in determining the existence of a violation under Article 10 (Freedom of expression). Conversely, under Feinberg's scheme, whilst Feinberg acknowledges a collective good of cultural heritage and a distinctive "city ambience" of parks and monuments, he tends to hold to his criminalization requirement for a "personal" grievance.[11] For collective, public harms he notes that most individuals can voice personal grievances only to the extent that they claim also to represent the interests of a wider collectivity.[12] Feinberg is also concerned that weighing a public or collective interest directly, rather than through the lens of individual claim rights, enlarges his conception of harm and wrong, opening the door to legal moralism dressed in harm principle clothes.[13] As a result, Feinberg's horizontal scheme is less open to criminalization of acts that breach generic public environment standards, absence a specific claim right grievance of one or more identifiable individuals that represents the clear collective view.

Although Feinberg's horizontal rights scheme generally limits the range of considerations that are taken into account in the case of non-interpersonal acts, as discussed in Chapter 3, Feinberg nonetheless develops a workaround – based on the wrongfulness of breach of a regulatory rule – to include some regulatory offences within his criminalization scheme. He applies this in the case, at least, of harm to important public institutions and practices such as interests in preserving law and order generally and avoiding depressions and epidemics.[14] Feinberg is thus able to support, for instance, criminalization of environmental pollution, tax evasion, perjury, and contempt of court. Whilst Feinberg therefore reaches the same criminalization position as the ECtHR, at least in the case of environmental pollution (*H. M.A.*) and contempt of court (*Dallas*), his approach to analysis does not offer the same flexibility as the vertical scheme of the ECtHR. Being unable to identify horizontal violations of a specific individual's rights to life, minimal health, economic sufficiency, or political liberty in such cases, Feinberg is effectively left solely with the test of whether a regulatory rule has, as its aim, the prevention of public harm. By contrast, the ECtHR has the possibility to engage in a more nuanced, if (across *in concreto* cases) somewhat unstructured, weighing of relevant societal and institutional considerations, as part of its vertical determination of the existence of a human rights violation, and resultant criminalization findings.

It is not entirely clear whether similar considerations would also apply to rights-based schemes proposed by more recent criminal law theorists. Tatjana Hörnle, for example, does not provide detail on the nature of her rights, although it would appear that they could be of the nature of horizontal claim rights. At the same time,

11 Feinberg, *Harmless Wrongdoing*, p.35.
12 *Ibid.*, p.37.
13 *Ibid.*
14 Feinberg, *Harm to Others*, p.225.

however, she acknowledges "important collective interests," which, she argues, can also be an independent object of protection alongside protective rights.[15] Hörnle certainly does not seem to be proposing a vertical rights-based system where the existence of a violation is determined with reference to the contours of the state's human rights obligations. Nonetheless, she does seem to acknowledge the need for a certain balancing between individual rights and collective interests in a manner that may be more akin to the approach of the ECtHR than that of Feinberg.

Dignity, vulnerability, and pluralism

In addition to the use of a primarily vertical state–individual analysis by international human rights law, a second key difference between the European Court and Feinberg relates to the importance of dignity, vulnerability, and pluralism to international human rights law. The concept of human dignity plays a central role in international human rights treaties and jurisprudence. In ECtHR criminalization cases, dignity reasoning is found closely linked with attacks on honour and reputation, defamation, and the humiliation, debasement, or objectification of another. In the majority of these cases, the affront to dignity is experienced directly by a specific individual, as a result of the actions of another. Whilst dignity in such cases is closely connected with harm or offense to others, it is clear that, for the ECtHR, dignity represents a separable, although often reinforcing, line of argument. The concept of human dignity features prominently, in particular, as reasoning in cases where the Court holds that an act should be a criminal offence. These include *C.R.* and *S.W.* (rape), *Rantsev* (human trafficking), and *Siliadin* (servitude).

Although international human rights courts, such as the ECtHR, are generally critical of paternalism, ECHR criminalization cases suggest that the Court does have a concern to protect those it perceives as vulnerable. Vulnerability-based reasoning is seen, for example, in the ECHR criminalization cases of *G* (strict liability rape), *Perrin* (obscene material), *Pretty* (assisting suicide), and *Vejdeland* (sexual-orientation hate speech). Where possible, the European Court also seeks to protect the principle of pluralism, understood by the Court as a diversity of values, opinions, and social groups, with the absence of predominance of particular values, opinions, or groups.[16] The protection of pluralism features strongly, for instance, in ECHR criminalization cases on conscientious objection (*Bayatyan*) and proselytism (*Kokkinakis*), where it is invoked by the Court as a shield against criminalization of such acts.

By contrast, criminal law theorists such as Feinberg who rely on a predominantly liberal approach do not typically accord equivalent weight to the three concepts. In so far as Feinberg's criminalization scheme, for example, is built upon wrongful harm, wrongful offense, and a limited number of non-grievance evils, Feinberg does not, unlike the ECtHR, explicitly recognize dignity, vulnerability, or plurality as separate relevant principles for criminalization. Rather, notions such as dignity for liberal

15 Hörnle, T., 2016, pp.304–305.
16 Nieuwhenhuis, A., 2007.

criminal law theorists tend to play more of a background role, rather than representing their own, independent grounds of reasoning. Nonetheless, Feinberg does touch on them each in a number of different ways. He appears to recognize one act, in particular, that can be thought of as an affront to dignity. Feinberg notes that victims of voyeurism experience embarrassment, mortification, humiliation, and an affront to their "dignity."[17] In that context, Feinberg views the experiential affront to dignity as contributing to the profound offense experienced by victims of voyeurism. As such, the affront to dignity does not provide any separable criminalization basis. Rather, it is the wrongful offense, as well as possible harm, of which dignity is but one component that justifies criminalization of the act.

Feinberg also elaborates on an understanding of dignity as being intimately tied with personal autonomy, in the context of his autonomy-based argument for the non-criminalization of assisted suicide, where voluntariness may be safely ascertained.[18] In the same way as with voyeurism, however, Feinberg views dignity as a theoretical component of another concept (in this case, autonomy), rather than as a separable ground of criminalization reasoning. Finally, in *Harmless Wrongdoing*, Feinberg makes one additional dignity-based connection between dignity and "exploitation." With reference to the exhibition of a person with deformities in a circus sideshow, Feinberg suggests that such an act involves a loss of dignity constituting an evil, the profit from which amounts to exploitation.[19] As Feinberg generally holds that a free-standing exploitation principle cannot be a good reason for criminalization, his dignity-based point here is interesting. The reference to dignity in this context comes close to a more autonomous, free-standing concept of objectification or debasement, irrespective of consent. Feinberg does not elaborate further, and certainly does not explicitly include such a principle as part of his criminalization scheme. Nonetheless, it is perhaps one hint in the direction of a rationale for criminalization of non-grievance evils, such as a gladiatorial contest, which trouble Feinberg outside of his harm and offense principles. In this regard, many contemporary theorists, including Hörnle, are critical of the identification of dignity as an objective value, preferring instead to solely associate dignity as a subjective component of autonomy.[20]

Feinberg's possible concession in *Harmless Wrongdoing* notwithstanding, it is clear that dignity plays a background role in many strands of criminalization theory. By contrast, for the ECtHR, although criminalization in dignity cases such as *C.R.* and *S.W.* (rape), *Rantsev* (human trafficking), and *Siliadin* (servitude) is, or could, equally be based on harm and personal integrity, the Court identifies dignity in its own sense, as part of the essence of a human rights violation.[21] This separability of dignity is also highlighted in *S.A.S.* (wearing of

17 Feinberg, *Offense to Others*, p.51 and p.60.
18 Feinberg, *Harm to Self*, p.358, and Chapter 19, Footnote 84.
19 Feinberg, *Harmless Wrongdoing*, p.202, Footnote 35.
20 Hörnle T., 2014, p.182.
21 See, for example, *Rantsev v. Cyprus and Russia*, ECHR, para 282.

clothing designed to conceal the face). Although, in that case, the ECtHR held that respect for dignity could not justify criminalization, it considered the point on its own merits, noting also that it did not have any evidence capable of leading it to consider that women who wear the full-face veil sought to "offend against" the dignity of others.[22] Whilst dignity arguments before the ECtHR tend to succeed where they align with experiential harm, offense, or violations of personal integrity, the fact that dignity *can* be considered as an autonomous concept by the ECtHR creates an additional dimension to the criminalization reasoning of the Court. This, in principle, opens the door to wider criminalization of acts that may be considered to constitute attacks on honour and reputation, defamation, or humiliation, debasement, or objectification. In this respect, other international human rights bodies have taken the concept further than the ECtHR in the direction of an objective value. Echoing Feinberg's link between dignity and exploitation, for example, the United Nations Human Rights Committee, although not in the criminal context, has held that a ban on consensual "dwarf tossing" was compatible with the ICCPR in order to protect public order, which brought into play considerations of human dignity that were compatible with the objectives of the Covenant.[23]

As regards vulnerability and pluralism within Feinberg's work, in the same way as for dignity, Feinberg does not ignore such concepts altogether but, at the same time, does not accord them a specific role within his criminalization scheme. Feinberg most usually refers to vulnerability in two main senses. Firstly, that of persons who are unable to look after their own interests and protect themselves, such as minors and persons with mental disabilities.[24] And secondly, as persons of reduced physical or mental resilience, as compared with the "average" person, but who nonetheless retain full capacity.[25] As regards the former, Feinberg largely excludes measures for the protection of such vulnerable persons from his detailed inquiry into the criminal law, on the basis that soft paternalistic measures to prevent self-regarding harmful conduct where the conduct is substantially non-voluntary are, in principle, acceptable.[26] In respect of the latter, Feinberg's general position is that the criminal law should be tailored to persons of "normal" fortitude. Thus, a person with a particular vulnerability can demand protection from the criminal law only from conduct that would harm the normal person in his position. Similarly, in the context of exploitation, Feinberg holds that even if an individual happens upon another in a condition of "vulnerability" and asks his consent to the terms of an exploitative "coercive offer," the acceptance of that offer, whilst short of perfect voluntariness, will usually be voluntary enough to relieve the individual of criminal responsibility.[27] As such,

22 *S.A.S. v. France*, ECHR, para 120.
23 *Manuel Wackenheim v. France*, UNHRC, para 7.4.
24 Feinberg, *Harm to Self*, p.6.
25 See, for example, Feinberg, *Harm to Others*, p.216; and Feinberg, *Harm to Self*, pp.170–180.
26 See Feinberg, *Harm to Self*, p.13.
27 Feinberg, *Harm to Self*, p.263.

Feinberg generally does not accord particular weight within his criminalization scheme to vulnerability that does not clearly reach the threshold of removal of capacity to consent. This is the case for both innate conditions of vulnerability and externally imposed conditions (such as imprisonment). In his discussion on assisted suicide, for example, whilst Feinberg discusses a number of challenges in establishing voluntariness, he does not consider the criminalization question in terms of the vulnerability of persons who may request such an act.

By contrast, for the ECtHR, vulnerability represents an important concept in its own right and is central to the Court's criminalization findings in a number of cases. In particular, in *Pretty* (assisting suicide), the ECtHR highlighted that whilst the applicant herself was not considered vulnerable, it was the vulnerability of "the class" (of terminally ill individuals) which provided the rationale for the criminal law.[28] Similarly, in *Egeland* (invasion of privacy), the ECtHR considered the compatibility with Article 10 (Freedom of expression) of a criminal conviction for photographing or recording an accused or convicted on his or her way to, or from, or when inside, the building in which the court hearing takes place without his or her consent.[29] In finding that the conviction was compatible with Article 10, the Court emphasized that the victim was at her most vulnerable psychologically and in a state of reduced self-control, a situation which lay at the core of the protection which the relevant statutory provision was intended to provide.[30] In both *Pretty* and *Egeland*, the Court's reliance on vulnerability-based reasoning supports criminalization that may not necessarily be supported by criminal theory such as Feinberg's harm and offense principles. Feinberg does not recognize, for example, any general vulnerability of terminally ill individuals as negating consent for the purposes of the harm principle. Similarly, whilst Feinberg acknowledges a conflict between a newspaper's interest in publishing news and a personal interest in privacy (as a welfare interest right), he does not consider the role of vulnerability in this context.[31] As a result, Feinberg's harm principle does not support criminalization of assisted suicide and may hesitate to legitimize criminalization of photographing defendants outside court. In the same way as for dignity, the use of vulnerability reasoning by the ECtHR opens a route to wider criminalization in scenarios that may be viewed as potentially exploitative than that allowed by Feinberg.

As regards pluralism, Feinberg is clear that he is committed to a pluralistic society. He holds that it is no reason whatever to restrict an individual's behaviour simply because the community disapproves of it, in the absence of harm or offense.[32] Feinberg's analysis where the different interests of individuals are in conflict, however, is concerned purely with the interpersonal balancing of interests, rather than a separate interest in maintaining a pluralistic society. Feinberg

28 *Pretty v. United Kingdom*, ECHR, para 74.
29 *Egeland and Hanseid v. Norway*, ECHR, para 19.
30 *Ibid.*, para 61.
31 Feinberg, *Harm to Others*, p.204.
32 *Ibid.*, p.122.

describes, for example, that when interests of quite different kinds are invaded to the same degree, legislators must consider their vitality, the degree to which they are reinforced by other interests, and their inherent moral quality.[33] Under this approach, Feinberg would address, for instance, the question of criminalization of proselytism as a matter of interest balancing between the interest of individuals in speaking freely about their faith and the interest of others in quiet enjoyment of their own beliefs or faith. This approach also tends to be followed by more recent criminal law theorists, who do not generally give independent weight to the value of pluralism.[34] By contrast, as the ECHR criminalization case of *Kokkinakis* (proselytism) shows, the safeguarding of multiple principles within society is itself a distinct consideration for the Court in some criminalization cases. This approach fits with the greater readiness of the ECtHR to accord weight to non-individual interests, such as those of the society or community. The exact impact of the European Court's approach to pluralism on criminalization outcomes is hard to ascertain, in particular in light of the Court's preference for community consensus over pluralism in *S.A.S.* (wearing of clothing designed to conceal the face). Nonetheless, as with dignity and vulnerability, the fact that the ECtHR gives independent weight to pluralism in criminalization case reasoning provides an additional objective in the Court's view of the criminal law. Under this approach, the aims of the criminal law become not just the balancing of individual interests but the balancing of interests with a view to maintaining or promoting, where possible, a plurality of interests.

Multi-factorial reasoning

Under an international human rights law approach, the question as to whether any particular act should be criminalized can engage a number of underlying concepts. As a result, ECHR criminalization cases typically contain more than one ground of reasoning. Reasoning and concepts employed by the ECtHR, such as harm, offense, autonomy, societal interests, and community consensus, are not limited to consideration under specific ECHR articles. Nonetheless, some concepts may tend to be used by the Court more frequently under certain articles. Across ECHR criminalization cases, for instance, the concept of offense is (as might be expected) most often considered under Article 10 (Freedom of expression); harm reasoning occurs most frequently under Articles 2 (Right to life), 3 (Prohibition of torture), 8, and 10; community consensus reasoning often features under Articles 8 and 10, and autonomy is relevant to a number of Convention articles, including 4 (Prohibition of slavery), 8, 9 (Freedom of religion), and 10. The structure of Convention rights, and associated limitation clauses, provides the framework within which the ECtHR can combine or balance different concepts and considerations. One common balance faced by the Court, for example, is between the principle of personal autonomy and the interests and views of society. Whilst the ECtHR faces some limitations in the framing of its

33 *Ibid.*, p.204.
34 See, for example, Wohlers, W., 2014.

analysis under ECHR rights, it is clear that its approach nonetheless enables a wide range of factors and concepts to be taken into account at the same time. In a complex ECHR criminalization case such as *Friend* (hunting a wild mammal with a dog), for instance, the Court's analysis can thus involve multiple concepts, considered under a number of different Convention rights. In that case, the Court considered whether the act was sufficiently close to the notion of personal autonomy; whether the measures served a community consensus as to the morality of hunting and killing animals for sport; whether the measures impacted the social dimension and way of life of the applicants; and whether the measures violated property rights.[35] These lines of underlying reasoning were considered under ECHR Articles 8 (Right to respect for private and family life), 11 (Freedom of assembly), and Protocol 1 (Right to property). Through such analysis, the acceptability of criminalization of hunting in *Friend* derived from all of the Court's findings that hunting was too far removed from personal autonomy; that the social dimension and way of life was maintained by drag or trail hunting; that the criminal prohibition served a legitimate aim of the protection of morals; and that property rights were not infringed.

By contrast, under a Feinbergian criminal theory approach to the same act, analytical options would likely be limited to determining whether, as a regulatory rule, a criminal offence of hunting had as its aim the prevention of public harm; and/or whether hunting caused wrongful offence to those who view it as morally repugnant; or even a discussion as to whether animals have welfare interests.[36] The first of these options may open the door for some degree of interest balancing under Feinberg's harm principle mediating maxim related to liberty.[37] Nonetheless, this maxim provides little practical guidance in assessing whether, for instance, restricting the liberty of persons who wish to engage in hunting is an acceptable trade-off for the protection of the interest of others (and possibly society) in animal welfare. Alternatively, Feinberg might simply argue that hunting (as long as not carried out on an owner's land without permission) does not directly set back the interests of any individual, let alone violate any welfare interest right, and should not therefore properly be the subject of the criminal law. Whilst this position would be consistent with the core of Feinberg's scheme, it leaves something of the sense that the issue has not been fully debated.

In seeking to limit the scope of the criminal law through the single gateways of the harm and offense principles, criminal theorists such as Feinberg risk, at the same time, effectively reducing the analytical power of their criminalization framework. In comparison with a multi-factorial international human rights law approach, Feinberg's lens of setbacks of interest and horizontal welfare interest rights is decidedly limited in addressing complex criminalization challenges such as hunting wild mammals with dogs. The limitations of Feinberg's approach are, to

35 *Friend, the Countryside Alliance and Others v. United Kingdom*, ECHR, paras 42, 43, 50, and 57.

36 See Feinberg, *Harm to Others*, pp.58–59.

37 Feinberg, *Harm to Others*, pp.205–214.

some extent, addressed by more recent criminal law theorists. The dual-element approach of Simester and von Hirsch, for example, allows the emphasis to be placed on either harm or wrongfulness as a starting point, with the second acting as a reciprocal constraint. In addition, Simester and von Hirsch do not hold to a general criterion or theory of wrongfulness, in contrast to Feinberg's reliance on welfare interest rights for the identification of wrongfulness. Rather, they are prepared for wrongfulness to take different forms in different cases, such as in immediate harms, remote harms, and offense.[38] What this approach gains in flexibility, it risks losing in specificity. Nonetheless, the increased range of options for analysing conduct that it presents does represent a move towards the more multi-factorial system of international human rights law.

Comparison of the international human rights law multi-factorial approach to criminalization with criminal theory further suggests that key concepts – such as autonomy, harm, and societal interests – whilst all featuring in both international human rights law reasoning and criminal theory, are often understood and applied in quite different ways. In part, this is due to structural variations, such as the difference between multi-factorial and "single gateway" approaches to criminalization.

The prevention of harm and offense to others, for example, is recognized by both Feinberg and the ECtHR as a reason in support of criminalization. For Feinberg, the prevention of harm to others represents the primary gateway for principled criminalization. As a result, Feinberg develops a complex theory of harm to others as a setback of interests that wrong the victim by violating his or her welfare rights. Combined with his understanding of autonomy and rights, Feinberg's concept of harm generally excludes harm to self. Its focus on harm to specific individuals also requires a complex construction for the notion of collective, or public, harm. Apart from these restrictions, however, in principle, for Feinberg, any act that can be held to set back interests and violate the specific welfare interest rights of another can cause Feinbergian harm and carry a good reason in favour of criminalization. This position also has parallels in the work of more recent criminal law theorists, who continue to emphasize the importance of harm to criminal law theory. Von Hirsch, for instance, holds that it is harm, as a safeguard of interests in resources, together with the reciprocal constraint of wrongfulness, that generally should be a requirement of criminalization.[39]

The European Court, on the other hand, does not elaborate any detailed concept of harm. It shows general awareness of harm as part of the heritage of criminalization theory, and appears to endorse the prevention of harm in general, as a reason in support of criminalization. It does not, however, place any particular emphasis on harm as an overarching or central principle for criminalization in the same way as Feinberg and other criminal law theorists. Rather,

38 Von Hirsch, A., 2014, p.252.
39 *Ibid.*, p.255.

harm reasoning is employed by the ECtHR to the extent that it is material to the determination of a human rights violation as part of its multi-factorial reasoning. The Court refers to the concept alongside other principles and in a general sense of bodily harm or negative consequences. In so far as the ECtHR understands harm mostly in terms of its common usage, as opposed to the specific harm definition developed by Feinberg, its harm reasoning is perhaps more predictable than Feinberg, but also more restricted. ECHR criminalization cases where harm reasoning is used to support the conclusion that an act *should* be a criminal offence mostly represent acts such as assault, domestic violence, intentional taking of life, and sexual offences against children. Thus, in *Öneryildiz* (negligence in dangerous activities), for example, the harmfulness of the activity in question was held by the ECtHR to be relevant to determining the responsibility of the state under Article 2 (Right to life).[40] The lack of adequate protection by law for deterring similar life-endangering conduct in future resulted in the finding of a violation of the procedural aspect of Article 2. In so doing, the Court highlighted the deterrent function of the criminal law in the case of life-endangering acts.

The fact that the Court's conception of harm is narrower than Feinberg's means that in almost all cases where the European Court employs harm reasoning to hold that an act should be or can be a criminal offence, Feinberg, and likely other criminal law theorists, would generally also find a harm-based argument in support of criminalization. Offences of domestic violence (*Opuz*), sexual acts against children (*Stubbings*), assault (*Beganović*), and rape (*G*), for example, are easily supported by harm arguments of both Feinberg and the European Court. Other cases, however, are not so straightforward and reveal the effect of the variation between Feinberg and the ECtHR in their understanding of harm on criminalization outcomes. In *Laskey* (assault in the context of sadomasochistic activities), for instance, the ECtHR, considering harm in its everyday sense, alongside other factors such as autonomy and societal interests, endorsed the idea that the state is entitled to regulate, through the operation of the criminal law, activities which involve the infliction of physical harm.[41] The Court applied this maxim at the level of justification for restricting the right to private and family life (ECHR Article 8), notwithstanding the argument of consent to the harm inflicted. By contrast, the fact that Feinberg specifically defines harm, as his single gateway to criminalization, with reference to an experiential setback of interests and the violation of welfare interest rights, means that Feinberg is more reluctant to identify harm in such cases.

The theme continues with respect to the concepts of societal interests and community consensus. The European Court relies heavily on societal interest and community consensus reasoning across criminalization cases as a key component of its multi-factorial reasoning. Such reasoning often supports the

40 *Öneryildiz v. Turkey*, ECHR, para 73.

41 *Laskey, Jaggard and Brown v. United Kingdom*, ECHR, para 43.

Court's finding that a particular act *can* or *should not* be an offence. Thus in *Norwood* (religious hate speech), for example, the ECtHR held that an applicant convicted for displaying a threatening, abusive, or insulting sign did not enjoy the protection of ECHR Article 10 (Freedom of expression), on the basis that the words and images on the poster in question were incompatible with the values of tolerance and social peace. Similarly, in *S.A.S.* (wearing of clothing designed to conceal the face), the Court held that the conviction was compatible with the Convention on the basis that the restriction on rights reflected an established consensus, as an indispensable element of community life within the society in question. Feinberg addresses at length similar archetypal cases in his discussion on profound offense in *Offense to Others*[42] and in his consideration of a like-minded community in *Harmless Wrongdoing*.[43] Both discussions demonstrate a greater hesitance than the European Court to give weight to societal or consensus considerations. To a large degree, this is due to the focus on identifying the existence, or not, of wrongful harm or offense as the single gateway reason to criminalization. In respect of offensive signs and symbols, Feinberg places significant weight on the practical "avoidability" of the offense. Using a largely consequentialist approach, Feinberg considers, for example, the "relative ease" by which malicious and spiteful insults could be avoided and finds that the scales would mostly tip towards criminalization only if the insulting behaviour became more frequent and a major nuisance.[44] Such practical factors appear at least as important to Feinberg as the actual content or expressive function of offensive material. Whilst Feinberg recognizes conceptual differences between pure insults and genuine political advocacy and debate, his general scheme of wrongful offense, as a single gateway to criminalization, is built around the experiential impact on others, rather than the (more deontological) concept of expression which is incompatible with societal values.[45] The relative balance towards a consequentialist approach means that Feinberg is not often convinced by an argument based on the potential or conceptual impact on society in general, requiring rather demonstration of a concrete effect on specified others.

A similar reticence to treat society or the community as a distinct interest is seen when Feinberg considers the balance between the interests of the community in a shared way of life and the interest of the individual in some nonconforming action.[46] In such a scenario, Feinberg favours personal interests in how individuals live their own lives, above other-regarding interests in how others live their lives. In other words, where the interests of a private individual in a particular action (that causes neither harm nor offense to others) clash with

42 Feinberg, *Offense to Others*, pp.86–95.
43 Feinberg, *Harmless Wrongdoing*, pp.51–63.
44 Feinberg, *Offense to Others*, p.87.
45 See, for example, Feinberg, *Offense to Others*, pp.14–21.
46 See, for example, the discussion in Feinberg, *Harmless Wrongdoing*, pp.55–64.

the interests of others in living in a world without such action, then, Feinberg holds, the personal interest should usually prevail. Feinberg supports this position from his starting point of individual autonomy, arguing that the added weight of the personal interests comes not from any necessary inherent moral superiority of self-regarding concerns but rather from the protection personal autonomy gives to the area that is one's own proper business.[47] Whilst *The Moral Limits* does not consider the specific example of wearing of clothing designed to conceal the face, Feinberg's reasoning strongly suggests that he would not accord an established consensus of open interpersonal relationships as an indispensable element of community life sufficient weight to override the individual interest in wearing clothing of one's choice.

Such variations in the nature and weight of societal interests and community consensus within the respective structural frameworks of Feinberg and the ECtHR result in different criminalization conclusions. In this regard, Feinberg's approach to societal interests and offensive behaviour is not necessarily identical to that of more recent criminal law theorists. Simester and von Hirsch, for example, place greater emphasis on the "wrong" caused by offensive behaviour than on the resulting affront, through the failure to treat others with due consideration and respect and to accord the victim full moral standing as a person.[48] They also recognize the need for conciliation between the individual's way of life and the society in which she lives. In this way, it is possible that Simester and von Hirsch may come to different conclusions to Feinberg in some instances regarding the criminalization of acts involving societal and community interests. This may bring criminal theory closer to the approach of the ECtHR in some ways, such as through Simester's and von Hirsch's openness to the possible criminal law protection of infringement of instrumental social conventions.[49] It also highlights the fact that criminal law theory itself lacks a single unified approach to such questions.

The margin of appreciation

Finally, differences between international human rights law and criminalization theory arise through the fact that criminalization outcomes in international human rights law are themselves influenced by the extent of international consensus on the particular criminalization question.

The margin of appreciation is a doctrine that is deeply embedded within the jurisprudence of the ECtHR as a whole, rather than in criminalization cases alone.[50] Nonetheless, one of the first ECtHR cases to discuss the margin of appreciation was a criminalization case: *Handyside* (obscene publications).

47 Feinberg, *Harmless Wrongdoing*, p.63.
48 Simester, A.P., and von Hirsch, A., 2011, p.99.
49 *Ibid.*, p.103.
50 Legg, A., 2012.

Handyside explained that a margin is given both to the domestic legislator and to the bodies, including judicial bodies, that are called upon to interpret and apply the laws in force.[51] Conceptually, the margin of appreciation doctrine aligns, in many respects, with community consensus reasoning that is also recognized, but largely rejected, by criminal law theorists such as Feinberg.

The doctrine has the result that the degree to which there is a common approach to the ECHR regarding the criminalization of a particular act is relevant to determining whether criminalization is permitted or not within the state in question. The doctrine operates at the level of restriction clauses to human rights, guiding the ECtHR's determination as to whether a restriction on rights meets a legitimate aim and is necessary in the circumstances. A common European consensus, in terms of similar patterns of practice or regulation across states parties to the ECHR, typically means a more limited latitude, or margin of appreciation, for a state in determining its own approach. Conversely, a lack of European consensus, either as to the relative importance of the interest at stake or as to the best means of protecting it, means that the margin will be wider. In addition, the margin is widened where sensitive moral or ethical issues are involved and narrowed where an important face of existence or identity is at stake.[52]

The margin of appreciation applied by the Court is seen to play a particular role where the Court finds that an act *can* be a criminal offence. In *İ.A* (blasphemy), for example, the Court emphasized that there was no uniform European conception of the requirements of the protection of the rights of others in relation to attacks on religious convictions. As a result, it accorded a wide margin of appreciation to the regulation of freedom of expression in connection with matters that may offend intimate personal convictions within the sphere of morals and religion. The ECtHR concluded that a conviction for blasphemy against God, one of the religions, one of the prophets, one of the sects, or one of the holy books, was within that margin.[53] In *A, B and C* (procuring miscarriage), the ECtHR decided that there was a consensus amongst states parties towards allowing abortion on broader grounds than accorded under Irish law, such as justifications on health and well-being grounds. However, the Court still accorded a wide margin of appreciation due to the "acute sensitivity" of the moral and ethical issues raised by the question of abortion. As a result, the ECtHR held that the prohibition in Ireland of abortion for health and well-being reasons, being based on the "profound moral views" of the Irish people as to the nature of life and the consequent protection to be accorded to the right to life of the unborn, did not exceed the margin of appreciation accorded.[54]

51 *Handyside v. United Kingdom*, ECHR, p.17.
52 Council of Europe, Undated. Online resource.
53 *İ.A. v. Turkey*, ECHR, paras 25–32.
54 *A, B and C v. Ireland*, ECHR, paras 232–236.

The margin of appreciation also comes to the fore in a limited number of ECHR criminalization cases where the Court finds that an act *should not* be a criminal offence. In *Bayatyan* (conscientious objection), for example, the Court accorded a limited margin of appreciation due to its finding that almost all of the member states of the Council of Europe which ever had or still had compulsory military service had introduced alternatives to such service in order to reconcile the possible conflict between individual conscience and military obligations.[55] As a result, the Court held that a conviction for draft evasion constituted a violation of Article 9 (Freedom of thought, conscience and religion). In *A.D.T.* (same-sex relations), the European Court adopted a narrow margin of appreciation on the basis that the case involved intimate aspects of private life, with the result that the maintenance in force of legislation criminalizing homosexual acts between men in private constituted a violation of Article 8 (Right to private life) of the Convention.[56]

Such cases illustrate a number of effects of the margin of appreciation doctrine on the ECtHR's criminalization findings. The first is that where little or no consensus exists at the international level as to whether a particular act should or should not be a criminal offence, international human rights law is more prepared to accept criminalization. This is especially so if the act involves ethical or moral issues. That this is the case is seen in a number of ECHR criminalization cases in which the Court finds that an act *can* be a criminal offence, including acts such as procuring miscarriage (*A, B and C*), blasphemy (*İ.A* and *Wingrove*), nudity in public (*Gough*), obscene publications (*Handyside*, *Müller*, and *Perrin*), hate speech (*Feret*, *Norwood*, *Osmani*, and *Vejdeland*), assisting suicide (*Pretty*), wearing of clothing designed to conceal the face (*S.A.S.*), and incest (*Stübing*). Because the margin of appreciation determines the overall context for determining the proportionality of a restriction on rights, this general result applies irrespective of whether the underlying reasoning is based on societal interests, autonomy, harm and offense, community consensus, or human dignity. A wider margin of appreciation allows more latitude for arguments based on any or all of these concepts. In so far as such reasoning includes community consensus at local or national (rather than international) level, a lack of consensus at international level effectively opens the door to allow more weight for the local consensus.

No equivalent approach to a wide margin of appreciation is readily identifiable within the work of criminal theorists such as Feinberg. Feinberg well recognizes and discusses the existence of communities, including families, ethnic communities, nations, and other communities that individuals are born into, as well as the promotion of abundant, diverse, and receptive social groups.[57] Feinberg is in favour of diverse communities and acknowledges that there may be multiple

55 *Bayatyan v. Armenia*, ECHR, para 123.
56 *A.D.T. v. United Kingdom*, ECHR, paras 37 and 38.
57 Feinberg, *Harmless Wrongdoing*, pp.120–122.

overlapping communities at different levels.[58] His discussion of the role of community consensus in criminalization, however, is limited primarily to the issue of conflict between a single defined community way of life and an individual interest in non-conforming conduct – a balance where Feinberg finds in favour of the individual. To the extent that Feinberg considers the impact of multiple communities with different values on criminalization theory, if anything, he tends in the opposite direction to the European Court. In *Harmless Wrongdoing*, he suggests that diverse groups can be bound more securely together by a "common" respect for established rights, rather than offering a greater latitude for criminalization according to local values.[59] Equally, the idea that acts where sensitive moral or ethical issues are involved should mean greater latitude for criminalization does not find support in Feinberg's work. Again, if anything, Feinberg has a particular concern for ensuring that legal moralism alone cannot form the basis of principled criminalization.

As such, the margin of appreciation doctrine of international human rights law tends to result in a greater emphasis than Feinberg's criminalization theory on local or national community context in matters of criminalization, where there is no consensus approach at the international level. This is the case at least for acts that engage rights with limitation clauses, such as the right to respect for private and family life, freedom of thought, conscience and religion, freedom of expression, and freedom of assembly and association. Together with the readiness of international human rights law to use criminalization reasoning based on societal interests and human dignity, the doctrine contributes significantly to the general permissiveness of international human rights law towards criminalization, including as regards complex moral and ethical acts.

On the other hand, a second effect of the margin of appreciation doctrine on criminalization outcomes is that where an international consensus *does* exist, this is highly persuasive for the criminal law of non-aligned states. Indeed, the five treaty-based criminalization requirements within international human rights law express the consensus of the international community that these specific acts *should* be criminalized across all countries. In human rights jurisprudence, the European consensus, and its resultant narrow margin, is more significant in respect of acts that *should not* be criminal offences, including same-sex relations (*A.D.T.* and *Dudgeon*), conscientious objection (*Bayatyan*), proselytism (*Kokkinakis*), and insulting a head of state (*Mondragon* and *Colombani*). In each of these cases, a narrow margin of appreciation is material to the finding of the Court that the act should *not* be a criminal offence.

As with the role of the wide margin of appreciation, no equivalent approach to the narrow margin of appreciation is seen explicitly within Feinberg's criminalization theory. Rather than building an account of commonly accepted, or rejected, criminal law into his theory, Feinberg, along with many other criminal

58 Feinberg, *Harmless Wrongdoing*, pp.105–107.
59 Feinberg, *Harmless Wrongdoing*, p.118.

law theorists, aims instead to construct a critical theory of criminalization which can provide for principled criminalization in the first place.[60] As such, to the extent that a majority of communities criminalize, or do not criminalize, a certain act, Feinberg's core harm and welfare interest-based theory, including its mediating maxims, does not have any specific mechanism for taking this into account in assessing the validity of criminalization of that act. When compared with Feinberg's criminalization theory, international human rights law, through the narrow margin of appreciation, thus adds a subjective dimension to questions of criminalization. It holds that common approaches to criminalization are material in determining the legitimacy of the criminal law.

Whilst the approach of the European Court in this regard is in strong contrast to the critical moral approach adopted by Feinberg and other theorists, such as Simester and von Hirsch, it does, of course, resonate in some ways with legal moralist conceptions of criminal law theory.[61] There may also be similarities with the use of flexible concepts such as *Rechtsgut* that can more easily be subject to interpretation and growth with the aim of recognizing commonly criminalized phenomena. Commentators on continental *Rechtsgut* theory note, for example, that criminal prohibitions of conduct grow surreptitiously and that the concept of the "legal good" accompanies and hides that growth. The legal good, in turn, assists the aim of criminalization and facilitates the protection of an interest through the criminal law.[62] Some conceptions of *Rechtsgut*, in particular, recognize ethical convictions of society that are adopted by the legal order. As such, criminal theory based on *Rechtsgut* can itself include elements of commonly accepted legal values, in a manner similar to which the European Court is informed by existing patterns of criminalization.

Summary

In sum, international human rights law does not merely reframe criminalization theory – at least in so far as a detailed comparison of the jurisprudence of the ECtHR, and Anglo-American criminal theorists, such as Joel Feinberg, suggests. Due to a significant influence of the liberal tradition on both, it is the case that a number of same concepts, including autonomy, harm, offense, societal interests, and community consensus, are explored by the ECtHR and Feinberg as relevant to criminalization. Each has, however, either a different understanding or places a different weight on each of these concepts. Feinberg, for instance, develops a highly particular understanding of harm, whereas the ECtHR uses the term in its everyday sense. The European Court is much more ready to accord weight to the interests of society or a community consensus, whereas Feinberg values demonstration of the concrete effect of an act on specified individuals.

60 Feinberg, *Harm to Others*, p.3.
61 See, for example, Moore, M., 1997.
62 Hassemer, W., 2014, pp.197–199.

Such differences are closely intertwined with four major structural differences between the approach of the ECtHR and criminal theorists in the Anglo-American tradition: (i) the use of a primarily "vertical" state–individual analysis by international human rights law, as opposed to a "horizontal" claim rights approach by theorists such as Feinberg and Hörnle; (ii) the use of dignity, vulnerability, and pluralism as separable analytical concepts by international human rights law, as opposed to their inclusion as background values in Feinberg's scheme; (iii) the use by international human rights law of multi-factorial reasoning, as opposed to the more restricted "single gateway" approach of theorists such as Feinberg; and (iv), the influence of existing criminalization practice through the margin of appreciation. These differences have the potential to result in divergent criminalization conclusions in a number of cases, for example, as regards consented-to acts, acts considered incompatible with an established community consensus, and acts of an exploitative nature.

Other, more recent, criminal law literature indicates that these four major differences may also be relevant to criminalization theory more widely. Criminal theory literature does not contain, for example, any prominent work that relies on a vertical rights-based theory. Similarly, whilst a number of theorists refer to concepts such as dignity, vulnerability, and pluralism, very few of these place a significant emphasis on these ideas in a separable way. When it comes to multi-factorial reasoning, a number of theorists do allow a multiple "filter" or "gated" approach; however, such theories are rarely developed to the same extent as the clear structure created for reasoning of the ECtHR. Finally, as regards the margin of appreciation, this can, on some levels, have equivalence to a legal moralist approach, although it is certainly not reflected in broader criminal theory literature in the same sense as applied by the ECtHR.

9 The value of international human rights law for criminal theory

The widespread and diverse criminalization jurisprudence of international human rights law has hitherto not been subject to rigorous analytical review. One reason for this is that international human rights criminalization cases, such as those considered by the ECtHR, are largely context-dependent and fact-driven. This book demonstrates that it is possible nonetheless to identify some lines of underlying reasoning employed by the ECtHR in criminalization cases, as well as features of its analytical framework. This reasoning and framework is certainly not akin to a full criminalization theory. Judgments of the ECtHR, and other international human rights courts and tribunals, tend to develop reasoning and precedent through an iterative process depending upon the *in concreto* cases that come before them. Judgements may not always be entirely consistent and can be variable in terms of the level of underlying reasoning for their decisions. The analysis in this book suggests, however, that when considering issues of criminalization, the ECtHR applies underlying reasoning based on a number of identifiable concepts, including societal interests, autonomy, harm and offense, community consensus, and human dignity. Many of these concepts are known to criminalization theory. However, specific features of an international human rights law approach, such as use of a "vertical" conception of rights, a multi-factorial approach to reasoning, and use of concepts such as dignity, vulnerability, and pluralism, mean that such reasoning does not merely reframe existing criminal theory.

How can these new insights into an international human rights law approach to criminalization best be made use of? One possibility could be to attempt the development of a full theoretical framework for the criminal law, based on the emerging jurisprudence of international human rights courts and tribunals. This would certainly face a number of challenges. The first is whether the framework of human rights, as contained in instruments like the ECHR, is sufficiently broad to apply to the vast range of human conduct that has been, or could be, in practice, criminalized by states. International human rights law was never directly intended as a framework for determining the proper nature and extent of the criminal law. Drafters of the Universal Declaration of Human Rights (UDHR) rather assumed that acts could be regarded as criminal by virtue of the "general principles of law" recognized by civilized nations. On the other hand, it is clear that aspirations for the UDHR, as the foundational document for contemporary international human rights, were aimed at the development of a system that addressed the situation of humankind in the most fundamental way. As the law of the state itself presents a key constraint on the exercise of human rights, the completeness of those rights as a system for assessing criminalization is thus not perhaps an unreasonable assumption. Nonetheless, the range of acts covered by today's criminal law is immense. It includes interpersonal acts leading to death, injury, sexual violation, or loss of property, as well as acts involving controlled substances, fraud, deception, or corruption, in addition to acts against public order and authority, public safety and state security, and the natural environment. It is far from clear that all of these acts engage human rights issues, such that they are amenable to an international human rights law analysis.

Instruments such as the ECHR do have a reasonably wide scope, covering at least any act that concerns death, injury, the establishment of relationships, issues of identity and personal development, personal integrity, the communication of information or ideas, or property. However, many acts will still likely fall outside the scope of specific rights, such as in the ECHR case of *Friend* (hunting a wild mammal with a dog), where the act was held to be too far removed from personal autonomy and interpersonal relations to engage the right to private life (ECHR Article 8). In that case, other rights were engaged, and the Article 8 result effectively formed part of the ECtHR's reasoning for confirming the acceptability of criminalization of hunting. It is quite conceivable, however, that any number of other acts, including acts against trade regulations, acts contrary to labour law, acts causing pollution or degradation of the environment, or market manipulation and insider trading, may not engage any internationally recognized human right. Criminal theorists who rely on notions of rights, such as Tatjana Hörnle, also acknowledge this point. Hörnle holds, for example, that whilst the rights of others should be the most important pillar supporting a theory of criminalization, it could not be the only pillar, because a rights-centred approach would not work for crimes such as counterfeiting money or bribing state officials. Due to the limited nature of rights she proposes that individual rights would need to be supplemented with recognition of "genuine collective interests."[1] Presumably such a system would elevate selected collective interests – including those recognized by international human rights law as grounds for restrictions on rights, such as national security, public safety, public order, health, or morals – to a level equivalent to the right itself for the purposes of a rights-based criminalization theory. Acts impinging upon the individual right or a collective interest would then be accorded a reason in favour of criminalization.

Under the approach of international human rights law, should a particular act not engage any substantive right, then this has the result that the act *can* legitimately be a criminal offence. This derives from the ECHR *Engel* principle that states are free to designate as a criminal offence an act or omission not constituting the normal exercise of one of the rights that the ECHR protects.[2] If no right is engaged, then the act *can* be a criminal offence, due to the general position that

1 Hörnle, T., 2016, p.305.
2 *Engel and Others v. The Netherlands*, ECHR, para 81.

states are free to exercise sovereignty to the extent that it does not contravene any international rule. With no particular right engaged, an international human rights court or tribunal would have no mechanism to apply reasoning and concepts such as harm, offense, dignity, societal interests, or community consensus. As a result, it is highly unlikely that international human rights law could offer a complete scheme for criminalization reasoning. If the first "filter" of international human rights law for the criminalization of any particular act is the engagement of one or more rights, then a wide range of acts do not receive adequate criminalization scrutiny. A criminalization framework based solely on international human rights law thus opens the door for criminalization of any number of trivial, and indeed not-so trivial, acts without good reason.

It is significant that this result is almost the exact opposite of the approach of most criminal theorists. Under Feinberg's scheme, for example, a good reason for criminalization only arises where there *is* a setback of interests, which is at the same time a violation of welfare interest rights. As welfare interest rights are the most basic requisites of a man's well-being, Feinberg's requirement – unlike international human rights law – effectively prevents the criminalization of trivial acts that do not infringe any welfare right of another. Other theorists who argue for a rights-based criminalization theory similarly adopt a "justificatory" scheme, where rights are placed within a system that requires substantive reasons *for* criminalization, in contrast to the permissive situation under the *Engel* principle. Hörnle's scheme, for example, identifies the rights of others as the class of objects that can justify protection by the criminal law, but is clear that these are to be used as an "entrance decision" for criminalization. Hörnle does not make reference to international human rights law as an inspiration for the nature and content of her rights. With respect to constitutional rights in national law, she clarifies that her notion of rights in criminal theory is not as rights granted by positive law but as an "understanding" which precedes the legal process of criminalization.[3] It is certainly true that criminal theory cannot be anchored, as Hörnle argues, in a simple, genuinely positivistic way. Nonetheless, as Hörnle also asserts, the notion of rights as granted in any given legal system should not be entirely ignored. This raises the question as to how the rights and reasoning of international human rights law could have value for criminal theory. If international human rights law cannot itself form a complete system for criminalization, what other contributions might it make to the development of criminal theory?

Use as a "test bed" for criminalization theory results could be one option. The outcomes of criminalization cases from the ECHR and other international human rights courts and tribunals might be used as a reference point for the "correctness" of criminal theory, in a similar way, for instance to that of intuition as a test for criminalization. The degree of global consensus in international human rights law that exists over and above any national criminal law makes this a particularly valuable comparison. The issue, however, is perhaps what should be done when such a test shows different outcomes as between

3 Hörnle, T., 2016, p.308.

criminal theory and international human rights law. Chapter 8 demonstrates that a number of differences are apparent in criminalization results, as between international human rights law and broadly liberal criminal theory in the tradition of Joel Feinberg. The ECtHR, for example, differs to liberal criminal theorists in areas such as the criminalization of assisted suicide and consented-to harm to self. International human rights law is also more ready than many criminal theorists to allow criminalization in favour of protecting a community interest or consensus, even of an intangible nature such as the perceived interest in communicating face-to-face.

Exactly what are the implications of these test results – is criminal theory simply wrong on such points? The value of the test lies, in fact, as much in the underlying reasons *why* different criminalization results are reached as much as it does in the indicator of outcome difference. The outcomes of international human rights law criminalization cases, whilst driven by individual context to a large extent, can tell us far more than results from a mere intuition test of criminal theory. They are rather derived from a principled framework with some identifiable underlying reasoning. Indeed, as discussed in Chapter 8, reasons for differences can be traced to a number of different methodological and conceptual approaches as between criminal theory and international human rights law. They include the differences between applying a theory based on vertical or horizontal rights, the weight placed on concepts such as dignity and vulnerability, the difference between single gateway or multi-factorial approaches, and whether weight is given to any existing consensus at different levels. As such, the other side of the coin to testing criminal theory against international human rights law criminalization outcomes is to consider what should be done about differences that arise. If the criminalization jurisprudence of international human rights law is considered as a valuable touchstone for what should, or should not, be a criminal offence, then lessons might be drawn from the underlying reasoning of international human rights law for criminal theory itself.

To this end, Table 9.1 summarizes attributes of the criminal theory of Joel Feinberg and the approach of the ECtHR to criminalization cases as the two primary points of reference for criminal theory and international human rights law considered in this book. It reviews, for each, a range of issues, including those discussed in detail in Chapter 8, but also attributes such as the default criminalization position; the genesis and approach; the philosophical background; scope of application; scheme outcome; primary gateway to criminalization; the position, nature, and role of rights; and the role of different concepts applied by each scheme.

Table 9.1 demonstrates that the inherent nature of a liberal criminal theory, such as that of Joel Feinberg, and the approach of international human rights law to criminalization are quite different. Nonetheless, there are a number of points of intersection where international human rights law could have value for criminal theory.

Table 9.1 Comparison of Attributes of Criminal Theory and an International Human Rights Law Approach to Criminalization

Attribute	*Criminal theory (Feinberg)*	*International human rights law (ECtHR)*
Default criminalization position	Presumption of liberty. Principled justification required for criminalization.	Criminalization of any act is permitted unless incompatible with a specific obligation under international human rights law. Criminalization of some acts is required.
Genesis and approach	Critical moral theory applied specifically to the question of criminalization.	System of international law designed to ensure respect for human rights, including delineating borders of exercise of state power and authority in that regard.
Philosophical background	Primarily consequentialist impact of an act on the individual, but with additional deontological rights-based theory.	Deontological rights-based heritage, but with consequentialist considerations, including through human rights limitation clauses.
Scope of application	In principle, all acts, although largely excluding *mala prohibita* (regulatory) acts.	Limited to acts engaging defined treaty-based human rights.
Scheme outcome	Identification of a good reason in support of criminalization of a specific act.	Identification of the acceptability of, or requirement for, criminalization, derived from legal findings on the existence of a human rights violation.
Primary gateway to criminalization	Wrongful harm, defined as a setback of interests that wrongs an individual by violating his or her welfare rights.	No single gateway. Consideration of criminalization issue dependent upon engagement of individual right and mode of framing of *in concreto* human rights case.
Position and role of rights	Scheme examines potential for act to directly violate individual welfare rights of another. Violation of welfare rights required to establish good reason for criminalization.	Compatibility of criminal law (or lack of) examined against contours of positive and negative state obligations for each separate human right engaged. Violation of rights not required for acceptability of criminalization.

(*Continued*)

Table 9.1 (Cont.)

Attribute	*Criminal theory (Feinberg)*	*International human rights law (ECtHR)*
Nature of rights	Horizontal individual claim rights derived from broad welfare interests. Rights not exhaustively listed.	State vertical obligations to ensure respect for, to protect, and to fulfil human rights. Rights set out in full in international treaties.
Primary concepts and reasoning	Autonomy, wrongful harm, wrongful offense, and non-grievance evils.	Societal interests, autonomy, harm and offense, community consensus, human dignity, vulnerability, and pluralism.
Role and concept of autonomy	Starting point for scheme. Used in identifying setback of interests and in weighing the necessity of criminalization under harm principle mediating maxims.	Principle underlying right to respect for private and family life and prohibition of slavery and forced labour. Invoked where notions of identity, choice, or self-determination are at stake. Weighed against other concepts.
Role and concept of harm	Wrongful harm is primary gateway to criminalization. Harm defined in specific sense as setback of individual interests.	Harm understood in everyday sense. Employed as a reason in support of criminalization alongside other concepts.
Role and concept of human dignity	Acknowledged as background factor, but no role as a separable ground of reasoning.	Foundational to international human rights law. Employed as a separable consideration alongside other concepts.
Individual/ societal considerations	Primacy given to consequentialist impact on the individual. Work-arounds for public harm based on accumulative harm and wrongfulness of breach of regulatory rules. Personal interests favoured above other-regarding interests.	Societal, community consensus, and other non-individual interests employed as separable considerations alongside other concepts.
Role and concept of pluralism	Acknowledged as background factor, but no role as a separable ground of reasoning.	Employed as a separable consideration alongside other concepts.
Approach to paternalism	Hard paternalism rejected as a good reason for criminalization. Soft paternalism accepted as a reason for use of the criminal law to prevent harm to self.	Paternalism not generally recognized as a reason in support of criminalization. Protection of vulnerability employed as a separable consideration alongside other concepts.

(*Continued*)

Table 9.1 (Cont.)

Attribute	*Criminal theory (Feinberg)*	*International human rights law (ECtHR)*
Multi-factorial reasoning	Act usually analysed under one of the primary concepts as a good reason for criminalization.	Possibility to apply all relevant concepts and reasoning.
Place of consent	Consent to an act against an individual largely determinative in preventing criminalization.	Consent not determinative but weighed against other considerations, including societal interests.
Criminalization consensus	Not given weight. Scheme aims to provide *de novo* basis for criminalization.	Lack of international consensus on criminalization leads to greater latitude for criminalization. Established international consensus persuasive in direction of alignment.

Rethinking rights

The most obvious area in which international human rights law could make a contribution would be in the nature of rights themselves, as applied by Feinberg, Hörnle, and others within criminal theory. As discussed in Chapter 8, differences in the vertical and horizontal nature of rights employed give rise to different criminalization outcomes between criminal theory and international human rights law. With inspiration from international human rights law, future development of criminal theory could consider notions of vertical rights or otherwise drawing from findings of rights violation in ECHR criminalization cases. Integrating findings from international human rights law jurisprudence into criminal theory is not straightforward, however. One particular challenge relates to the connection between a rights violation and the criminalization outcome. In Feinberg's scheme, a violation of welfare interest rights is required for criminalization. The connection is not, however, linear for international human rights law. Rather, the relationship between criminalization outcomes and human rights violations depends upon the way in which a case is framed before the human rights court or tribunal, as well as the contours of state obligations under each right engaged. The "delinking" of a rights violation and permissible criminalization is seen, for example, where the ECtHR confirms the acceptability of criminalization through a conviction case. The ECtHR holds, for instance, that acts such as blasphemy, nudity in public, copyright infringement, or failing to wear a motorcycle helmet all *can* be a criminal offence.[4] Convictions for these acts engage substantive

4 *İ.A. v. Turkey*, ECHR; *Gough v. United Kingdom*, ECHR; *Fredrik Neij and Peter Sunde Kolmisoppi v. Sweden*, ECHR; and *X v. United Kingdom*, ECHR.

rights, but do not necessarily constitute human rights violations in and of themselves. Whereas Feinberg always tests the act directly against the claims of individuals, when the issue comes before an international human rights court or tribunal as a conviction case, the ECHR considers (for rights with restriction clauses) whether the criminal law measure is proportionate to the legitimate aim pursued, having regard to the margin of appreciation, for each right engaged.

Thus, in the case of nudity in public, for example, Feinberg asks whether public nudity without reasonable justification (such as sunbathing) shocks, embarrasses, or inconveniences others, violating their right "to be free of offended states."[5] The ECtHR, by contrast, in the conviction case of *Gough*, asked whether a criminal conviction is proportionate to preventing antisocial conduct that is likely to be alarming and morally and otherwise offensive to the general public, having regard to a wide margin of appreciation.[6] In some respects, *Gough* is the reverse of Feinberg's test: whether public nudity violates rights on the one hand (Feinberg) versus whether the criminalization of public nudity violates rights on the other (*Gough*). The question could of course also have been brought before the ECtHR as a positive criminalization case, asking whether nudity in public constitutes a violation of the positive obligations of international human rights law if not prohibited by criminal law. Either way, the international human rights court can confirm the permissibility of criminalization of public nudity without necessarily finding a human rights violation. The complex relationship between violations of international human rights law and criminalization outcomes suggests that it would not be possible to simply replace, in their entirety, notions of rights in criminal theory, such as Feinberg's welfare rights, with international human rights directly. Notwithstanding the limited range of conduct that would engage international human rights law, the finding of a violation (or not) in the replaced scheme of international human rights would not, alone, point to a clear criminalization conclusion.

Nonetheless, a more limited innovation may be considered. Could, for example, horizontal claim rights as used in criminal theory by Feinberg and Hörnle be transformed into vertical rights, as between the state and the individual? This could have the effect of enabling consideration of a wider range of considerations within the rights-based analysis whilst keeping the substantive content of a notion such as the violation of welfare interest rights as a central pillar. Any development of Feinberg's theory in this direction could still use the primary gateway of harm. Acts qualifying for criminalization, however, could be those that cause a setback of interests (possibly to individuals or society at large) and which give rise to a violation of (existing Feinbergian) welfare interests to life, minimal health, economic sufficiency, political liberty, and so on, but as defined with reference to a broader vertical violation scheme. In a vertical scheme, to be constructed and defined, an act perpetrated by an individual would be tested against the contours of the state obligation to ensure respect for the relevant welfare interests engaged. This violation scheme, in

5 Feinberg, *Offense to Others*, p.40.
6 *Gough v. United Kingdom*, ECHR, para 176.

a manner similar to the approach of international human rights law, might take into account limitations due to societal, communal, or other interests. These interests could also include, for instance, the consent of an individual to an act, but this would not be determinative in the way envisaged by Feinberg's current horizontal claim rights. In this way, any such reformulation of rights within Feinberg's scheme could have far-reaching consequences for the relative importance of paternalism and societal interests within the scheme.

Equivalent transformation of horizontal rights into vertical rights within Hörnle's scheme, which uses rights rather than harm as the primary entry point for criminalization, could also enable the integration of broader considerations with the focus of a rights violation. To constitute a complete criminalization scheme, as Hörnle proposes, collective interests would also need to be recognized at the same level of individual rights. Options may therefore exist for results from international human rights law that protect interests such as public health, safety, or order, to be recognized as separable grounds for criminalization, as balanced against criminalization demands resulting from individual rights. It is worth noting, in this regard, that Simester and von Hirsch largely reject the option of using rights in such a way. They argue that it is hard to see what rights when conceived as objects of protection add to the terms "interest" or "resource." They further point out that damage to collective interests can result in harm to individuals without necessarily violating individual rights.[7] This latter point is of course exactly the problem encountered, and addressed, to some extent, by Feinberg in respect of his welfare interest rights in the context of setbacks to public interests. It indicates the challenges in covering all relevant conduct that might be considered for criminalization through a rights-based scheme. Indeed, the starting point for this discussion was that international human rights law may not easily function as a direct replacement for criminalization theory in its entirety.

In this regard, one novel contribution that international human rights law could still make might be as an additional "sensor" for particularly sensitive criminalization. Feinberg and other liberal criminal theorists operate a largely "flat" criminalization scheme, in that all acts are essentially treated in the same way. Either sufficiently good reasons exist to tip the scales in favour of criminalization for a particular act, or not. There may be merit in developing a principle within criminal theory of identification of acts that require a greater degree of scrutiny due to their engagement of internationally recognized human rights. Combined with a primary reason in support of criminalization, such as Feinberg's harm theory, or a variant thereof, engagement of international human rights law could function to screen acts that require particular consideration. In this respect, the engagement of a human right would signal either that the act was linked to the exercise of a specific right that may not easily be restricted by the criminal law or that the act would itself infringe upon the right of another and so be a strong candidate for criminalization. In essence, the "sword" and "shield" functions of international human rights law might be used as flags for

7 Simester, A.P., and von Hirsch, A., 2016, p.368.

acts in which there is an especially strong argument for or against criminalization. Criminal theory might then be directed to an additional set of considerations, gates or filters, in order to fully test the acceptability of criminalization of that particular act.

Balancing considerations

A second area of focus might address the limitations of "single gateway" theories of criminalization, such as Feinberg's wrongful harm. Table 9.1 details how acts are usually analysed by Feinberg primarily under this one principle. Acts that do not cause harm (or offense), for Feinberg, are almost all excluded from legitimate criminalization, due usually to arguments based on his foundational principle of individual autonomy. By contrast, once a right is engaged, international human rights law allows multi-factorial analysis of an act with reference to a wider range of considerations than harm alone. Of course, in this respect, criminal theorists such as Feinberg explicitly take the critical moral view that there is (subject to a few limited exceptions for some non-grievance evils) coincidence between what is truly immoral and what is harmful in the sense so defined. As a result, for Feinberg, it is important that harm represents the primary principle for determining the moral limits of the criminal law. This is the case, not least, because Feinberg wishes to exclude legal moralism from the proper scope of the criminal law.

Both an international human rights law approach to criminalization and other criminal theorists, however, challenge the view that a single master principle is necessarily achievable or desirable. Simester and von Hirsch, for instance, adopt a more flexible approach to the identification of harm and wrongfulness. They hold that certain actions, such as murder and vandalism, are wrongs because of the harm they produce. In other words, the wrong derives from the harm. On the other hand, they argue that some actions, such as perjury and blackmail, are wrongs independently of the harms they directly cause. Such a dual-element theory already provides for a greater freedom of analysis than allowed by Feinberg. A number of theorists further suggest that the proper task for a theory of criminalization is to assemble and clarify the different kinds of consideration that should be relevant in different contexts, including in the form of "filters" or "gates" that could be applied to discern which actions can justifiably be made criminal. In this sense, the multi-factorial approach of international human rights law aligns more closely with, for instance, the view of Andrew Ashworth: that there are a range of principles and values that ought to be considered when deciding whether or not to make conduct criminal. Where criminalization theory is developed towards a filter or gate approach, international human rights law could provide guidance on relevant concepts that should be taken into account. As indicated in Table 9.1, international human rights law employs a wide range of underlying concepts, including societal interests, autonomy, harm and offense, community consensus, and human dignity, each of which is recognized as a separable ground of reasoning. Within the framework utilized by the ECtHR, these concepts are employed in the determination of the existence (or not) of a human rights violation, which in turn allows criminalization conclusions to be drawn. Whilst the definition of each concept, and the way in which, it is employed is tied, in principle, to the process of determining a rights violation, questions concerning the criminal law are central to that determination. As such, it is not inconceivable that concepts and reasoning drawn from such cases could inform the development of criminalization theory even if separated from their original context of ECtHR jurisprudence. The manner in which the European Court identifies a serious restriction of the autonomy of one individual by another as a reason in support of criminalization, for example, might inform one such theoretical filter within criminalization theory.

In this regard, amongst the concepts employed, it is clear that international human rights law places far greater weight on societal interests and community consensus as a reason in support of criminalization than theorists such as Feinberg, who prioritize individual autonomy and harm. This is due also to Feinberg's conscious decision to construct his framework based on setbacks of interest and violations of individual claim rights. The extent to which interests other than individual interests are recognized and protected by the criminal law is central to many debates within criminalization theory as a whole.[8] Beyond commentators who prioritize harm theory, for example, a number of theorists are advocates of forms of legal moralism. Other criminal law theorists recognize and promote the principle of "welfare" within criminalization theory and emphasize the social context in which the law must operate and give weight to collective goals.[9] Continental criminal law theories are also flexible in this regard, including both a wide concept of legal goods and, in some cases, legally protected values.[10]

Within this wider criminal theory context, international human rights law may be employed as a source of inspiration, in particular, for the balance between individual autonomy and collective, or societal, interests. Limitations on individual rights for a range of interests, including community and societal interests, are themselves embedded in the wording of the European Convention. In the criminalization context, the ECtHR has explored this balance across a range of acts, including, amongst others, criminal law regulating hate speech, conscientious objection, compulsory health screening, and building planning regulations. The diverse case law and *in concreto* approach of the ECtHR to such questions makes the identification of principles that could inform criminalization theory in this area quite challenging. Starting points may include, however, the readiness of international human rights law to allow criminal law protection for some societal coordination-type interests necessary to facilitate the coexistence of persons who will encounter each other in day-to-day life or need to share resources, as well as for the prevention of conflict and the infliction of harm or offense on indeterminate others or groups of persons.

8 See, for example, Duff, R.A., 2010.
9 Ashworth, A., and Horder, J., 2013, p.26.
10 Hassemer, W., 2014.

As discussed in Chapter 3, liberal theorists such as Feinberg do incorporate notions of societal interest within criminal theory to some extent. Feinberg makes a number of concessions towards societal interests and public harms, including in cases such as environmental pollution. In *Harmless Wrongdoing*, Feinberg appears to broaden his theory to include public harmful acts that set back convergent interests. Moving away from wrongfulness as determined by the violation of individual claim rights, Feinberg identifies, in this context, wrongfulness deriving from the violation of each individual's interest in the shared convergent interest.[11] This entry point could conceivably provide one route by which international human rights law could contribute perspectives to Feinberg's criminalization theory in particular, on the nature and balance of shared societal interests, such as public order or social peace, whose protection provides reason for protection by the criminal law.

Similarly, both Feinberg and theorists such as von Hirsch, whilst largely rejecting legal moralism, nonetheless do not rule out that there may be some very particular cases where wrongfulness alone could suffice for criminalization. Feinberg acknowledges, for example, that the prevention of some limited non-grievance evils may have weight on the criminalization scales. It is possible that international human rights law may help identify elements of wrongfulness that provide a reason in favour of criminalization for such cases. Feinberg's gladiatorial contest example, as well as his discussion on duelling for instance, contains elements of concepts, such as human dignity and vulnerability, that are employed by the ECtHR as separable reasoning, alongside societal interests and harm and offense. In so far as criminal law theorists, including Feinberg, find themselves needing to construct a number of exceptions to core harm-based theories, international human rights law, through its recognition of a wider range of relevant concepts, and exploration of the interrelations between them, may aid in further defining an approach to those exceptions. A systematic recognition and development of applicable concepts for acts that do not obviously cause harm could strengthen criminalization theory, drawing out and fully defining such cases, rather than minimizing them or developing *ad hoc* solutions. The application of additional concepts, such as human dignity and vulnerability, may also more tightly define why exceptions are made for some non-grievance acts and not others.

Criminalization outcomes

Thirdly, international human rights law may inspire further thought as to how criminalization outcomes themselves are defined. Criminal theory is often characterized in terms of a binary approach that either "allows" or "forbids" criminalization of a particular act. On closer examination, however, Feinberg's scheme, at least, contains gradations of argument. His harm principle, for instance, is never an absolute argument for criminalization but rather a "good reason" in support of penal legislation that applies where there is probably no other means that is equally effective

11 See Feinberg, *Harmless Wrongdoing*, p.33.

at no greater cost to other values.[12] Further, as regards non-grievance evils, Feinberg, in *Harmless Wrongdoing*, holds that the need to prevent evils of any description is at least "some kind of reason," putting at least some amount of weight, however slight, on the decisional scales.[13] Such other considerations are, for Feinberg, considerations that are at most sometimes (but rarely) good reasons, depending on exactly what the non-grievance evil is whose prevention is supposed to support criminalization.[14] Feinberg's framework then is best viewed, as he himself alludes to, as a system of weighing scales. The scales start due to the presumption of liberty, weighted against criminalization, but may tip towards, and sometimes decisively towards, criminalization as a result of different considerations, including the need to prevent wrongful harm, wrongful offense, or a limited number of non-grievance evils. In a similar manner, theorists such as Simester and von Hirsch recognize the need for a "balancing" approach in weighing issues such as the degree of restriction of choice against magnitude and likelihood of harm.[15]

Within international human rights law, ECHR criminalization cases reviewed for this book were classified as finding that an act *should* be, *can* be, or *should not* be a criminal offence. Again, however, this is, in many ways, an oversimplification of the ECtHR's underlying reasoning. It is, of course, the case that a human rights court or tribunal must find a (binary) violation or non-violation of applicable human rights. However, across human rights jurisprudence, as a whole, gradations of criminalization argument within judgments can be discerned in a similar way to Feinberg's scales. Significantly, however, international human rights law introduces the notion that some acts *should* be a criminal offence. Neither Feinberg's theory nor other modern criminalization theories tend to speak to any obligation to criminalize where a state chooses *not* to do so. By contrast, international human rights law brings this perspective through positive human rights obligations. Where criminalization is viewed by international human rights law as necessary for the protection of a specific human right, then, in many respects, this could be considered as significant as when no good reason for criminalization exists. Options for reflecting this perspective in criminalization theory may represent one potential contribution of international human rights law to the field. Specifically interpreting "a very good" reason in support of criminalization on Feinberg's scales as akin to an "obligation" to criminalize, for example, could align criminal theory with international consensus on the need for key criminal offences, such as trafficking in persons and torture.

The role of consensus

International human rights law has the potential to inspire multiple directions of development of criminal theory. One final direction in this regard relates to the

12 Feinberg, *Harm to Others*, p.26.
13 Feinberg, *Harmless Wrongdoing*, p.322.
14 Feinberg, *Harmless Wrongdoing*, p.323.
15 Simester, A.P., and von Hirsch, A., 2011, p.56.

overall aim of criminalization theory. It returns to the classical Devlin-Hart debate and the proper role of legal moralism and community consensus within the criminal law. At its core, Feinberg's theory is concerned with "principled" criminalization: that the moral limits of the criminal law should be defined by a critical morality, and not by the standards and principles of any given society. Whereas international human rights law has a deontological starting point, it is clear from ECHR criminalization cases, through the doctrine of the margin of appreciation, as well as recognition of a national or local community consensus, that international human rights courts nonetheless give significant weight to prevailing thought and standards. Across countries, states are encouraged to align their criminal law with the international consensus. Within countries, in some circumstances, states may legitimately make use of the criminal law to protect or uphold an established consensus, indispensable element of community life, or choice of society. On the other hand, where there are divergent views as to what should, or should not, be a criminal offence, international human rights law allows even greater latitude for criminalization, rather than requiring deeper justification and scrutiny for an offence in respect of which there is no common agreement. In effect, international human rights law recognizes that, in some instances, criminalization *may* be locally driven and legitimately different as between countries and contexts, as opposed to aligned with underlying critical moral principles.

This position is by no means new. MacCormick argues persuasively that the criminal law, in so far as it is concerned with fending off harmful behaviour, is necessarily geared to protection of what are legitimate interests according to a certain dominant political morality.[16] The decisions of the European Court, including on criminalization, represent, in line with the dual nature of law approach, the application of fundamental legal and human rights principles, but derived from a negotiated instrument applied within a complex and changing sociopolitical environment. Whether the perspective of international and local consensus as having weight in criminalization decisions should, or could, be integrated into criminal theory is a complex question. Where the international consensus is that an act should *not* be criminal, as in the ECHR cases of *Bayatyan* (conscientious objection) and *A.D.T.* (same-sex relations), there is perhaps a pragmatic argument that this consensus could add weight to existing primary grounds of reasoning in criminalization theory. Where there is a lack of international consensus, and a resultant wide margin of appreciation in international human rights law, however, it is quite challenging to reconcile the approach of offering greater latitude for criminalization with a commitment to a principle-based criminalization theory. At the national level, the comparative weakness of local community consensus as a ground in support of criminalization means that it may often need to associate with other grounds of reasoning other than harm, such as offense or societal interests, in order to make an argument for criminalization.

16 MacCormick, N., 1984, p.30.

With this in mind, it is perhaps conceivable that a greater role for a notion of community consensus could be considered within the development of criminal theory, at least in restricted circumstances. From the liberal perspective, such a move would of course be open to the criticism that it represents a step towards legal moralism. On the other hand, in the same vein as international human rights law, a relatively defined and controlled concept of community consensus within a multi-factorial or multi-gated criminal theory could offer formal recognition within criminal theory of the role, in practice, of national and international values and principles, and the politically contingent nature of much of criminal legislation.[17]

Summary

Overall, international human rights law can bring significant value to criminalization theory. Whereas international human rights law cannot act, by itself, as a developed criminal theory, it can be used as a touchstone for criminal theory results. This in turn leads to possible routes for further development of criminal theory, inspired by an international human rights law approach. Observations made here include possibilities for the redefinition of the structure of existing claim rights theories based on the vertical individual–state approach of international human rights law; use of the content of and interrelationship between concepts, such as harm, offense, societal interests, and human dignity, from international human rights law jurisprudence within the development of a multi-filter or gated model of criminalization; the engagement of international human rights to identify acts where there is an especially strong argument for or against criminalization; the inclusion of a criminalization obligation into criminal law theory; and the possible integration of international consensus on criminalization and local community consensus into criminalization theory.

These observations are necessarily of a very general nature. As international human rights law jurisprudence on criminalization expands, its potential value to criminal theory will certainly increase. Further characterization of underlying reasoning in criminalization cases will provide greater understanding of the way in which rights can be applied to the criminal law. Testing of criminal theories against the outcomes of international human rights criminalization cases will deepen understanding of where and why difference arise. This, in turn, has the potential to lead to refinement of criminal theories and new options for further evolution of a theory of principled criminal law.

17 See Ashworth, A., 2013. p.40.

10 Conclusion

Decisions and standards on the correctness of criminalization are increasingly globalized. In today's interconnected world, developments in the criminal law of any one individual country are no longer the concern of merely that country. The substantive content of its criminal law has wide implications for the state in areas such as international cooperation in criminal matters through the doctrine of dual criminality, perceptions of that country in the international arena, and its participation in regional and global economic and social systems. A wide range of multilateral treaties impose criminalization obligations. At the regional level, regional organizations such as the European Union exercise extensive criminalization powers through supranational legislation.[1] At the international level, "suppression" conventions such as the United Nations Convention against Transnational Organized Crime, the United Nations Convention against Corruption, and the Single Convention on Narcotic Drugs aim to harmonize the criminal law approach of countries to acts that have transnational implications. In a wider global context, issues of crime and criminalization feature in global commitments to sustainable development, in the form of the United Nations Sustainable Development Goals.[2]

Near the heart of this multilateral system sits international human rights law. Although not intended, in its contemporary form, as a system of general regulation of criminalization, international human rights law nonetheless plays a highly significant role in the international context within which states craft their own national criminal law. In a manner similar to the suppression conventions, international human rights treaties contain a number of direct criminalization obligations. International human rights courts and tribunals have developed extensive jurisprudence on when state obligations in such treaties may require, permit, or prohibit criminalization of certain acts. Academic attention to this body of law is increasing. One recent analysis of *de*criminalization and the United Nations human rights bodies, for example, identified a broad set of 26

1 See Ouwerkerk, J.W., 2017.

2 United Nations, General Assembly, 2015. UN Doc. A/RES/70/1. See also Blaustein, J. *et al.*, 2018.

offence groups in respect of which recommendations had been made by those human rights bodies in the direction of decriminalization.[3] These included many identified in this book, such as abortion, proselytism, blasphemy, apostasy, witchcraft, refusal of military service, defamation, and status offences.

The notion of a global approach to criminalization is not necessarily alien to criminal theory. Criminal theorists have always purported to seek to identify an independent critical moral approach to the criminal law that is applicable, in principle, across a range of national and social contexts. That said, criminal theorists have a strong tendency to draw examples from and test their theories against their own national systems, whether Anglo-American or continental. As a result, influential criminal theories, such as that of Joel Feinberg, have a distinct national essence – in Feinberg's case, from the criminal law of the United States. As the international multilateral system develops, together with its influence on criminal law worldwide, however, a strong argument emerges for examining the impact on and value of international law and standards for criminal theory. This is not limited to justifications for an approach that aims at global harmonization of criminal law. International law, and in particular international human rights law, is as much about defining circumstances when states may legitimately depart from or vary certain standards under proportionate conditions, as it is about defining core equivalent standards, such as criminalization of torture, trafficking in persons, slavery, or genocide. The concepts and reasoning employed by international human rights law in deciding where states have latitude in criminalization therefore influence in practice, both directly and indirectly, the decisions of countries in promulgating national criminal laws. If criminal theory is to remain persuasive in influencing the criminalization policy of states in practice in today's global world, it ignores international human rights law at its peril.

This book represents one of the first truly in-depth characterizations of the place of criminalization within international human rights law. A number of commentators have previously noted and explored key human rights cases that address criminalization. However, the identification and analysis of a sizeable group of criminalization cases from the European Court of Human Rights (ECtHR), in terms of the manner in which criminalization is addressed, the criminalization outcome, and underlying concepts and reasoning employed, enable a novel picture of an emerging international human rights criminalization jurisprudence. This is made possible through the use of a systematic and semi-quantitative approach to characterizing European Convention on Human Rights (ECHR) cases. By classifying grounds of reasoning in ECtHR judgments and presenting broad associations between grounds of reasoning, criminalization outcomes, and the act in question across a large number of cases, the approach aims to account for, to the extent possible, the otherwise highly contextual nature of individual decisions. If further developed, such an approach could

3 Keehn, E.N., 2018.

allow continued analysis of the criminal law boundaries decided by the ECtHR in Europe and elsewhere, revealing whether criminalization trends are generally becoming more permissive or restrictive across a range of acts.

In reviewing human rights jurisprudence and framing the analysis of international human rights law and criminalization, the issue is best viewed from the perspective of state obligations, in line with the position of states as the primary subjects of international law. In a very real sense, the rights of the individual under international human rights law – in particular, the contours of its content and its violability – are described not solely by the effect on the individual himself or herself but by the nature and extent of the corresponding state obligations. State norms of behaviour that delineate the right entail both negative and positive obligations, with the result that international human rights law has a role in both neutralizing and triggering the criminal law, acting as a shield and sword.

In international human rights law jurisprudence, consideration of the criminal law arises not only directly where the existence or absence of criminalization is argued to violate individual rights but also indirectly within a broader discourse on crime and security, the right to security of person, crime investigatory and prosecutorial obligations, and the rights of victims of crime. The general security of person obligation, for example, developed within the Inter-American human rights system, describes a general right to security from crime or interpersonal or social violence, with a corresponding state obligation requiring a legal framework to meet the need to prevent or suppress crime and violence. In practice this is largely a discourse on specific crime types, including violent threats to life, serious assault, kidnapping, rape, and possibly, crimes against property. Similarly, in the European human rights system, the specific crime prevention obligation confirms criminalization requirements in cases such as serious bodily assault, murder, and serious domestic violence. Criminalization requirements in the case of serious human rights violations can also be derived from the general crime investigatory obligation, which describes the duty to have in place an effective machinery for investigating complaints of human rights violations, combined with the duty to ensure that there is a thorough and effective investigation capable of leading to the identification and punishment of those responsible.

An international human rights tribunal, such as the ECtHR, addresses issues of criminalization through these multiple routes. Criminalization results in ECtHR jurisprudence thus derive from all of the European specific crime prevention obligation, direct positive and negative criminalization obligations, and the general crime investigatory obligation. In the most direct instances, an applicant submits that a specific criminal law is incompatible with Convention rights (the negative criminalization obligation) or that the positive obligations of the Convention require that a specific act should be a criminal offence. Conviction cases require careful delineation as to whether a challenge to a criminal conviction is dependent only upon the facts of the particular conviction to hand or represent a wider challenge to the legitimacy of the underlying criminal law. Criminalization outcomes from investigatory and procedural obligation cases are derived from positive obligations to investigate and provide a remedy. These typically derive from cases where an applicant who has been the victim of a particular act claims that the response of the state does not meet its positive obligations under the ECHR.

Being limited to the specific rights contained in international human rights law, it is unlikely that all acts that are, or could be, subject to the criminal law will engage an international human rights court or tribunal. As a result, ECHR criminalization cases cluster around a number of act groups, such as acts leading to harm to the person, injurious acts of a sexual nature, or acts against public order. These acts are most often examined under Articles 8 (Right to respect for private and family life) and 10 (Freedom of expression) of the ECHR. The broad picture which emerges from this jurisprudence is one of general permissiveness towards criminalization by international human rights law. In only around 15 per cent of cases reviewed does the ECtHR suggest that an act should *not* be a criminal offence. Comparison of criminalization outcomes from the ECtHR with findings of United Nations human rights treaty bodies shows reasonable alignment, albeit with some differences that arise from the different procedural and structural frameworks of the two human rights systems within which criminalization issues come to be considered.

The broad permissiveness of international human rights law towards criminalization is due, in part, to the operation of the margin of appreciation doctrine that allows latitude to states in some circumstances. It is also due, however, to the fact that the European Court accepts a range of concepts and reasoning as weighing in favour of criminalization, rather than being restricted to a single primary "gateway" to criminalization. These include concepts of harm, offense, and the protection of individual autonomy that are well known to liberal criminal theory. They also include, however, reasoning based on broader considerations, including societal interests, community consensus, human dignity, vulnerability, and the protection of pluralism. Criminalization outcomes reached by the ECtHR are typically based on a number of these concepts, all of which are found in varying combinations in a multi-factorial analysis. In any one case, some concepts reinforce each other, whilst others work on opposing sides of criminalization arguments. In line with a broadly liberal theory of interpretation, the Court places value on the protection of individual autonomy, including in the face of possible paternalistic arguments. It is often prepared to defer, however, to arguments that criminal law is required for the protection of societal interests in health, safety, and security. In some cases, these extend to community conceptions of morality or commonly accepted behaviour, although a public element to the act is usually inherent to such cases. Whilst the Court does not rely overtly on paternalistic reasoning, a number of cases suggest a strong influence in the ECtHR's criminalization reasoning of the related ground of vulnerability. Human dignity, in addition, represents a complex ground of reasoning that is invoked by the ECtHR in respect of acts which may humiliate, debase, or objectify an individual. Where the Court finds that human dignity and a risk of serious harm, in the broad sense of detrimental effects, are at stake, this represents a particularly strong argument for criminalization and can lead the Court to find that the act *should be* a criminal offence.

Whereas all criminal theorists will instantly recognize the names of concepts employed by the ECtHR in criminalization cases, many will find that the content of these concepts differ from the sense of existing criminal theories. Autonomy, for instance, is the starting point of many criminalization schemes, including that of Joel Feinberg. It is used in identifying a setback of interests for the purposes of Feinberg's wrongful harm and in weighing the necessity of criminalization under the harm principle mediating maxims. By contrast, in international human rights law, autonomy is a principle underlying the right to respect for private and family life and the prohibition of slavery and forced labour. It is invoked usually only where notions of identity and choice of self-determination are at stake. Such variations in understandings of autonomy contribute to differing conclusions in the case of criminalization of assisted suicide and consented-to harm, as between Feinberg and the ECtHR. Similar variations exist as regards understandings of harm, offense, and the role of societal interests in criminalization decisions. In respect of harm, in particular, the ECtHR employs a more general understanding of the term, as opposed to Feinberg's technical construct of a wrongful setback of interests.

Many of these variations, as well as other structural differences between an international human rights law approach to criminalization and liberal criminal theory, can be attributed to the use of horizontal claim rights by criminal theorists, as opposed to a vertical individual–state conception of rights under international human rights law. The vertical conception of rights enables the human rights court or tribunal to take into account a large number of other concepts, such as societal interests and community consensus, that are not so easily recognized by criminalization theories that focus on experiential violation of individual horizontal rights. This difference in the structure of rights also impacts on the importance given to consent within each criminalization scheme. Criminalization theories that rely on horizontal claim rights typically hold that such rights cannot be violated where a person consents to an infringement. By contrast, in international human rights law, a (vertical) rights violation may still arise, even in the presence of consent to the act. Such differences make it clear that criminalization cases in international human rights jurisprudence do not merely reframe existing liberal criminal theory through a human rights lens. Rather, international human rights courts and tribunals adopt their own unique approach.

The analysis of international human rights law reasoning and criminalization outcomes provides strong material that is of value for existing criminal theory – in particular in light of the influence of multilateralism and international human rights law on national laws. Once the objection of the contextual nature of international human rights court and tribunal decisions is removed, as far as possible through aggregate analysis, however, other considerations that may trouble liberal criminal theorists come to light. Even in respect of perhaps the most core offence, the killing of one individual by another, criticism arises regarding coercive overreach and the coherence of ECtHR jurisprudence on requirements for criminalization under ECHR Article 2 (Right to life).[4] Perhaps most significantly, differences between criminalization results from criminal theory and international human rights law often derive from the acceptance by international human rights law of notions such as protection of morals, community consensus, vulnerability, and more nebulous concepts such as human dignity – notions that criminal theorists such as Feinberg generally do not find as good reasons in support of criminalization. Even given that international human rights law influences the direction of national criminal law with reference to such principles, should this be a reason to retest or rethink liberal criminal theories that generally reject such ideas? The inclusion of "morals" as a ground in many restriction clauses of international human rights treaties reflects the reality that, at their core, human rights treaties codify foundational moral and ethical commitments of states. Human rights derive their power, in part, from their resonance with local histories, traditions, and values. In so far as international human rights law recognizes genuinely foundational values – what some commentators refer to as an "intertextual morality" – as relevant to criminalization decisions, there is an argument that this should also be a valid consideration in criminal theory.[5] Indeed, *if* international human rights law is able to distinguish, using a multi-factorial weighing approach, between "moral" views that are merely – in Hart's words – what make the "man on the Clapham omnibus sick" and a genuine interest in the protection of community interests, vulnerability, or human dignity, then this may add value to a developed criminal theory. Such considerations are, in practice, relevant to modern criminalization dilemmas, such as those involving end of life or cross-cultural considerations. Critical issues such as artificial intelligence and climate change will also likely shortly demand appropriately justified criminal law provisions. Although frequently challenging to define and apply in practice, such concepts should not be shied away from in a criminal theory that is fit for purpose in today's world.

As recognized by a number of contemporary criminal theorists, single gateway theories such as those of Feinberg may not in practice fare as well as multi-gated or filter theories that start with criminalization principles but recognize also normative and pragmatic limiting factors. Continental theories, such as *Rechtsguttheorie*, similarly offer a higher degree of flexibility in terms of relevant criminalization considerations. International human rights law itself, due not least to its limitation in the range of acts that engage internationally recognized rights, cannot, and should not, act as a replacement framework for criminal theory. Nonetheless, as this book shows, it could inspire the further development of criminal theory, in particular where theories follow a multi-gated approach and are able to take into account multiple relevant considerations in favour of, or against, criminalization. Insofar as not

4 Mavronicola, N., 2017.
5 See, for example, Thoreson, R., 2018.

all acts that could be criminalized likely engage human rights provisions, international human rights law could perhaps operate as one "gate" that identifies acts where special consideration is needed due to the particular implications of criminalization for human rights. Many possibilities exist, including, as above, further reflection in criminal theory of concepts such as community consensus, vulnerability, and human dignity, based on notions and balances found in international human rights law jurisprudence. In particular, where rights are already employed in existing criminal theory, consideration may be given to a vertical state–individual structure for such rights that allows the right to be more effectively balanced against wider societal considerations.

Overall, this work will have achieved its intended function if it has succeeded in highlighting the importance of international human rights law to matters of criminalization and is able to inspire further cross-disciplinary study. As recognized by some of the founding documents of contemporary international human rights law, a broad theory of governance, use of law and the social contract, has particular power in defining the proper nature and extent of the exercise of state power. As international human rights lawyers, moral legal philosophers, practical criminal lawyers, and legal theorists become increasingly specialized, and their respective fields expand, there is a danger that work becomes progressively isolated. By contrast, research at the interface of each offers invaluable opportunities for deepening our understanding and developing governance systems that genuinely fulfil the requirements of fairness and justice.

References

Books and book chapters

Addo, M.K., 2010. *The Legal Nature of International Human Rights.* Leiden and Boston: Martinus Nijhoff Publishers.

Alldridge, P., and Brants, C., 2001. *Personal Autonomy, the Private Sphere and Criminal Law: A Comparative Study.* Oxford: Hart Publishing.

Ashworth, A., 2013. *Positive Obligations in Criminal Law.* Oxford: Hart Publishing.

Ashworth, A., and Horder, J., 2013. *Principles of Criminal Law* (7th ed). Oxford: Oxford University Press.

Baker, D.J., 2011. *The Right Not to Be Criminalized: Demarcating Criminal Law's Authority.* Abingdon and New York: Routledge.

Barrett, D., and Nowak, M., 2009. The United Nations and Drug Policy: Towards a Human Rights-Based Approach. In: Constantinides, A., Zaikos, N. (eds.), *The Diversity of International Law: Essays in Honour of Professor Kalliopi K. Koufa.* Leiden: Brill/Martinus Nijhoff.

Bossuyt, M.J., 1987. *Guide to the "Travaux Préparatoires" of the International Covenant on Civil and Political Rights.* Dordrecht, Boston and Lancaster: Martinus Nijhoff Publishers.

Cassese, A., 2005. *International Law* (2nd ed). Oxford: Oxford University Press.

Coliver, S. (ed.), 1992. *Striking a Balance: Hate Speech, Freedom of Expression and Non-Discrimination.* London: Article 19.

Daes, E.-I., 1990. *Freedom of the Individual under Law: An Analysis of Article 29 of the Universal Declaration of Human Rights.* New York: United Nations.

Duff, R.A., 2007. *Answering for Crime.* Oxford: Hart.

Du Hert, P., Gutwirth, S., Snacken, S., and Dumortier, E., 2007. La Montée de l'Etat Penal: Que Peuvent les Droits de l'Homme? In: Cartuyvels, Y., Dumont, H., Ost, Fr., Van de Kerchove, M., and Van drooghencroeck, S. (eds.), *Les Droits de l'Homme: Bouclier ou Épée du Droit Penal?* Bruxelles: FUSL/Bruylant.

Elias, R., 1991. Crime Control as Human Rights Enforcement. In: Pepinsky, H., Quinney, R. (eds.), *Criminology as Peacemaking.* Bloomington: Indiana University Press.

Feinberg, J., 1984. *The Moral Limits of the Criminal Law, Harm to Others.* Oxford: Oxford University Press.

Feinberg, J., 1985. *The Moral Limits of the Criminal Law, Offense to Others.* Oxford: Oxford University Press.

Feinberg, J., 1986. *The Moral Limits of the Criminal Law, Harm to Self.* Oxford: Oxford University Press.

Feinberg, J., 1988. *The Moral Limits of the Criminal Law, Harmless Wrongdoing.* Oxford: Oxford University Press.

Gardner, J., 1998. On the General Part of the Criminal Law. In: Duff, R.A. (ed.), *Philosophy and the Criminal Law*. Cambridge: Cambridge University Press.

Gewirth, A., 1978. *Reason and Morality.* Chicago: University of Chicago Press.

Gewirth, A., 1982. *Human Rights: Essays on Justification and Applications.* Chicago: University of Chicago Press.

Gewirth, A., 1996. *The Community of Rights.* Chicago: Chicago University Press.

Griffin, J., 2008. *On Human Rights.* Oxford: Oxford University Press.

Hassemer, W., 2014. The Harm Principle and the Protection of "Legal Goods" (*Rechtsgüterschutz*): A German Perspective. In: Simester, A.P., du Bois-Pedain, A. (eds.), *Liberal Criminal Theory. Essays for Andreas von Hirsch.* Oxford and Portland, Oregon: Hart Publishing, pp. 197–199.

Hefendehl, R., von Hirsch, A., and Wohlers, W. (eds), 2003. *Die Rechtsguttheorie: Legitimiationsbasis des Strafrechts oder dogmatisches Glasperlenspiel*? Baden-Baden: Nomos.

Hörnle, T., 2014. "Rights of Others" in Criminalisation Theory. In: Simester, A.P., du Bois-Pedain, A. (eds.), *Liberal Criminal Theory. Essays for Andreas Von Hirsch.* Oxford and Portland, Oregon: Hart Publishing.

Husak, D., 2007. *Overcriminalization. The Limits of the Criminal Law*. Oxford: Oxford University Press.

International Council on Human Rights Policy, 2003. *Crime, Public Order and Human Rights.* Versoix, Switzerland: ICHRP.

International Council on Human Rights Policy, 2010. *Modes and Patterns of Social Control. Implications for Human Rights Policy.* Geneva: ICHRP.

International Press Institute, 2015. *Out of Balance: Defamation Law in the European Union*. Vienna: IPI.

Jescheck, H.H., and Weigand, T., 1996. *Lehrbuch des Strafrechts – Allgemeiner Teil* (5th ed). Berlin: Duncker & Humblot.

Lauterwein, C.C., 2016. *The Limits of Criminal Law: A Comparative Analysis of Approaches to Legal Theorizing.* New York: Routledge.

Lazarus, L., 2012. Positive Obligations and Criminal Justice: Duties to Protect or Coerce? In: Zedner, L., Roberts, J.V. (eds.), *Principles and Values in Criminal Law and Criminal Justice: Essays in Honour of Andrew Ashworth.* Oxford: Oxford University Press.

Legg, A., 2012. *The Margin of Appreciation in International Human Rights Law.* Oxford: Oxford University Press.

Letsas, G. 2007. *A Theory of Interpretation of the European Convention on Human Rights.* Oxford: Oxford University Press.

Locke, J., 1980. *Second Treatise of Government.* Indianapolis: Hackett (originally published 1690).

MacCormick, N., 1984. *Legal Right and Social Democracy: Essays in Legal and Political Philosophy.* Oxford: Oxford University Press.

Mégret, F., 2018. Nature of Obligations. In: Moeckli, D., Shah, S., and Sivakumaran, S. (eds.), *International Human Rights Law*. Oxford: Oxford University Press.

Mégret, F., and Calderón, J.-P.S., 2015. The Move Towards a Victim-Centred Concept of Criminal Law and the Criminalisation of Inter-American Human Rights Law. In: Haeck, Y., Ruiz-Chiriboga, O., and Burbano Herrera, C. (eds.), *The Inter-American Court of Human Rights: Theory and Practice, Present and Future.* Mortsel: Intersentia.

Mill, J.S., 1974. *On Liberty.* Harmondsworth: Penguin (originally published 1859).

Moore, M., 1997. *Placing Blame.* Oxford: Oxford University Press.

Oppenheim, L., 1905. *International Law: A Treatise.* Volume I (Peace), (1st ed).

Organization of American States, Inter-American Commission on Human Rights, 2009. *Report on Citizen Security and Human Rights.* OEA/Ser.L/V/II. Doc. 57. Washington: OEA.

Powell, R.L. 2008. *Security and the Right to Security of Person.* DPhil Thesis. Oxford: University of Oxford.

Rawls, J., 1971. *A Theory of Justice.* Cambridge, MA: Belknap.

Renzo, M., 2013. Responsibility and Answerability in the Criminal Law. In: Duff, R. A., Farmer, L., Marshall, S.E., Renzo, M., and Tadros, V. (eds), 2014. *The Constitution of the Criminal Law.* Oxford: Oxford University Press.

Roxin, C., 1998. *Strafverfahrensrecht* (25th ed). Munich: C.H. Beck.

Roxin, C., 2006. *Strafrecht Allgemeiner Teil Band I: Grundlagen. Der Aufbau der Verbrechenslehre* (4th ed). Munich: C.H. Beck.

Seibert-Fohr, A., 2009. *Prosecuting Serious Human Rights Violations.* Oxford: Oxford University Press.

Simester, A.P., 2012. Enforcing Morality. In: Marmor, A. (ed.), *The Routledge Companion to Philosophy of Law.* New York: Routledge.

Simester, A.P., and Shute, S., 2002. *Criminal Law Theory, Doctrines of the General Part.* Oxford: Oxford University Press.

Simester, A.P., and von Hirsch, A., 2011. *Crimes, Harms and Wrongs: On the Principles of Criminalisation.* Oxford: Hart Publishing.

Temperman, J., 2015. *Religious Hatred and International Law: The Prohibition of Incitement to Violence or Discrimination.* Cambridge: Cambridge University Press.

United Nations Office on Drugs and Crime, 2012. *Manual on Mutual Legal Assistance and Extradition.* New York: United Nations.

Vermeulen, G. 2009. *EULOCS. The EU Level Offence Classification System.* Antwerpen: Maklu.

Von Hirsch, A., 1993. *Censure and Sanctions.* Oxford: Oxford University Press.

Wohlers, W., 2014. Criminal Liability for Offensive Behaviour in Public Spaces. In: Simester, A.P., du Bois-Pedain, A. (eds.), *Liberal Criminal Theory. Essays for Andreas Von Hirsch.* Oxford and Portland, Oregon: Hart Publishing.

Journal articles

Addo, M.K., 1997. Does Hohfeld Still Matter? *Bracton Law Journal* 29, 7–12.

Alexander, L., 1994. Harm, Offense and Morality. *Canadian Journal of Law and Jurisprudence* 7(2), 199–216.

Alexy, R., 2010. The Dual Nature of Law. *Ratio Juris* 23(2), 167–182.

Ambos, K., 2007. Towards a Universal System of Crime: Comments on George Fletcher's Grammar of Criminal Law. *Cardozo Law Review* 28, 2647–2673.

Ambos, K., 2013. Punishment without a Sovereign? The *Ius Puniendi* Issue of International Criminal Laws: A First Contribution towards a Consistent Theory of International Criminal Law. *Oxford Journal of Legal Studies* 33(2),293–315.

Ambos, K., 2015. The Overall Function of International Criminal Law: Striking the Right Balance between the *Rechtsgut* and the Harm Principles. *Criminal Law and Philosophy* 9, 301–329.

Ambos, K. 2017. Review Essay: Liberal Criminal Theory. *Criminal Law Forum* 28, 589–628.

Baker, D.J., 2007. The Moral Limits of Criminalizing Remote Harms. *New Criminal Law Review* 10, 370–391.

Baker, D.J., 2009. A Critical Evaluation of the Historical and Contemporary Justifications for Criminalising Begging. *The Journal of Criminal Law* 73, 212–240.

Bendor, A.L., and Dancig-Rosenberg, H., 2016. Unconstitutional Criminalization. *New Criminal Law Review* 19(2), 171–207.

Bassioni, M.C., 1982. The Proscribing Function of International Criminal Law in the Processes of International Protection of Human Rights. *Yale Journal of World Public Order* 9, 193–214.

Bassiouni, M.C., and Badr, G.M., 2002. The Shari'ah: Sources, Interpretation and Rule-Making. *UCLA Journal of Islamic and Near Eastern Law* 1, 135–181.

Bengoetxea, J., and Jung, H., 1991. Towards a European Criminal Jurisprudence? The Justification of Criminal Law by the Strasbourg Court. *Legal Studies* 11(3), 239–280.

Blau, J., and Moncada, A., 2007. It Ought to Be a Crime: Criminalizing Human Rights Violations. *Sociological Forum* 22(3),364–371.

Blaustein, J., Pino, N.W., Fitz-Gibbon, K., and White, R., 2018. Criminology and the UN Sustainable Development Goals: The Need for Support and Critique. *British Journal of Criminology* 58, 767–786.

Boister, N., 2002. Human Rights Protections in the Suppression Conventions. *Human Rights Law Review* 2(2), 199–227.

Boister, N., 2003. Transnational Criminal Law? *European Journal of International Law* 14(5), 953–976.

Chwaszcza, C., 2010. The Concept of Rights in Contemporary Human Rights Discourse. *Ratio Juris* 23(3), 333–364.

Craven, M., 2000. Legal Differentiation and the Concept of the Human Rights Treaty in International Law. *European Journal of International Law* 11(3), 489–519.

Demenchonok, E., 2009. The Universal Concept of Human Rights as a Regulative Principle: Freedom versus Paternalism. *The American Journal of Economics and Sociology* 68(1), 273–301.

Donnelly, J., 1982. Human Rights and Human Dignity: An Analytic Critique of Non-Western Conceptions of Human Rights. *The American Political Science Review* 76(2), 303–316.

Donnelly, J., 2007. The Relative Universality of Human Rights. *Human Rights Quarterly* 29, 281–306.

Du Bois-Pedain, A., 2014. The Wrongfulness Constraint in Criminalization. *Criminal Law and Philosophy* 8(1), 149–169.

Dubber, M.D., 2005. Theories of Crime and Punishment in German Criminal Law. *The American Journal of Comparative Law* 53, 679–708.

Duff, R.A., 2010. Towards a Theory of Criminal Law? *Proceedings of the Aristotelian Society Supplementary Volume LXXXIV*, 1–28.

Duff, R.A., 2014. Towards a Modest Legal Moralism. *Criminal Law and Philosophy* 8, 217–235.

Edwards, J.R., and Simester, A.P., 2014. Wrongfulness and Prohibitions. *Criminal Law and Philosophy* 8, 171–186.

Fletcher, G.P., 1985. The Right and the Reasonable. *Harvard Law Review* 98, 949–982.

Freeman, M., 1994, The Philosophical Foundations of Human Rights. *Human Rights Quarterly* 16, 491–514.

Guinchard, A., 2005. Fixing the Boundaries of the Concept of Crime: The Challenge for Human Rights. *International and Comparative Law Quarterly* 54, 719–734.

Guzman, A.T., and Meyer, T.L., 2010. International Soft Law. *Journal of Legal Analysis* 2, 171–225.

Hannum, H., 1996. The Status of the Universal Declaration of Human Rights in National and International Law. *Georgia Journal of International and Comparative Law* 25, 287–397.

Higgins, R., 1992. The Relationship between International and Regional Human Rights Norms and Domestic Law. *Commonwealth Law Bulletin* 18(4),1268–1275.

Hohfeld, W., 1913. Some Fundamental Legal Conceptions as Applied in Judicial Reasoning. *Yale Law Journal* 23(1),16–59.

Hohfeld, W., 1917. Fundamental Legal Conceptions as Applied in Judicial Reasoning. *Yale Law Journal* 26(8), 710–770.

Hörnle, T., 2016. Theories of Criminalization. Comments on A.P. Simester/Andreas Von Hirsch: Crimes, Harms and Wrongs. On the Principles of Criminalisation. *Criminal Law and Philosophy* 10, 301–314.

Huneeus, A., and Madsen, M.R., 2018. Between Universalism and Regional Law and Politics: A Comparative History of the American, European and African Human Rights Systems. *International Journal of Constitutional Law* 16, 136–160.

Kedian, M.K., 1999. Customary International Law and International Human Rights Litigation in United States Courts: Revitalizing the Legacy of the Paquete Habana. *William & Mary Law Review* 40(4),1395–1425.

Klein, S.R., 1999. Redrawing the Criminal-Civil Boundary. *Buffalo Criminal Law Review* 2, 681–723.

Lacey, N., 2009. Historicising Criminalisation: Conceptual and Empirical Issues. *Modern Law Review* 72(6), 936–960.

Lagodny, O., 1999. The Case of Substantive Criminal Law before the Bars of Constitutional Law – An Overview from the Perspective of the German Legal Order. *European Journal of Crime, Criminal Law and Criminal Justice*, 7(3), 277–288.

Langley, E.E., and Nardi, Jr., D.J., 2010. The Irony of Outlawing AIDS: A Human Rights Argument against the Criminalization of HIV Transmission. *The Georgetown Journal of Gender and the Law* 11, 743–794.

López-Rey, M., 1978. Crime and Human Rights. *Federal Probation* 42, 10–15.

Ludwikowski, R.R., 1990. The French Declaration of the Rights of Man and Citizen and the American Constitutional Development. *American Journal of Comparative Law Supplement* 38, 445–462.

Marks, S.P., 1998. From the "Single Confused Page" to the "Decalogue for Six Billion Persons": The Roots of the Universal Declaration of Human Rights in the French Revolution. *Human Rights Quarterly* 20, 459–514.

Matravers, M., 2016. Symposium on Andrew Simester and Andreas von Hirsch, Crimes, Harms and Wrongs: On the Principles of Criminalisation. *Criminal Law and Philosophy*, 10(2), 297–394.

Mavronicola, N., 2017. Taking Life and Liberty Seriously: Reconsidering Criminal Liability under Article 2 of the ECHR. *Modern Law Review*, 80(6), 1026–1051.
McCrudden, C., 2008. Human Dignity and Judicial Interpretation of Human Rights. *European Journal of International Law* 19(4), 655–724.
Nieuwhenhuis, A., 2007. The Concept of Pluralism in the Case-Law of the European Court of Human Rights. *European Constitutional Law Review* 3, 367–384.
O'Flaherty, M., 2006. The Concluding Observations of United Nations Human Rights Treaty Bodies. *Human Rights Law Review* 6(1), 27–52.
O'Flaherty, M., and Higgins, N. 2015. International Human Rights Law and "Criminalization". *Japanese Yearbook of International Law* 58, 45–70.
Ouwerkerk, J.W., 2017. Criminalization Powers of the European Union and the Risks of Cherry-Picking between Various Legal Bases: The Case for a Single Legal Framework for EU-Level Criminalization. *Columbia Journal of European Law* 23, 503–550.
Orakhelashvili, A., 2001. The Position of the Individual in International Law. *California Western International Law Journal* 31(2), 241–276.
Radbruch, G., 1946. Gesetzliches Unrecht und Übergesetzliches Recht (Statutory Lawlessness and Supra-Statutory Law). *Süddeutsche Juristenzeitung* 1, 105–108.
Rawls, J., 1980. Kantian Constructivism in Moral Theory. *The Journal of Philosophy* 77(9), 515–572
Richards, D.A.J., 1979a. Commercial Sex and the Rights of the Person: A Moral Argument for the Decriminalization of Prostitution. *University of Pennsylvania Law Review* 127(5), 1195–1287.
Richards, D.A.J., 1979b. Human Rights and the Moral Foundations of the Substantive Criminal Law. *Georgia Law Review* 13, 1395–1446.
Richards, D.A.J., 1981a. Drug Use and the Rights of the Person: A Moral Argument for Decriminalization of Certain Forms of Drug Use. *Rutgers Law Review* 33, 607–686.
Richards, D.A.J., 1981b. Rights, Utility and Crime. *Crime and Justice* 3, 247–294.
Schonscheck, J., 1994. *On Criminalization: An Essay in the Philosophy of the Criminal Law*. Dordrecht: Kluwer.
Simester, A.P., and von Hirsch, A., 2002. Rethinking the Offense Principle. *Legal Theory* 8, 269–295.
Simester, A.P., and von Hirsch, A., 2011. On the Legitimate Objectives of Criminalisation. *Criminal Law and Philosophy*, 367–379.
Snodgrass-Godoy, A. 2005. *La Muchacha Respondona*: Reflections on the Razor's Edge between Crime and Human Rights. *Human Rights Quarterly* 27, 597–624.
Stevens, A., 2001. Drug Policy, Harm and Human Rights: A Rationalist Approach. *International Journal of Drug Policy* 22, 233–238.
Stewart, H., 2001. Harms, Wrongs, and Set-Backs in Feinberg's Moral Limits of the Criminal Law. *Buffalo Criminal Law Review* 5, 47–67.
Sunstein, C.R., 1996. The Expressive Function of Law. *University of Pennsylvania Law Review* 144, 2021–2053.
Thoreson, R., 2018. The Limits of Moral Limitations: Reconceptualizing Morals in Human Rights Law. *Harvard International Law Journal* 59, 197–244.
Tulkens, F., 2011. The Paradoxical Relationship between Criminal Law and Human Rights. *Journal of International Criminal Justice* 9, 577–595.
Von Hirsch, A., 2014. Harm and Wrongdoing in Criminalisation Theory. *Criminal Law and Philosophy* 8, 245–256.
Williams, G., 1955. The Definition of Crime. *Current Legal Problems* 8, 107–130.

Online resources

Council of Europe, Undated. The Margin of Appreciation. Available from: www.coe.int/t/dghl/cooperation/lisbonnetwork/themis/echr/paper2_en.asp [Accessed 1 April 2019].

Crown Prosecution Service, Undated. Offences against the Person, Incorporating the Charging Standard. Available from: www.cps.gov.uk/legal-guidance/offences-against-person-incorporating-charging-standard [Accessed 1 April 2019].

European Commission, 2006. Commission Decision Setting up a Group of Experts on the Policy Needs for Data on Crime and Criminal Justice (7 August 2006). Available from: https://eur-lex.europa.eu/LexUriServ/LexUriServ.do?uri=OJ:L:2006:234:0029:0032:EN:PDF [Accessed 1 April 2019].

International Commission of Jurists, 1997. Maastricht Guidelines on Violations of Economic, Social and Cultural Rights. Available from: http://hrlibrary.umn.edu/instree/Maastrichtguidelines_html [Accessed 1 April 2019].

Keehn, E.N., 2018. Decriminalization and the U.N. Human Rights Bodies. Research Working Paper Series HRP 18-002. Available from: http://hrp.law.harvard.edu/wp-content/uploads/2018/03/Emily-Keehn_HRP-18_002.pdf [Accessed 1 April 2019].

Oxford Human Rights Hub, 2015. A Duty to Prosecute Hate Speech under the European Convention on Human Rights? Available from: http://ohrh.law.ox.ac.uk/a-duty-to-prosecute-hate-speech-under-the-european-convention-on-human-rights/ [Accessed 1 April 2019].

United Nations, 2004. UN Convention on the Rights of People with Disabilities, Third Session of the Ad Hoc Committee, Daily Summary of Discussions Related to Article 12. Available from: www.un.org/esa/socdev/enable/rights/ahc3sum12.htm [Accessed 1 April 2019].

United Nations Office on Drugs and Crime, 2015. International Classification of Crime for Statistical Purposes. Available from: www.unodc.org/documents/data-and-analysis/statistics/crime/ICCS/ICCS_English_2016_web.pdf [Accessed 1 April 2019].

United Nations Treaty Collection, 2019. Chapter IV: Human Rights, 2. International Convention on the Elimination of All Forms of Racial Discrimination. Available from: https://treaties.un.org/Pages/ViewDetails.aspx?src=IND&mtdsg_no=IV-2&chapter=4&clang=_en [Accessed 1 April 2019].

United Nations documents

United Nations, 1948. The Universal Declaration of Human Rights (UDHR). General Assembly resolution 217A (10 December 1948). UN Doc. A/810, 71.

United Nations, 1976. Report on the Fifth United Nations Congress on the Prevention of Crime and the Treatment of Offenders (1-12 September 1975). UN Doc. A/CONF.56/10.

United Nations, 2008. International Human Rights Instruments Volume I (27 May 2008). UN Doc. HRI/GEN/1/Rev.9 (Vol. I).

United Nations, Ad Hoc Committee on a Comprehensive and Integral International Convention on Protection and Promotion of the Rights and Dignity of Persons with Disabilities, 2003. Compilation of proposals for a Comprehensive and Integral International Convention to Promote and Protect the Rights and

Dignity of Persons with Disabilities (16 June 2003). UN Doc. A/AC.265/2003/CRP/13.

United Nations, Commission on Narcotic Drugs and Commission on Crime Prevention and Criminal Justice, 2010. Drug control, crime prevention and criminal justice: A Human Rights Perspective (3 March 2010). UN Doc. E/CN.7/2010/CRP.6–E/CN.15/2010/CRP.1.

United Nations, Committee against Torture, 2010. Concluding Observations on the Second Periodic Report of the Republic of Moldova (29 March 2010). UN Doc. CAT/C/MDA/CO/2.

United Nations, Committee against Torture, 2011a. Concluding Observations on the Third Periodic Report of Mauritius (15 June 2011). UN Doc. CAT/C/MUS/CO/3.

United Nations, Committee against Torture, 2011b. Concluding Observations on the Second Periodic Report of Kuwait (28 June 2011). UN Doc. CAT/C/KWT/CO/2.

United Nations, Committee against Torture, 2011c. Concluding Observations on the Fourth to Sixth Periodic Reports of Paraguay (14 December 2011). UN Doc. CAT/C/PRY/CO/4-6.

United Nations, Committee on Economic, Social and Cultural Rights, 2005. Concluding Observations on the Initial Report of the People's Republic of China (including Hong Kong and Macao) (13 May 2009). UN Doc. E/C.12/1/Add.107.

United Nations, Committee on Economic, Social and Cultural Rights, 2011. Concluding Observations on the Fifth Periodic Report of Germany (20 May 2011). UN Doc. E/C.12/DEU/CO/5.

United Nations, Committee on Economic, Social and Cultural Rights, 2012. Concluding Observations on the Second to Fourth Periodic Reports of Peru (30 May 2012). UN Doc. E/C.12/PER/CO/2-4.

United Nations, Committee on Enforced Disappearances, 2014. Concluding Observations on the Report Submitted by Belgium under Article 29, Paragraph 1, of the Convention (15 October 2014). UN Doc. CED/C/BEL/CO/1.

United Nations, Committee on the Elimination of Discrimination against Women, 2002. Report of the Committee on the Elimination of Discrimination against Women (2 May 2002). UN Doc. A/57/38 (SUPP).

United Nations, Committee on the Elimination of Racial Discrimination, 2005. Concluding Observations on the Tenth, Eleventh, Twelfth and Thirteenth Period Reports of Luxembourg (18 April 2005). UN Doc. CERD/C/LUX/CO/13.

United Nations, Committee on the Elimination of Racial Discrimination, 2009. Concluding Observations on the Consolidated Seventeenth to Nineteenth Reports of Poland (14 September 2009). UN Doc. CERD/C/POL/CO/19.

United Nations, Committee on the Elimination of Racial Discrimination, 2013. General Comment 35. Combating Racist Hate Speech (26 September 2013). UN Doc. CERD/C/GC/35.

United Nations, Committee on the Elimination of Racial Discrimination, 2014. Concluding Observations on the Nineteenth to Twenty-First Periodic Reports of Cameroon (26 September 2014). UN Doc. CERD/C/CMR/CO/19-21.

United Nations, Committee on the Elimination of Racial Discrimination, 2015. Concluding Observations on the Fourteenth and Fifteenth Periodic Reports of Guatemala (11 May 2015). UN Doc CERD/C/GTM/CO/14-15.

United Nations, Committee on the Rights of the Child, 1993. Report Adopted by the Committee at Its 74th Meeting (5 March 1993). UN Doc. CRC/C/16.
United Nations, Committee on the Rights of the Child, 2007. Concluding Observations on the Initial Report of Costa Rica under Article 12 (1) of the Optional Protocol to the Convention on the Rights of the Child on the Sale of Children, Child Prostitution and Child Pornography (2 February 2007). UN Doc. CRC/C/OPSC/CRI/CO/1.
United Nations, Committee on the Rights of the Child, 2009. Concluding Observations on the Second Periodic Report of the Democratic Republic of Congo (10 February 2009). UN Doc. CRC/C/COD/CO/2.
United Nations, Committee on the Rights of the Child, 2010a. Concluding Observations on the Third and Fourth Periodic Reports of Nigeria (21 June 2010). UN Doc. CRC/C/NGA/CO/3-4.
United Nations, Committee on the Rights of the Child, 2010b. Concluding Observations on the Initial Report of Sierra Leone Submitted Article 8 of the Optional Protocol to the Convention on the Rights of the Child on the Involvement of Children in Armed Conflict (14 October 2010). UN Doc. CRC/C/OPAC/SLE/CO/1.
United Nations, Committee on the Rights of the Child, 2011. Concluding Observations on the Initial Report of Belarus Submitted Article 8 of the Optional Protocol to the Convention on the Rights of the Child on the Involvement of Children in Armed Conflict (28 April 2011). UN Doc. CRC/C/OPAC/BLR/CO/1.
United Nations, Commission on Human Rights, 1993. Note by the Secretariat, Rights of the Child (20 December 1993). UN Doc. E/CN.4/1994/91.
United Nations, Commission on Human Rights, 1994a. Report of the Second International Workshop on National Institutions for the Promotion and Protection of Human Rights (1 March 1994). UN Doc. E/CN.4/1994/45/Add.1.
United Nations, Commission on Human Rights, 1994c. Report of the Secretary-General, Comments on the Preliminary Draft Optional Protocol to the Convention on the Rights of the Child on Involvement of Children in Armed Conflicts (21 June 1994). UN Doc. E/CN.4/1994/WG.13/2.
United Nations, Commission on Human Rights, 1994d. Report of the Secretary-General, Comments on the Preliminary Draft Optional Protocol [To the Convention on the Rights of the Child on Involvement of Children in Armed Conflicts] (14 September 1994). UN Doc. E/CN.4/1994/WG.13/2/Add.1.
United Nations, Commission on Human Rights, 1996. Report of the Working Group on Its Second Session, Question of a Draft Optional Protocol to the Convention on the Rights of the Child on the Sale of Children, Child Prostitution and Child Pornography, as Well as Basic Measures Needed for Their Eradication (25 March 1996). UN Doc. E/CN.4/1996/101.
United Nations, Commission on Human Rights, 1998a. Report of the Working Group on Its Fourth Session, Question of a Draft Optional Protocol to the Convention on the Rights of the Child on the Sale of Children, Child Prostitution and Child Pornography, as Well as the Basic Measures Needed for Their Eradication (24 March 1998). UN Doc. E/CN.4/1998/103.
United Nations, Commission on Human Rights, 1998b. Report of the Sessional Working Group on the Administration of Justice (19 August 1998). UN Doc. E/CN.4/Sub.2/1998/19.
United Nations, Commission on Human Rights, 1999a. Report of the Working Group on a Draft Optional Protocol to the Convention on the Rights of the Child

on the Sale of Children, Child Prostitution and Child Pornography on Its 5th Session (25 March 1999). UN Doc. E/CN.4/1999/74.

United Nations, Commission on Human Rights, 1999b. Report of the Secretary-General, Comments on the Report of the Working Group (8 December 1999). UN Doc. E/CN.4/2000/WG.13/2/Add.1.

United Nations, Commission on Human Rights, 2002. Report Submitted by Mr. Manfred Nowak, Independent Expert Charged with Examining the Existing International Criminal and Human Rights Framework for the Protection of Persons from Enforced or Involuntary Disappearances, Pursuant to Paragraph 11 of Commission Resolution 2001/46 (8 January 2002). UN Doc. E/CN.4/2002/71.

United Nations, Commission on Human Rights, 2003. Final Report of the Special Rapporteur, Miguel Alfonso Martínez, on the Study Requested by the Commission in Its Resolution 2000/63, and Submitted Pursuant to Economic and Social Council Decision 2002/277 (17 March 2003). UN Doc. E/CN.4/2003/105.

United Nations, Commission on Human Rights, 2004. Report of the Intersessional Open-Ended Working Group to Elaborate a Draft Legally Binding Normative Instrument for the Protection of All Persons from Enforced Disappearance (23 February 2004). UN Doc. E/CN.4/2004/59.

United Nations, Commission on Human Rights, 2005a. Compilation of the Essential Aspects of Replies Received on the Pre-Draft Declaration on Human Social Responsibilities. Report of the Office of the High Commissioner for Human Rights (7 February 2005). UN Doc. E/CN.4/2005/99.

United Nations, Commission on Human Rights, 2005b. Report of the Intersessional Open-Ended Working Group to Elaborate a Draft Legally Binding Normative Instrument for the Protection of All Persons from Enforced Disappearance (10 March 2005). UN Doc. E/CN.4/2005/66.

United Nations, Economic and Social Council, 1946a. Commission on Human Rights and Sub-Commission on the Status of Women (22 February 1946). UN Doc. E/27.

United Nations, Economic and Social Council, 1946b. Commission on Human Rights, Draft Declaration on Human Rights and Letter of Transmittal, Cuban Delegation (22 April 1946). UN Doc. E/HR/1.

United Nations, Economic and Social Council, 1946c. Commission on Human Rights, Report of the Commission on Human Rights to the Second Session of the Economic and Social Council (21 May 1946). UN Doc. E/38/Rev.1.

United Nations, Economic and Social Council, 1947a. Commission on Human Rights, Summary Record of the Second Meeting (29 January 1947). UN Doc. E/CN.4/SR.2.

United Nations, Economic and Social Council, 1947b. Commission on Human Rights Drafting Committee. Outline of International Bill of Rights (Prepared by the Division of Human Rights) (4 June 1947). UN Doc. E/CN.4/AC.1/3.

United Nations, Economic and Social Council, 1947c. Commission on Human Rights Drafting Committee. International Bill of Rights. Documented Outline (11 June 1947). UN Doc. E/CN.4/AC.1/3/Add.1.

United Nations, Economic and Social Council, 1947d. Commission on Human Rights, Second Session, Summary Record of Thirty-Seventh Meeting (13 December 1947). UN Doc. E/CN.4/SR.37.

United Nations, Economic and Social Council, 1963. Commission on Human Rights, Report of the Nineteenth Session (5 April 1963). UN Doc. E/CN.4/857.

United Nations, Economic and Social Council, 1983. Economic and Social Council Resolution 1983/38, Question of the Human Rights of All Persons Subjected to Any Form of Detention or Imprisonment, in Particular Torture and Other Cruel, Inhuman or Degrading Treatment or Punishment (27 May 1983). UN Doc. E/RES/1983/38.

United Nations, Economic and Social Council, 1984. Report of the Working Group on a Draft Convention against Torture and Other Cruel, Inhuman or Degrading Treatment or Punishment, Questions of the Human Rights of All Persons Subjected to Any Form of Detention or Imprisonment, Torture and Other Cruel, Inhuman or Degrading Treatment of Punishment (9 March 1984). UN Doc. E/CN.4/1984/72.

United Nations, General Assembly, 1963. Report of the Third Committee, Draft Declaration on the Elimination of All Forms of Racial Discrimination (20 November 1963). UN Doc. A/PV.1261.

United Nations, General Assembly, 1965. Report of the Third Committee, Draft International Convention on the Elimination of All Forms of Racial Discrimination (21 December 1965). UN Doc. A/PV.1406.

United Nations, General Assembly, 1980. Protection of Human Rights in Chile (15 December 1980). UN Doc. A/RES/35/188.

United Nations, General Assembly, 1981. Declaration on the Inadmissibility of Intervention in the Domestic Affairs of States and the Protection of Their Independence and Sovereignty, General Assembly Resolution 2131 (XX) (21 December 1965). UN Doc. A/RES/20/2131.

United Nations, General Assembly, 1993. Declaration on Protection of All Persons from Enforced Disappearance (12 February 1993). UN Doc. A/RES/47/133.

United Nations, General Assembly, 2000. Report of the Independent Expert on the Right to Development, Arjun Sengupta, Pursuant to General Assembly Resolution 454/175 and Commission on Human Rights Resolution 2000/5 (17 August 2000). UN Doc. A/55/306.

United Nations, General Assembly, 2005. Report of the Economic and Social Council for 2005 (15 August 2005). UN Doc. A/60/3/Rev.1.

United Nations, General Assembly, 2009. Report of the Special Rapporteur on Freedom of Religion or Belief, Asma Jahangir (28 December 2009). UN Doc. A/HRC/13/40/Add.3.

United Nations, General Assembly, 2012. Study of the Human Rights Council Advisory Committee on Promoting Human Rights and Fundamental Freedoms through a Better Understanding of Traditional Values of Humankind (6 December 2012). UN Doc. A/HRC/22/71.

United Nations, General Assembly, 2015. Transforming Our World: The 2030 Agenda for Sustainable Development (25 September 2015). UN Doc. A/RES/70/1.

United Nations, Human Rights Committee, 1996. Communication No. 550/1993 (16 December 1996). UN Doc. CCPR/C/58/D/550/1993.

United Nations, Human Rights Committee, 2003. Concluding Observations on the Fourth and Fifth Reports of Sri Lanka (1 December 2003). UN Doc. CCPR/CO/79/LKA.

United Nations, Human Rights Committee, 2004a. General Comment 31, Nature of the General Legal Obligation on States Parties to the Covenant (26 May 2004). UN Doc. CCPR/C/21/Rev.1/Add.13.

United Nations, Human Rights Committee, 2004b. Concluding Observations on the Fifth Periodic Report of Morocco (1 December 2004). UN Doc. CCPR/CO/82/MAR.

United Nations, Human Rights Committee, 2005. Concluding Observations on the Initial Report of Tajikistan (18 July 2005). UN Doc. CCPR/CO/84/TJK.

United Nations, Human Rights Committee, 2006. Concluding Observations on the Second Periodic Report of the Central African Republic (27 July 2006). UN Doc. CCPR/C/CAF/CO/2.

United Nations, Human Rights Committee, 2007. Concluding Observations on the Third Periodic Report of the Sudan (29 August 2007). UN Doc. CCPR/C/SDN/CO/3.

United Nations, Human Rights Committee, 2008a. Concluding Observations on the Fifth Periodic Report of Japan (18 December 2008). UN Doc. CCPR/C/JPN/CO/5.

United Nations, Human Rights Committee, 2008b. Concluding Observations on the Third Periodic Report of Ireland (30 July 2008). UN Doc. CCPR/C/IRL/CO/3.

United Nations, Human Rights Committee, 2009a. Concluding Observations on the Third Periodic Report of Rwanda (7 May 2009). UN Doc. CCPR/C/RWA/CO/3.

United Nations, Human Rights Committee, 2009b. Concluding Observations on the Sixth Periodic Report of the Russian Federation (24 November 2009). UN Doc. CCPR/C/RUS/CO/6.

United Nations, Human Rights Committee, 2011a. Concluding Observations on the Fourth Periodic Report of Togo (18 April 2011). UN Doc. CCPR/C/TGO/CO/4.

United Nations, Human Rights Committee, 2011b. General Comment 34. Article 19: Freedoms of Opinion and Expression (12 September 2011). UN Doc. CCPR/C/GC/34.

United Nations, Human Rights Committee, 2012. Concluding Observations on the Second Periodic Report of Armenia (31 August 2012). UN Doc. CCPR/C/ARM/CO/2.

United Nations, Human Rights Committee, 2013a. Annual Report of the United Nations High Commissioner for Human Rights (11 January 2013). UN Doc. A/HRC/22/17/Add.4.

United Nations, Human Rights Committee, 2013b. Concluding Observations on the Initial Report of Macao, China (29 April 2013). UN Doc. CCPR/C/CHN-MAC/CO/1.

United Nations, Human Rights Committee, 2013c. Concluding Observations on the Third Periodic Report of Paraguay (29 April 2013). UN Doc. CCPR/C/PRY/CO/3.

United Nations, Human Rights Committee, 2013d. Concluding Observations on the Initial Report of Mauritania (21 November 2013). UN Doc. CCPR/C/MRT/CO/1.

United Nations, Human Rights Committee, 2014a. Concluding Observations on the Third Periodic Report of Latvia (11 April 2014). UN Doc. CCPR/C/LVA/CO/3.

United Nations, Human Rights Committee, 2014b. Concluding Observations on the Fourth Periodic Report of Ireland (19 August 2014). UN Doc. CCPR/C/IRL/CO/4.

United Nations, Human Rights Committee, 2014c. Concluding Observations on the Second Periodic Report of Kuwait (18 November 2011). UN Doc. CCPR/C/KWT/CO/2.

United Nations, Human Rights Committee, 2015a. Concluding Observations on the Initial Report of Côte d'Ivoire (28 April 2015). UN Doc. CCPR/C/CIV/CO/1.

United Nations, Human Rights Committee, 2015b. Concluding Observations on the Third Periodic Report of Croatia (30 April 2015). UN Doc. CCPR/C/HRV/CO/3.

United Nations, Security Council, 2004. The Rule of Law and Transitional Justice in Conflict and Post-Conflict Societies. Report of the Secretary-General (23 August 2004). UN Doc. S/2004/616.

United Nations, Statistical Commission, 2015. Report on the Forty-Sixth Session (27 March 2015). UN Doc. E/2015/24 – E/CN.3/2015/40.

United Nations, Sub-Commission on the Promotion and Protection of Human Rights, 2000. Decision 2000/111 (18 August 2000). UN Doc. E/CN.4/2001/2.

Treaties and legislation

Association of Southeast Asian Nations, 2012. ASEAN Human Rights Declaration (19 November 2012). 21st ASEAN Summit.

Council of Europe, 1950. European Convention for the Protection of Human Rights and Fundamental Freedoms (ECHR) (4 November 1950).

French National Constituent Assembly, 1789. Declaration of Rights and Duties of Man and Citizen (26 August 1789).

French National Constituent Assembly, 1795. Declaration of Rights and Duties of Man and Citizen, Constitution of the Year III (22 August 1795).

International Committee of the Red Cross (ICRC), 1949a. Geneva Convention (I) for the Amelioration of the Condition of the Wounded and Sick in Armed Forces in the Field (12 August 1949). 75 UNTS 31.

International Committee of the Red Cross (ICRC), 1949b. Geneva Convention (II) for the Amelioration of the Condition of Wounded, Sick and Shipwrecked Members of Armed Forces at Sea (12 August 1949). 75 UNTS 85.

International Committee of the Red Cross (ICRC), 1949c. Geneva Convention (III) Relative to the Treatment of Prisoners of War (12 August 1949). 75 UNTS 135.

International Committee of the Red Cross (ICRC), 1949d. Geneva Convention (IV) Relative to the Protection of Civilian Persons in Time of War (12 August 1949). 75 UNTS 287.

International Committee of the Red Cross (ICRC), 1977a. Protocol Additional to the Geneva Conventions of 12 August 1949, and Relating to the Protection of Victims of International Armed Conflicts (Protocol I) (8 June 1977). 1125 UNTS 3.

International Committee of the Red Cross (ICRC), 1977b. Protocol Additional to the Geneva Conventions of 12 August 1949, and Relating to the Protection of Victims of Non-International Armed Conflicts (Protocol II) (8 June 1977). 1125 UNTS 609.

League of Arab States, 2004. Arab Charter on Human Rights (22 May 2004). 26th Summit of Heads of States of the League of Arab States.

League of Nations, 1926. Slavery Convention (25 September 1926).

Organization of African Unity, 1981. African Charter on Human and Peoples' Rights (27 June 1981). OAU Doc. CAB/LEG/67/3 rev. 5.

Organization of American States, 1948. American Declaration on the Rights and Duties of Man (2 May 1948). Ninth International Conference of American States.

Organization of American States, 1969. American Convention on Human Rights (22 November 1969). Inter-American Specialized Conference on Human Rights.
Organization of American States, 1994a. Inter-American Convention on the Prevention, Punishment, and Eradication of Violence against Women (Convention of Belém Do Pará) (9 June 1994).
Organization of American States, 1994b. Inter-American Convention on Forced Disappearance of Persons (9 June 1994).
Organization of American States, 2013. Inter-American Convention against All Forms of Discrimination and Intolerance (5 June 2013). General Assembly of the Organization of American States A-69.
United Nations, 1945. Charter of the United Nations and Statute of the International Court of Justice (24 October 1945). 1 UNTS XVI.
United Nations, 1948. Convention on the Prevention and Punishment of the Crime of Genocide (9 December 1948). General Assembly resolution 260A (III).
United Nations, 1964. International Convention on the Elimination of All Forms of Racial Discrimination (ICERD) (21 December 1965). General Assembly resolution 2106 (XX).
United Nations, 1966a. International Covenant on Civil and Political Rights (ICCPR) (16 December 1966). General Assembly resolution 2200A (XXI).
United Nations, 1966b. International Covenant on Economic, Social and Cultural Rights (ICESCR) (16 December 1966). General Assembly resolution 2200A (XXI).
United Nations, 1979. Convention on the Elimination of All Forms of Discrimination against Women (CEDAW) (18 December 1979). General Assembly resolution 34/180.
United Nations, 1984. Convention against Torture and Other Cruel, Inhuman or Degrading Treatment or Punishment (CAT) (10 December 1984). General Assembly resolution 39/46.
United Nations, 1988. United Nations Convention against Illicit Traffic in Narcotic Drugs and Psychotropic Substances (20 December 1988). United Nations Conference for the Adoption of a Convention against Illicit Traffic in Narcotic Drugs and Psychotropic Substances.
United Nations, 1989a. Convention on the Rights of the Child (CRC) (20 November 1989). General Assembly resolution 44/25.
United Nations, 1989b. Second Optional Protocol to the International Covenant on Civil and Political Rights, Aiming at the Abolition of the Death Penalty (ICCPR-OP2) (15 December 1989). General Assembly resolution 44/128.
United Nations, 1990. International Convention on the Protection of the Rights of All Migrant Workers and Members of Their Families (ICMW) (18 December 1990). General Assembly resolution 45/158.
United Nations, 1998. Rome Statute of the International Criminal Court (17 July 1998). United Nations Diplomatic Conference of Plenipotentiaries on the Establishment of an International Criminal Court, 15 June- 17July 1998 (Rome Conference). UN Doc. A/CONF.183/9.
United Nations, 2000a. Optional Protocol to the Convention on the Rights of the Child on the Involvement of Children in Armed Conflict (OP-CRC-AC) (25 May 2000). General Assembly resolution A/RES/54/263.
United Nations, 2000b. Optional Protocol to the Convention on the Rights of the Child on the Sale of Children, Child Prostitution and Child Pornography (OP-CRC-SC) (25 May 2000). General Assembly resolution A/RES/54/263.

United Nations, 2000c. United Nations Convention against Transnational Organized Crime (UNTOC) (15 November 2000). General Assembly resolution 55/25.

United Nations, 2000d. Protocol to Prevent, Suppress and Punish Trafficking in Persons, Especially Women and Children, Supplementing the United Nations Convention against Transnational Organized Crime (15 November 2000). General Assembly resolution 55/25.

United Nations, 2003. United Nations Convention against Corruption (UNCAC) (31 October 2003). General Assembly resolution 58/4.

United Nations, 2006a. Convention on the Rights of Persons with Disabilities (CRPD) (13 December 2006). General Assembly resolution A/RES/61/106.

United Nations, 2006b. International Convention for the Protection of All Persons from Enforced Disappearance (CPED) (20 December 2006). General Assembly resolution A/RES/61/177.

United Nations, 1949. Convention for the Suppression of the Traffic in Persons and of the Exploitation of the Prostitution of Others (2 December 1949). General Assembly resolution A/RES/317(IV).

United Nations, 1961. Single Convention on Narcotic Drugs of 1961 as Amended by the 1972 Protocol (30 March 1961). United Nations Conference for the Adoption of a Single Convention on Narcotic Drugs.

United States Constitutional Convention, 1787. United States Constitution (17 September 1787).

Cases

A v. United Kingdom (Application no. 25599/94), ECHR. 18 September 1997.

A, B and C v. Ireland (Application no. 25579/05), ECHR. 16 December 2010.

Acmanne and others v. Belgium (Application no. 10435/83), ECHR. 10 December 1984.

A.D.T. v. United Kingdom (Application no. 35765/97), ECHR. 31 July 2000.

Aksu v. Turkey (Application no. 4149/04), ECHR. 15 March 2012.

Altuğ Taner Akçam v. Turkey (Application no. 27520/07), ECHR. 25 October 2011.

Angelova and Iliev v. Bulgaria (Application no. 55523/00), ECHR. 26 July 2007.

Animal Defenders International v. United Kingdom (Application no. 48876/08), ECHR. 22 April 2013.

Antonov v. Ukraine (Application no. 28096/04), ECHR. 3 November 2011.

Armellini and Others v. Austria (Application no. 14134/07), ECHR. 16 April 2015.

Ashlarba v. Georgia (Application no. 45554/08), ECHR. 15 July 2014.

Bautista de Arellana v Colombia (Communication No 563/1993), UNHRC. 27 October 1995.

Bayatyan v. Armenia (Application no. 23459/03), ECHR. 7 May 2011.

Beganović v Croatia (Application no. 46423/06), ECHR. 25 September 2009.

Belgium v. Senegal (Questions relating to the Obligation to Prosecute or Extradite, I.C.J. 422), ICJ. 20 July 2012.

Bevacqua and S. v. Bulgaria (Case no. 71,127/01), ECHR. 12 June 2008.

Bladet Tromso and Stensaas v. Norway (Application no. 21980/92), ECHR. 20 May 1999.

Blumberga v. Latvia (Application no. 70930/01), ECHR. 14 October 2008.

Bozhkov v. Bulgaria (Application no. 3316/04), ECHR. 19 April 2011.

Brenda Rowley v. United Kingdom (Application no. 31914/03), ECHR. 22 February 2005.
Calvelli and Ciglio v Italy (Application no. 32967/96), ECHR. 17 January 2002.
Çelik v. Turkey (no.2) (Application no. 39326/02), ECHR. 27 May 2010.
Colombani and Others v. France (Application no. 51279/99), ECHR. 25 June 2002.
C.N. v. United Kingdom (Application no. 4239/08), ECHR. 13 November 2012.
C.R. v. United Kingdom (Application no. 20190/92), ECHR. 22 November 1995.
Cristiàn Daniel Sahli Vera et al *v. Chile* (Case 12.219), IACHR. March 10, 2005.
Cumpana and Mazare v. Romania (Application no. 33348/96), ECHR. 17 December 2004.
Dąbrowski v. Poland (Application no. 18235/02), ECHR. 19 December 2006.
Dallas v. United Kingdom (Application no. 38395/12), ECHR. 11 February 2016.
Decision 2012-647, French Constitutional Council. 28 February 2012.
Decision 90-145, German Federal Constitutional Court, 9 March 1994.
Delfi AS v. Estonia (Application no. 64569/09), ECHR. 16 June 2015.
Dickson v. United Kingdom (Application no. 44362/04), ECHR. 4 December 2007.
Dudgeon v. United Kingdom (Application no. 7525/76), ECHR. 22 October 1981.
Đurđević v. Croatia (Application no.52442/09), ECHR. 19 July 2011.
Egeland and Hanseid v. Norway (Application no. 34438/04), ECHR. 16 April 2009.
Ehrmann v. France (Application no. 27777/10), ECHR. 7 June 2011.
Engel and Others v. The Netherlands (Application no. 5100/71; 5101/71; 5102/71; 5354/72; 5370/72), ECHR. 8 June 1976.
Erdoğdu v. Turkey (Application no. 25723/94), ECHR. 15 June 2000.
Feret v. Belgium (Application no. 15615/07), ECHR. 16 July 2009.
Fredrik Neij and Peter Sunde Kolmisoppi v. Sweden (Application no. 40397/12), ECHR. 19 February 2013.
Friend, the Countryside Alliance and Others v. United Kingdom (Application no. 16072/06 and Application no. 27809/08), ECHR. 24 November 2009.
G v. United Kingdom (Application no. 37334/08), ECHR. 30 August 2011.
Garyfallou Aebe v. Greece (Application no. 93/1996/712/909), ECHR. 24 September 1997.
Geert Drieman and Others v. Norway (Application no. 36678/96), ECHR. 4 May 2000.
Goiburú et al. *v. Paraguay* (Ser.C No.153), IACHR. 22 September 2006.
González et al. *("Cotton Field") v. Mexico* (Ser.C No.205), IACHR. 16 November 2009.
Gough v. United Kingdom (Application no. 49327/11), ECHR. 28 October 2014.
Handyside v. United Kingdom (Application no. 5493/72), ECHR. 7 December 1976.
Hansen v. Denmark (Application no. 28971/95), ECHR. 16 March 2000.
H.M.A. v. Spain (Application no. 25399/94), ECHR. 9 April 1996.
İ.A. v. Turkey (Application no. 42571/98), ECHR. 13 September 2005.
Lohé Issa Konaté v. Burkina Faso (Application no. 004/2013), African Court on Human and Peoples' Rights. 5 December 2014.
Janowski v. Poland (Application no. 25716/94), ECHR. 21 January 1999.
Jessica Lenahan (Gonzales) et al. *v. United States* (Case 12.626), IACommHR. 21 July 2011.
José Antonio Coronel and others v. Colombia (Communication No. 778/1997), UNHRC, 24 October 2002.
Jussila v. Finland (Application no. 73053/01), ECHR. 23 November 2006.

K.A. and A.D. v. Belgium (Application nos. 42758/98 and 45558/99), ECHR. 17 February 2005.
Karataş v Turkey (Application no. 23168/94), ECHR. 8 July 1999.
Kaya v. Turkey (Application no. 22729/93), ECHR. 19 February 1998.
Keenan v. United Kingdom (Application no. 27229/95), ECHR. 3 April 2001.
Kokkinakis v. Greece (Application no. 14307/88), ECHR. 25 May 1993.
Konstantin Markin v. Russia (Application no. 30078/06), ECHR. 22 March 2012.
Kontrova v. Slovakia (Application no. 7510/04), ECHR. 31 May 2007.
K.U. v. Finland (Application no. 2872/02), ECHR. 2 December 2008.
Kudrevičius and Others v. Lithuania (Application no. 37553/05), ECHR. 15 October 2015.
L. and V. v. Austria (Application no. 39392/98 and 39829/98), ECHR. 9 January 2003.
Laskey, Jaggard and Brown v. United Kingdom (Application nos. 21627/93, 21826/93 and 21974/93), ECHR. 19 February 1997.
Lawrence v. Texas, 539 U.S. 558 (2003).
Leyla Şahìn v. Turkey (Application no. 44774/98), ECHR. 10 November 2005.
Lindon, Otchakovsky-Laurens and July v. France (Application nos. 21279/02 and 36448/02), ECHR. 22 October 2007.
Mahmut Kaya v. Turkey (Application no. 22535/93), EHCR. 28 March 2000.
Maktouf and Damjanovic v. Bosnia and Herzegovina (Applications nos. 2312/08 and 34179/08), ECHR. 18 July 2013.
Mamère v. France (Application no. 12697/03), ECHR. 7 February 2007.
Manuel Wackenheim v. France (Application no. 854/999), UNHRC. 15 July 2002.
María Eugenia Morales de Sierra (Case 11.625), IACommHR. 19 January 2001.
Mastromatteo v. Italy (Application no.37703/97), ECHR. 24 October 2002.
McCann and Others v. United Kingdom (Application no. 18984/91), ECHR. 27 September 1995.
M.C. v. Bulgaria (Application no. 39272/98), ECHR. 4 December 2003.
Milanović v. Serbia (Application no. 44614/07), ECHR. 14 December 2010.
M.K. v. Austria (Application no. 28867/95), ECHR. 2 July 1997.
Modinos v. Cyprus (Application no. 15070/89), ECHR. 22 April 1993.
Müller and Others v. Switzerland (Application no. 10737/84), ECHR. 24 May 1988.
Nicaragua v. United States (Case concerning Military and Paramilitary Activities in and against Nicaragua, ICJ Rep. 1986), ICJ. 27 June 1986.
Norris v. Ireland (Application no. 10581/83), ECHR. 26 October 1988.
Norwood v. United Kingdom (Application no. 23131), ECHR. 16 November 2004.
Odièvre v. France (Application no. 42326/98), ECHR. 13 February 2003.
O'Keefe v. United Kingdom (Application no. 10610/05), ECHR. 11 December 2007.
Öneryildiz v. Turkey (Application no. 48939/99), ECHR. 30 November 2004.
Opuz v. Turkey (Application no. 33401/02), ECHR. 9 June 2009.
Osman v. United Kingdom (Application no.23452/94), ECHR. 28 October 1998.
Osmani v Former Yugoslav Republic of Macedonia (Application no. 50841/99), ECHR. 11 October 2001.
Otegi Mondragon v. Spain (Application no. 2034/07), ECHR. 15 March 2011.
Özgür Gündem v. Turkey (Application no. 23144/93), ECHR. 16 March 2000.
Palusinski v. Poland (Application no. 62414/00), ECHR. 3 October 2006.
Parrillo v. Italy (Application no. 46470/11), ECHR. 27 August 2015.

Paul and Audrey Edwards v. United Kingdom (Case no. 46477/99), ECHR. 14 March 2002.
Perevedentsevy v. Russia (Application no. 39583/05), ECHR. 24 April 2014.
Perinçek v. Switzerland (Application no. 27510/08), ECHR. 15 October 2015.
Perrin v. United Kingdom (Application no. 5446/03), ECHR. 18 October 2005.
Pretty v. United Kingdom (Application no. 2346/02), ECHR. 29 April 2002.
Prince v. South Africa (Communication no. 1474/2006), UNHRC. 14 November 2007.
R v. Adomako (1994) 3 All ER 79.
Radio France and Others v. France (Application no. 53984/00), ECHR. 30 March 2004.
Rantsev v. Cyprus and Russia (Application no. 25965/04), ECHR. 7 January 2010.
Renaud v. France (Application no. 13290/07), ECHR. 25 February 2010.
Rujak v. Croatia (Application no. 57942/10), ECHR. 2 October 2012.
Salabiaku v. France (Application no. 10519/83), ECHR. 7 October 1988.
S. and G. v United Kingdom (Application no. 17634/91), ECHR. 2 September 1991.
S.A.S. v. France (Application no. 43835/11), ECHR. 1 July 2014.
Siliadin v. France (Application no. 73316/01), ECHR. 26 July 2005.
Šilih v. Slovenia (Application no. 71463/01), ECHR. 9 April 2009.
Söderman v. Sweden (Application no. 5786/08), ECHR. 12 November 2013.
Stoll v. Switzerland (Application no. 69698/01), ECHR. 10 December 2007.
Stubbings and Others v. United Kingdom (Application nos. 22083/93 and 22096/93). 22 October 1996.
Stübing v. Germany (Application no. 43547/08), ECHR. 12 April 2012.
Şükran Aydin and Others v. Turkey (Application nos. 49197/06, 23196/07, 50242/08, 60912/08 and 14871/09), ECHR. 22 January 2013.
S.W. v. United Kingdom (Application no. 20166/92), ECHR. 22 November 1995.
Ulla Annikki Karttunen v. Finland (Application no. 1685/10), ECHR. 10 May 2011.
United Kingdom v. Albania (the Corfu Channel case, ICJ Rep. 4), ICJ. 9 April 1949.
Van Colle v. United Kingdom (Application no. 7678/09), ECHR. 13 November 2012.
Van der Heijden v. The Netherlands (Application no. 42857/05), ECHR. 3 April 2012.
Vejdeland and Others v. Sweden (Application no. 1813/07), ECHR. 9 May 2015.
Velásquez Rodriguez (Ser.C No.4), IACHR. 29 July 1988.
Vo v. France (Application no. 53924/00), ECHR. 8 July 2004.
Willem v. France (Application no. 10883/05), ECHR. 16 July 2009.
Wingrove v. United Kingdom (Application no. 17419/90), ECHR. 25 November 1996.
X and Y v. The Netherlands (Application no. 8978/80), ECHR. 26 March 1985.
X v. United Kingdom (Application no. 7992/77), ECHR. 12 July 1978.

Table of ECHR criminalization cases by crime classification, outcome, and reasoning[1]

Applicant	*Party*	*Date*	*Subject*	*ICCS crime classification*	*Article*	*Outcome*	*Concepts and reasoning in judgment*	*Concept classification*
A	UK	23/09/98	Assault – reasonable chastisement	020112	3	Should be an offence	Degree of severity	Seriousness
							Vulnerability deserving protection	Vulnerability
							Human dignity	Human dignity
							Effective deterrence	Deterrence
							Causing non-trivial injuries	Harm
							Personal integrity	Personal integrity
A, B and C	Ireland	16/12/10	Procuring miscarriage	0106	8	Can be an offence	Possibility to obtain restricted service in other states	Availability of other remedies
							Community consensus of morality	Community consensus
							Risk of harm	Harm
Acmanne	Belgium	10/12/84	Refusing compulsory health screening	0902	8	Can be an offence	Endangerment of others	Harm
							Protection of health	Societal interests

							Social duty to general interest	Societal interests
A.D.T.	UK	02/08/00	Gross indecency between more than two men	08029	8	Should not be an offence	Offense through mere knowledge	Offense
							Purely private nature	Essential private life
							Public health interests	Societal interests
							Protection of morals	Community consensus
Akçam	Turkey	27/10/11	Denigrating the nation	0809	10	Should not be an offence	Broadness of offense, shock, disturbing nature	Offense
							Protecting and preserving values	Community consensus
Angelova	Bulgaria	28/07/07	Racially motivated murder or injury	*	2	Need not be an offence	Possibility of aggravated sentences	Availability of other remedies
							Assert condemnation of racism	Discrimination
							Maintain confidence of minorities	Discrimination
Antonov	Ukraine	03/11/11	Causing death by dangerous driving	010321	2	Can be an offence	Availability of other remedies	Availability of other remedies
							Mens rea – intentionality	Mens rea
Armellini	Austria	16/04/15	Defamation	0209	10	Can be an offence	Damage to personal and professional reputation	Reputation
Ashlarba	Georgia	15/07/14	Membership of criminal group	09051	7	Can be an offence	Harm principle	Harm
							Impact on society at large	Societal interests

(*Continued*)

(Cont.)

Applicant	*Party*	*Date*	*Subject*	*ICCS crime classification*	*Article*	*Outcome*	*Concepts and reasoning in judgment*	*Concept classification*
Aydin	Germany	27/01/11	Supporting banned organization	09069	10	Can be an offence	Incitement to violence or hatred	Hatred
							Protection of public order and safety	Societal interests
							Threat to national security	Societal interests
Bayatyan	Armenia	07/07/11	Conscientious objection	0904	9	Should not be an offence	Community consensus	Community consensus
							Deeply and genuinely held beliefs	Autonomy
							Pluralism and broadmindedness	Pluralism
							Protection of public order	Societal interests
							Tolerance	Societal interests
							Balance between interests of society and individual	Societal interests
							Sharing of societal burden	Societal interests
Beganović	Croatia	27/06/09	Assault	02011	3	Should be an offence	Causing non-trivial injuries	Harm
							Personal integrity	Personal integrity
							Minimum level of severity	Seriousness
							Causing anxiety and fear	Harm
Blumberga	Latvia	14/10/08	Burglary	05012	P1	Can be an offence	Availability of other remedies	Availability of other remedies

							Protection of property rights	Property rights
Bozhkov	Bulgaria	19/04/11	Defamation	0209	10	Can be an offence	Intentionality – reckless disregard	Mens rea
							Protection of the reputation or rights of others	Reputation
Calvelli	Italy	17/01/02	Medical negligence	02062	2	Need not be an offence	Availability of other remedies	Availability of other remedies
							Mens rea – intentionality	Mens rea
							Public aspect of wrong	Societal interests
Colombani	France	25/06/02	Insulting foreign heads of state	0809	10	Should not be an offence	Discrimination	Discrimination
							Additional protection for king	Discrimination
							Defence of truth	Offense
							Protection of honour or reputation	Reputation
							Maintenance of state relations	Societal interests
							Human dignity	Human dignity
C.R.	UK	22/11/95	Rape – marital	03011	7	Should be an offence	Essentially debasing character	Human dignity
							Respect for human dignity and human freedom	Human dignity
Cumpana	Romania	17/12/04	Insult and defamation	0209	10	Can be an offence	Chilling effect	Autonomy
							Statements of value or fact	Offense

(*Continued*)

(Cont.)

Applicant	*Party*	*Date*	*Subject*	*ICCS crime classification*	*Article*	*Outcome*	*Concepts and reasoning in judgment*	*Concept classification*
							Protection of the reputation or rights of others	Reputation
Dallas	UK	11/02/16	Contempt of court (internet research by jury member)	08062	7	Can be an offence	Mens rea – intentionality	Mens rea
							Prejudice to the administration of justice	Societal interests
Drieman	Norway	04/05/00	Obstructing lawful whaling	0809	10,11	Can be an offence	Coercion	Autonomy
							Intentionality	Mens rea
							Rights of others	Rights of others
							Prevention of disorder and protection of the rights of others	Societal interests
Dudgeon	UK	22/10/8122/10/81	Buggery	08029	8	Should not be an offence	Protection from offense and injury	Harm
							Offense through mere knowledge	Offense
							Private manifestations of human personality	Essential private life
							Harm to vulnerability deserving protection	Vulnerability
							Valid consent	Autonomy
							Community consensus of morality	Community consensus
Egeland	Norway	16/04/09	Invasion of privacy	02111	8,10		Community consensus	Community consensus

						Can be an offence	Consent	Autonomy
							Intrusiveness	Essential private life
							Protection of the reputation or rights of others	Rights of others
							Fair administration of justice	Societal interests
							Victim in reduced state of self control	Vulnerability
Ehrmann	France	07/06/11	Failure to comply with building planning regulations	08049	10	Can be an offence	Prevention of disorder	Societal interests
							Quality of the environment	Societal interests
							Protection of cultural heritage	Societal interests
							Harmonization of social life	Societal interests
							Protection of common good and respect for collective intent	Societal interests
							Public nature	Societal interests
Feret	Belgium	10/12/12	Incitement to racism, hatred, and discrimination	080322	10	Can be an offence	Incitement to hatred	Hatred
							Protection of the reputation or rights of others	Rights of others
							Risk of causing social tension	Societal interests

(*Continued*)

(Cont.)

Applicant	*Party*	*Date*	*Subject*	*ICCS crime classification*	*Article*	*Outcome*	*Concepts and reasoning in judgment*	*Concept classification*
							Direct incitement to violence (lack of)	Harm
Friend	UK	24/11/09	Hunting a wild mammal with a dog	10042	8,9,11	Can be an offence	Protection of morals	Community consensus
							Essence of identity and personal autonomy	Autonomy
							Protection of property rights	Property rights
							Public nature of activity	Societal interests
							Preservation of social dimensions	Societal interests
G	UK	30/08/11	Strict liability – rape	03011	6,8	Can be an offence	Harm principle	Harm
							Intimate aspect of private life	Essential private life
							Protection of rights and freedoms of others	Rights of others
							Vulnerability deserving protection	Vulnerability
Gough	UK	28/10/14	Nudity in public	080329	10	Can be an offence	Non-consent to offense	Autonomy
							Offense and alarm to members of the public	Offense
							Differing sensibilities and location	Offense
							Prevention of disorder	Societal interests

							Protection of matters of public interest	Societal interests
							Community consensus – accepted public behaviour	Community consensus
Handyside	UK	07/12/76	Obscene publications	08022	10	Can be an offence	Encouragement to indulge in harmful activities	Harm
							Vulnerability deserving protection	Vulnerability
							Community consensus of morality	Community consensus
Hansen	Denmark	16/03/00	Strict liability – transport regulations	09021	6	Can be an offence	Seriousness of act and risk	Seriousness
H.M.A.	Spain	09/04/96	Environmentally harmful emissions	10011	6	Can be an offence	Causal relationship with consequences	Causation
							Mens rea – intentionality or negligence	Mens rea
							Foreseeability and avoidability	Mens rea
							Knowingly and wilfully omitting to display requisite care	Mens rea
							Acts of omission	Omission
İ.A	Turkey	13/09/05	Blasphemy	080321	10	Can be an offence	Offense through actual experience	Offense
							Gratuitous offence or profanity	Offense

(*Continued*)

(Cont.)

Applicant	*Party*	*Date*	*Subject*	*ICCS crime classification*	*Article*	*Outcome*	*Concepts and reasoning in judgment*	*Concept classification*
							Improper attacks on objects of religious veneration	Offense
							Prevention of disorder and protection of morals and rights of others	Societal interests
							Intimate personal convictions	Autonomy
Janowski	Poland	21/01/99	Insulting a civil servant	02099	10	Can be an offence	Public nature of insult	Offense
							Whether actions warrant insult	Offense
							Use of abusive language	Offense
							Protection of the reputation or rights of others	Reputation
K.A.	Belgium	17/02/05	Assault – sadomasochism	02011	8	Can be an offence	Risk of harm	Harm
							Personal autonomy	Autonomy
							Consent	Autonomy
							Purely private nature	Essential private life
							Protection of health and rights and freedoms of others	Rights of others
Karttunen	Finland	10/05/11	Child pornography	030221	10	Can be an offence	Protection against harm and abuse	Harm
							Good intentions	Mens rea
							Protection of morals and rights of others	Rights of others

							Vulnerability deserving protection	Vulnerability
							Community consensus of morality	Community consensus
Kokkinakis	Greece	25/05/93	Proselytism	080321	9	Should not be an offence	Identity of individual and conception of life	Autonomy
							Coercion	Autonomy
							Manipulation and brainwashing	Autonomy
							Pluralism and state neutrality	Pluralism
							Protection of rights and freedoms of others	Rights of others
							Respect for human dignity and human freedom	Human dignity
K.U.	Finland	02/03/09	Malicious misrepresentation involving welfare of a minor	07019	8	Should be an offence	Deterrence	Deterrence
							Act caused increased vulnerability to harm	Harm
							Physical, moral, and psychological welfare of child	Harm
							Debilitating effect on victim	Harm
							Public interest	Societal interests
							Wrongdoing	Wrongdoing
Kudrevičius	Lithuania	15/10/15	Serious breach of public order	08019	11	Can be an offence	Mens rea – intentionality	Mens rea
							Needs and rights of others	Rights of others

(*Continued*)

(Cont.)

Applicant	*Party*	*Date*	*Subject*	*ICCS crime classification*	*Article*	*Outcome*	*Concepts and reasoning in judgment*	*Concept classification*
							Less serious than physical violence	Seriousness
							Disruption to ordinary life	Societal interests
Laskey	UK	20/01/97	Assault – sadomasochism	02011	8	Can be an offence	Protection of health or morals	Community consensus
							Harm principle	Harm
							Consent	Autonomy
							Respect for autonomy	Autonomy
							Demeaning activities	Human dignity
							Public health interests	Societal interests
Lindon	France	22/10/07	Defamation	0209	10	Can be an offence	Intention to stir up violence and hatred	Hatred
							Good faith defence	Mens rea
							Underlying intention to stigmatize	Mens rea
							Distinction between fact and value judgment	Offense
							Sufficient factual basis/verification	Offense
							Minimum degree of moderation and propriety	Offense
							Protection of reputation or rights of others	Reputation

							Impugning the honour or reputation of a person	Reputation
							Protection of political debate and a democratic society	Societal interests
Lindon	France	22/10/07	Defamation	0209	10	Can be an offence	Human dignity	Human dignity
L. and V.	Austria	09/01/03	Consensual male homosexual acts aged 14–18	08029	8,14	Should not be an offence	Equality of treatment	Discrimination
							Protection of sexual development	Autonomy
							Protection of the rights of others and protection of morals	Community consensus
M.C.	Bulgaria	04/03/04	Rape – resistance	030112	3,8	Should be an offence	Criminalization as last resort	Availability of other remedies
							Consent	Autonomy
							Respect for autonomy	Autonomy
							Personal integrity	Personal integrity
M.K.	Austria	02/07/97	Sexual offences against children	03021	8,14	Can be an offence	Consent	Autonomy
							Protection of the rights of others and protection of morals	Rights of others
							Vulnerability deserving protection	Vulnerability
Mondragon	Spain	15/03/11	Insulting the king	0809	10	Should not be an offence	General restraint in use of criminal law	Availability of other remedies
								Discrimination

(*Continued*)

(Cont.)

Applicant	*Party*	*Date*	*Subject*	*ICCS crime classification*	*Article*	*Outcome*	*Concepts and reasoning in judgment*	*Concept classification*
							Discrimination – higher degree of protection for King	
							Incitement to violence or hatred (lack of)	Hatred
							Innermost core of human dignity	Human dignity
							Chilling effect	Autonomy
							Statements of value or fact	Offense
							Protection of the reputation or rights of others	Reputation
Müller	Switzerland	24/05/88	Obscene publications	08022	10	Can be an offence	Community consensus of morality	Community consensus
							Sense of sexual propriety	Community consensus
							Offense through actual experience	Offense
							Ordinary sensitivity	Offense
							Vulnerability deserving protection	Vulnerability
Neij	Sweden	19/02/13	Copyright infringement – file sharing	0503	10	Can be an offence	Mens rea – knowledge and notice	Mens rea
							Protection of property rights	Property rights

							Protection of the rights of others	Rights of others
Norris	Ireland	26/10/88	Buggery	08029	8	Should not be an offence	Community consensus of morality	Community consensus
							Detrimental effects on life of person affected	Harm
							Offense through mere knowledge	Offense
							Intimate aspect of private life	Essential private life
Norwood	UK	16/11/04	Hate speech – religion	080322	10	Can be an offence	Vehement attack against a group	Offense
							Tolerance	Offense
							Social peace	Societal interests
							Discrimination	Discrimination
O'Keefe	Ireland	28/01/14	Sexual offences against children	03021	3,8	Can be an offence	Effective deterrence	Deterrence
							Harm principle	Harm
							Grave act	Seriousness
Öneryildiz	Turkey	30/11/04	Negligence by authorities in dangerous activities	02071	2	Should be an offence	Effective deterrence	Deterrence
							Harm principle	Harm
							Mens rea – knowledge	Mens rea
							Failure to take measures to avert risk	Omission
							Seriousness of act and risk	Seriousness
Opuz	Turkey	09/06/09		020112	2		Physical and psychological violence	Harm

(*Continued*)

(Cont.)

Applicant	*Party*	*Date*	*Subject*	*ICCS crime classification*	*Article*	*Outcome*	*Concepts and reasoning in judgment*	*Concept classification*
			Domestic violence – min harm requirement			Should be an offence	Level of harm – sickness or unfitness for work	Harm
							Threats to harm	Harm
							Verbal abuse	Offense
							Seriousness of act and risk	Seriousness
Osman	UK	28/10/98	Intentional taking of life	0101	2	Should be an offence	Harm principle	Harm
							Effective deterrence	Deterrence
Osmani	FYROM	11/10/01	Stirring up national, racial, and religious hatred	080322	10	Can be an offence	Content and context of speech	Offense
							Not personal, political, or intellectual opinion	Offense
							Prevention of disorder and protection of the rights of others	Rights of others
							Risk of disorder and conflict	Societal interests
							Encouragement to violence	Harm
Palusinski	Poland	03/10/06	Incitement to use of drugs	0609	10	Can be an offence	Protection of health and morals	Community consensus
							Encouragement to indulge in harmful activities	Harm
Perìnçek	Switzerland	15/10/15	Wide denial of genocide in general	1109	8,10	Should not be	Incitement to violence or hatred (lack of)	Hatred

						an offence	Offense as an attack on dignity and identity	Human dignity
							Direct link between events and denial (lack of)	Offense
							Identification of actual victims affected	Offense
							Protection of the reputation or rights of others	Rights of others
							Capacity to lead to harmful consequences	Harm
Perrin	UK	18/10/05	Obscene publications	08022	10	Can be an offence	Availability of other remedies	Availability of other remedies
							Consent	Autonomy
							Vulnerability deserving protection	Vulnerability
Pretty	UK	29/04/02	Assisting suicide	0104	2,3,8	Can be an offence	Harm principle	Harm
							Respect for human freedom	Autonomy
							Autonomy but not general self-determination	Autonomy
							Ability to take informed decision	Autonomy
							Protection of life and rights of others	Rights of others
							Public health and safety	Societal interests
							Vulnerability deserving protection	Vulnerability

(*Continued*)

(Cont.)

Applicant	*Party*	*Date*	*Subject*	*ICCS crime classification*	*Article*	*Outcome*	*Concepts and reasoning in judgment*	*Concept classification*
							Humiliates or debases an individual	Human dignity
Radio France	France	30/03/04	Defamation of a public official	02099	10	Can be an offence	Public nature of defamation – reach and repetition	Offense
							Immediate and powerful impact of audiovisual media	Offense
							Protection of the reputation or rights of others	Reputation
							Damage to honour and dignity	Human dignity
Rantsev	Cyprus	07/01/10	Human trafficking	0204	4	Should be an offence	Ownership and commodification of humans	Human dignity
							Restriction of movement	Autonomy
Rowley	UK	22/02/05	Corporate manslaughter	01032	2	Need not be an offence	Availability of other remedies	Availability of other remedies
							Need to provide proximate fault	Causation
							Mens rea – intentionality	Mens rea
Rujak	Croatia	02/10/12	Insult	0209	10	Can be an offence	Sole intent to insult	Mens rea
							Protection from offense	Offense
							Vulgar and offensive language	Offense
S and G	UK	02/09/91	Outraging public decency	08029	10		Community consensus of morality	Community consensus

						Can be an offence	Consent	Autonomy
Salabiaku	France	07/10/98	Strict liability – drug trafficking	060132	6	Can be an offence	Gravity of offense	Seriousness
S.A.S.	France	01/07/14	Wearing of clothing designed to conceal the face	08012	8,9,10	Can be an offence	Principle of interaction between individuals	Community consensus
							Protection of public safety and respect for minimum set of values	Societal interests
							Promoting harmony of groups	Societal interests
							Human dignity	Human dignity
							Pluralism	Pluralism
Siliadin	France	26/07/05	Servitude	02039	4	Should be an offence	Servitude as a particularly serious denial of freedom	Autonomy
							Poor living conditions of servitude	Human dignity
							Vulnerability deserving protection	Vulnerability
							Effective deterrence	Deterrence
Šilih	Slovenia	09/04/09	Medical negligence	02062	2	Need not be an offence	Availability of other remedies	Availability of other remedies
							Intentionality	Mens rea
Söderman	Sweden	12/11/13	Voyeurism – filming	030129	8	Should be an offence	Sexual purpose	Mens rea
							Personal integrity	Personal integrity

(*Continued*)

(Cont.)

Applicant	*Party*	*Date*	*Subject*	*ICCS crime classification*	*Article*	*Outcome*	*Concepts and reasoning in judgment*	*Concept classification*
							Fundamental values and essential aspects of private life	Essential private life
Stoll	Switzerland	10/12/07	Publishing secret official deliberations	0904	10	Can be an offence	Community consensus	Community consensus
							Prevention of disclosure of information received in confidence	Harm
							Public interest in being informed weighed against public interest in debate	Societal interests
							Protection of diplomatic confidentiality and activity	Societal interests
							Considerable damage to country's interests	Societal interests
Stubbings	UK	22/10/96	Sexual offences against children	03021	8	Should be an offence	Deterrence	Deterrence
							Debilitating effect on victim	Harm
							Essential aspects of private lives	Essential private life
							Vulnerability deserving protection	Vulnerability
							Wrongdoing	Wrongdoing
							Discrimination	Discrimination
Stübing	Germany	12/04/12	Incest	08029	8	Can be an offence	Community consensus of morality	Community consensus
							Sexual self-determination	Autonomy

							Protection of morals and rights of others	Rights of others
							Damage to family structures and society	Societal interests
Şükran	Turkey	22/01/13	Use of languages in election campaigns	08079	10	Should not be an offence	Essential values of a democratic society	Community consensus
							Prevention of disorder	Societal interests
S.W.	UK	22/11/95	Rape – marital	03011	7	Should be an offence	Respect for human dignity and human freedom	Human dignity
							Debasement	Human dignity
Vejdeland	Sweden	09/02/12	Hate speech – sexual orientation	080322	10	Can be an offence	Discrimination	Discrimination
							Incitement to hatred (not incl. call to violence)	Hatred
							Insulting, ridiculing, slandering specific groups of the population	Offense
							Protection of the reputation or rights of others	Reputation
							Serious and prejudicial allegations	Seriousness
							Views imposed on vulnerable recipients	Vulnerability

(*Continued*)

(Cont.)

Applicant	*Party*	*Date*	*Subject*	*ICCS crime classification*	*Article*	*Outcome*	*Concepts and reasoning in judgment*	*Concept classification*
Vo	France	08/07/04	Non-intentional homicide – unborn child	*	2	Need not be an offence	Availability of other remedies	Availability of other remedies
							Community consensus of morality (lack of)	Community consensus
Willem	France	16/07/09	Incitement to discrimination	02109	10	Can be an offence	Discrimination	Discrimination
							Protection of the rights of others	Rights of others
Wingrove	UK	25/11/96	Blasphemy	080321	10	Can be an offence	Community consensus of morality (lack of)	Community consensus
							Discrimination	Discrimination
							Intimate personal convictions	Autonomy
							Consent	Autonomy
							Offense through actual experience	Offense
							Protection of the rights of others	Rights of others
							High degree of profanation	Seriousness
X	UK	12/07/78	Failing to wear a motorcycle helmet	0907	9	Can be an offence	Protection of health	Harm
							Paternalism	Paternalism

X and Y	Netherlands	26/03/85	Rape – inability to consent	030112	8	Should be an offence	Effective deterrence Fundamental values and essential aspects of private life	Deterrence Essential private life

1 The group of ECHR criminalization cases was identified by full free-text search of HUDOC (http://hudoc.echr.coe.int/) using search terms "criminalization," "criminalisation," "criminal law," "penal law," "criminal code," "criminal prohibition," "penal code," "conviction," "convicted," "prohibited by law," and "sentenced." All results were reviewed and cases involving possible criminalization issues were retained for further consideration. HUDOC keyword search filters for "positive obligations" and "criminal offence" were selected and all results reviewed. Cases involving possible criminalization were retained for further consideration. All ECHR case law information notes from 1998 to 2016 were reviewed, and cases involving possible criminalization issues were identified for further consideration. Identified cases were read in full and retained where clear criminalization conclusions could be identified. Where multiple cases were identified dealing with the same act, a maximum of four cases, representing those with the clearest concepts, reasoning, and criminalization cases, were retained. Key concepts and reasoning were recorded using language from the judgment. Concepts and reasoning were reviewed and subjected to a first round of classification that grouped similar concepts and reasoning. The first round of classification was further refined through a second round of classification that again grouped related concepts, leading to a final classification of 23 criminalization reasoning categories.

* *Angelova and Iliev v. Bulgaria* concerns the offence of racially motivated murder or injury. This act does not have a separate category with ICCS, as motive is dealt with by means of a horizontal disaggregation variable. *Vo v. France* concerns the offence of non-intentional homicide of an unborn child. This act does not exist within the ICCS, as it includes only illegal feticide.

Index

Page numbers followed by n denotes notes.